THE MICROECONOMICS OF CONSUMER BEHAVIOR

REVISED EDITION

DAVID B. EASTWOOD
THE UNIVERSITY OF TENNESSEE

1997

DAME
PUBLICATIONS, INC.

Consulting Editor:
E. Thomas Garman
Virginia Polytechnic Institute and State University

Cover Design: Carol Pickens

Cover Photo: Corel Professional Photos (modified)

Graphic Artists: Amanda Austin
                  Carol Pickens

Desktop Publishing: RaeNelle Belch

Artist: Cindy Romero

©DAME PUBLICATIONS, INC.–**1997**
Houston, TX 77074

ISBN 0-87393-424-5

Library of Congress Card No. 95-69658

Printed in the United States of America.

• Preface •

Consumers are the driving force in all economies. We supply the labor for production and distribution, and we are the largest segment of users of goods and services. Each day people are confronted with choices about what to buy, how to spend time, and how to generate income. The constant decision making is supported by a set of criteria that serve as strategies to evaluate the options.

Economics is concerned with these criteria. Underlying economic principles are associated with all decision making situations, and they provide the framework for understanding the pressures confronting each person. This book presents these microeconomic principles and shows how they can be applied to real world situations. The economic logic does not vary. Regardless of a person's age, the objective is to maximize well-being, and this has been and will continue to be the basic motivation. As a result, the principles for identifying the best alternatives are relevant for all consumers in a wide variety of seemingly diverse settings.

The approach integrates basic economics and its application so the reader can see how to use the logic, as opposed to a discussion of specific solutions for specific situations. Books that stress the latter approach have several shortcomings. First, it is not possible to cover every choice problem. Second, the personal nature of consumer decisions can lead to differences in the optimal alternative. Third, markets are dynamic. New consumer issues evolve as other recede. New products and services emerge while some fade away. Fourth, public policies and programs that affect consumers wax and wane as governments react to social pressures.

This book is designed primarily for courses that are intended to be introductions to the ways in which consumers, acting as individual units, comprise the heart of an economic system. Emphasis centers on a presentation of the economic logic used by a consumer unit as it attempts to manage its resources to be as well off as possible. The approach should help readers understand their own choices and thereby increase the likelihood of making better selections. In addition, through a discussion of the microeconomics of consumer choice, businesses can become more responsive to consumers, and the public sector can provide programs and policies that facilitate the exchange process on behalf of consumers.

Material has been organized to accommodate a one semester or a one or two quarter format. Selected chapters or parts can be deleted for specific courses, depending on student backgrounds. The book has been written for students with little or no background in economics. Consequently, it can be used either at the undergraduate or graduate level. Possible chapter sequences for various types of courses are noted below.

Undergraduate introductory consumer economics or economics:
   Chapters 1-8, 11, and 14
Undergraduate intermediate consumer economics or marketing:
   Chapters 4-17 and appendices
Graduate consumer economics or marketing:
   Chapters 1-17 and appendices

This book has several notable features. First, material not found in any other introductory text is presented. Economists have been devoting a great deal of attention to consumer behavior, but most of the relevant literature requires a high level of sophistication in economics. This text translates these advances into introductory presentations that cover the insights provided by the emerging theories. Second, applications are stressed through the examples in the chapters and in the study questions. Third, key words are initially presented in special type and their definitions appear at the end of each chapter.

There are several important differences between this book and the first edition. Many examples and applications include more recent studies and settings. The material on characteristics and household production frameworks has been moved to part III where the models of consumer choice are presented. Relationships between the traditional and derived demand approaches are explained. The discussion of adult equivalence scales and sociodemographic variables is now part of Chapter 9 in section III. In addition, sections of other chapters have been revised or replaced.

Part I introduces some basic economic concepts that are used throughout the book and should be read by students who have little or no background in economics. The population growth application is to show how the concepts can be used to analyze a problem which should be familiar.

Part II is intended to interest students further. They should be able to relate to their dual roles. Many demographic changes have received attention in the popular press, and they are covered by other disciplines in introductory courses. The goal is to show readers, especially in Chapter 6, that microeconomics can provide some valuable insights into the causes of the sociodemographic changes. However, the discussion in that chapter also notes that more complete explanations must be postponed until some basics about consumer choice have been covered.

Part III presents the basics of decision making. Introduction to the major economic approaches to maximizing well-being subject to constraints is provided.

Part IV turns to the relationship between consumers as buyers and market structure. Applied demand analysis provides an excellent framework for covering instances of market system failure from a consumer perspective as well as a useful tool for evaluating public intervention.

The last part of the book extends the analysis to decision making over time, which is presented as a direct extension of the one period choice analysis presented in Part III.

• Table of Contents •

PART III: AN ECONOMIC APPROACH TO THE DECISION TO PURCHASE

PART IV: CONSUMERS AND MARKET STRUCTURE

PART V: CONSUMER DECISIONS AND TIME

Chapter 1

What is Consumer Economics All About?

Decisions, decisions, decisions! We seem to be confronted constantly with having to make choices. How do you go about choosing? Are there any underlying principles that you follow? Economists think so, and this book is an introduction into their way of analyzing decision making. That is, it presents an economic perspective. Basic economic guidelines are identified, and they become the structure for understanding and evaluating consumer behavior. The focus is on people and their activities in an economy. Decisions about what to buy and how to allocate resources (e.g., money, time, skills) are described from an economic viewpoint. One basic objective is assumed to be at the heart of consumer behavior: a person's motivation is to be as well off as possible given constraints of the economy in which the individual lives.

From the start, keep in mind that this book is neither an encyclopedia of the latest buying tips nor a compendium of current consumer activist issues. While such approaches have their merit, they quickly become outdated. Goods and services evolve, so buying tips become obsolete. The economic environment is always in transition as new businesses emerge, others cease operation, and international trade expands. Our public sector also changes rules and regulations, taxes, and the provision of goods and services to various segments of the population. Sweeping changes in elected governments and associated mandates for change bring about new interactions between consumers and the economy in which they live. In spite of the dynamic features of the world, there are basic decision making principles that can always be applied.

The goal is to develop the economic structure for evaluating consumer behavior and analyzing consumer issues. Economic theory provides clear statements and models of the way consumer decisions ought to be made. Results also become guidelines for decision making. Applying these models to situations in the marketplace highlights consumer problems and become the framework for advocating programs and policies to benefit consumers.

An **economy** is an organization for the production and distribution of goods and services. It comprises the institutions, laws, infrastructure (roads, electricity, etc.),the production of goods and services, management of resources, and the conditions under which exchange takes place. **Consumer economics** focuses on the roles of people acquiring goods and services and managing their resources in an economy.

Consumer theory rests on the premise that an individual's observed behavior is not the result of a random process. If it was, there would be no reason for proceeding any further. Each of us has better things to do than study something that is completely random. The starting point is the assumption that a consistent, rational model of consumer behavior can be constructed with the aid of some elementary economic principles. This model can then serve as a reference for describing how each person makes decisions. Such a perspective leads to an overview of the economic framework which can be used to understand how an individual functions in a market system. The analysis includes not only decisions to buy goods and services but also decisions about resource allocation to generate income (e.g., time).

● What is a Consumer Unit? ●

Before proceeding any further, an important concept must be introduced. What is the appropriate unit of analysis for a theory of consumer behavior? Should it be an **individual?** This may seem reasonable at first. However, a little more thought reveals some problems. Are children consumers? It is difficult to imagine that many children are in positions to make their own decisions. Or consider a spouse who purchases food for a family. Certainly that person's behavior is motivated by more than his or her own welfare.

This suggests that perhaps the appropriate unit of analysis is the family. What is the definition of a family? The U.S. Bureau of the Census is a source of basic data on families, and it defines a **family** as two or more people related by blood, marriage, or adoption residing together. There are two major deficiencies with this description in terms of its use as a definition of a consumer unit. First, individuals are excluded. Second, there are many people living together who are not related by blood, marriage, or adoption, but nevertheless act as a single unit.

A **household** is defined by government agencies as one or more persons residing together. It includes individuals, families, and persons living together but not related by blood, marriage, or adoption. This may appear to be close to the idea of a consumer unit. However, the fact that people are living together is no guarantee that they are acting as a single unit with respect to resource allocation and consumption. For example, if you are living off campus with several friends while attending college, are your resources and spending entirely pooled?

Recently, many government agencies (e.g., U.S. Bureau of the Census and U.S. Bureau of Labor Statistics) have developed the following definition of a consumer unit. A **consumer unit** comprises either (1) all members of a particular household who are related by blood, marriage, adoption, or other legal arrangements; (2) a person living alone or sharing a household with others or living as a roomer in a private home or lodging house or in permanent living quarters in a hotel or motel, but is financially independent; or (3) two or more persons living together who use their incomes to make joint expenditure decisions.[1]

This working definition is very close to the conceptual notion that a consumer is one or more persons collectively deciding how to allocate resources (which is more than income) to generate goods and services that are used to satisfy needs and desires. Whether they are residing together is not the key criterion. Rather, it is whether people act as a unit in terms of interactions with the economy.

Unfortunately, there is no practical way of identifying units that fit the definition exactly. Real-world applications are restricted to available data on individuals, families, and households. This does not mean, however, that all is lost. One can assume that the same motivation is at work whether the consumer unit is an individual, family, or household. Each is trying to achieve the highest level of satisfaction possible, subject to economic constraints.

---

[1]   U.S. Department of Labor, Bureau of Labor Statistics. *Consumer Expenditure Survey, 1990-91.* Bulletin 2425 (September, 1993).

STUDY QUESTIONS

What Is a Consumer Unit?

1.   Identify the similarities and differences in the definitions of a family, household, and consumer unit.
2.   Based on your own experience, to what types of consumer groups have you belonged?

● One Measure of Consumer Power ●

Since our interest centers on consumers' interactions in an economy, let's begin with an overview of the U.S. economy and consumers' roles. As a group consumers represent a dominant force. A popular measure of economic activity is the **gross domestic product** or GDP. It is the value of all final goods and services produced within the borders of an economy during a period of time. This means that the GDP is a measure of the rate of production, or a flow over a period of time. The period of time is usually a year, or the GDP is typically stated in terms of a twelve month period.

Production flows from diverse activities cannot be combined directly. The number of cars produced by Ford cannot be combined with the number of patients served by a hospital because the quantities are different. Converting them into a common unit can be accomplished easily by expressing production in terms of dollars. That is, simply multiply the quantities produced per time period by their prices so dollar values are generated. These can be added together.[2]

Only final activities are included in the GDP. The concept of final production can be explained by continuing with the Ford example. The value of the final product, a car, reflects the values of the goods and services used to make it. The cost of steel, plastic, labor, computer chips, etc., that go into making the car determine the price. Therefore, only the final product needs to be included in the GDP. If the values of the intermediate goods are added into the GDP calculation, there would be double-counting.

Final users can be separated into four major groups: consumers, business, government, and international trade. Together, the final users comprise the aggregate demand for the economy's production. Most final economic activity is in the form of final goods and services for consumers (Csm). Final goods for business are investment expenditures (Inv). Government expenditures represent purchases by the public sector (Gov). Exports (X) are goods produced here but sold abroad. Imports (M) are produced outside the domestic economy and sold within. Expenditures of consumers, business, and government include purchases of imports, so they need to be subtracted in order to measure domestic economic activity.

---

[2]   Let q be the quantity produced of a final good and p be the price per unit. Then pq is the total dollar value of the final production. Adding together all dollar values for the n goods produced yields the GDP for a particular year, t.
$$GDP_t = p_{1,t}q_{1,t} + \ldots + p_{n,t}q_{n,t}.$$

The relationship just described among the final users of an economy's production are represented by the equation shown below.

Csm represents personal **consumption** expenditure which includes purchases by individuals and nonprofit institutions. Rental values of owner-occupied housing are included as part of Csm. Inv denotes gross business investment. It is additions to or the replacement of real productive assets. Gov measures purchases of goods and services by all levels of government. X-M represents the difference between goods and services exported and imported. The subscript t is used to identify the particular year (production period).

(1) $GDP_t = Csm_t + Inv_t + Gov_t + (X_t - M_t)$.

Recent data for the GDP and its major components in terms of final users are presented in the chapter appendix. Equation (1) for $t = 1959$ is

$$494.2 = 318.1 + 78.8 + 99.0 - 1.7$$

Figure 1-1 displays the GDP and its user components associated with equation (1). Overall economic activity, measured in current dollars, has increased rapidly over the 1959-93 time period, and especially since the early 1970s. Csm has also increased, although it has not kept pace with the GDP, as reflected in the increased vertical distance between the two lines. Gov has always been larger than Inv, and the difference between them has grown. The rise in Gov is one indication of concern with the increasing role of the public sector in the U.S. economy.

Changes in the GDP are caused by a combination of factors. There could be changes in the rates of production of existing goods and services (e.g., the number of Fords produced in each year). New goods emerge and others cease to be produced, so the number of goods and services (the subscript n) included in the summation changes. More resources to produce goods and services may become available over time. Population growth results in more labor for production, and increases in the capital stock also permit more production. Furthermore, as technology improves over time, resources can be used more productively. Prices could also increase or decrease over time.

When economic activity is measured, changes in the GDP attributable to changes in prices should be omitted. One way to accomplish this is to value production by the prices of some agreed-upon reference period, instead of valuing production by current period prices. Then, changes in the GDP are a consequence of changes in quantities alone and reflect changes in real economic activity. The measure is called the **real gross domestic product** (RGDP).[3] Because the effect of price changes has been minimized by this calculation, the resulting data are appropriate for the purpose of presenting an overview of the relative size of consumer sector over time.

---

[3]   The Conceptual relationship for the RGDP using 1987 prices is
$RGDP_t = p_{1,1987}q_{1,t} + \cdots + p_{n,1987}q_{n,t}$.

Figure 1-1: GNP and Demand Components in Current Dollars: 1959-1993

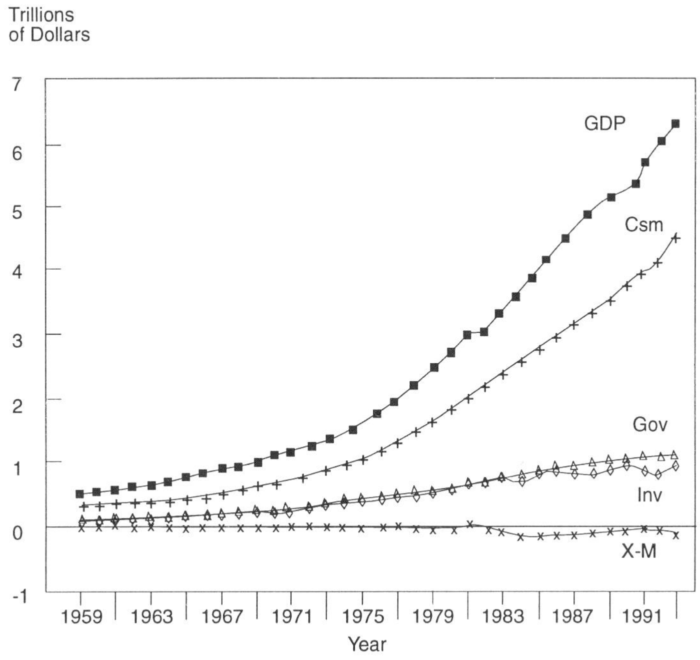

GDP and Csm, measured in current dollars, have increased rapidly since 1959. Gov and Inv have not grown as quickly. The difference between X and M shows a slight decline.

Figure 1-2 shows the RDGP and its demand components for the 1959-1993 period, and the actual data are in the appendix to Chapter 1. Although these series also rise over time, their increases are less than those in Figure 1-1. This is to be expected because prices increased over the time period, but they have been held constant in the "real" data.

One way of visualizing current versus real dollar valuations is found in Figure 1-3. It presents the GDP and RDGP from Figures 1-1 and 1-2. They cross in 1987 because the calculations have to be identical. Rising series are shown, which means that after an adjustment to remove the effect of price changes, real economic activity, as measured in constant 1987 dollars, has increased overall and for each of the major components: real consumption (RCsm), real investment (RInv), and real government (RGov). Prior to 1987, the constant dollar figures are larger than the comparable ones in current dollars. The reason for this is that prices prior to 1987 have been replaced with 1987 prices. Since the 1987 prices are higher, the "real" data must be larger. Just the opposite holds for the data following 1987, because subsequent prices are greater than those of 1987.

How does the economic activity of the consumer sector compare to the overall economy through time? One way of answering is to compare RCsm to RGDP (see Figure 1-4). RCsm divided by RGDP

Figure 1-2: RDGP and Demand Components in Constant (1987) Dollars: 1959-1993

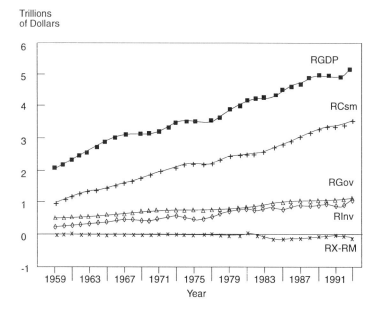

RGDP and Rcsm, measured in 1987 dollars, have risen, but not as rapidly as current dollar values (see Figure 1-1). RGov and RInv have not grown as rapidly. The difference between RX and RM shows a small decrease.

is the share of aggregate demand associated with consumption. Two important points are revealed. First, consumption activity typically accounts for more than 60 percent of real domestic production. Thus, as a group, consumers are the largest economic agent. Second, the share is remarkably stable, which is one indication that consumer behavior is not the result of a completely random process.

Additional support for the second point is provided in other series shown in Figure 1-4. The appendix to Chapter 1 contains the data. In the U.S. market system, the ability of consumers to purchase goods and services depends to a very large extent on the amount of consumer income. Real disposable income (RDInc), measures income after taxes and after adjustments for inflation. Division of RCsm by RDInc yields a measure of the percent of disposable income that consumers as a group use to buy goods and services. This ratio is the top line in Figure 1-4. It is approximately 90 percent throughout the period, which suggests a very stable relationship. Three major categories of consumer spending relative to overall consumption are also shown. Consumer spending for durables (RDur) and services (RServ) as percents of total consumption have increased while the share attributable to nondurables (RNondur) has declined.

Figure 1-3: Current Versus Real (1987) Dollars, 1959-1993

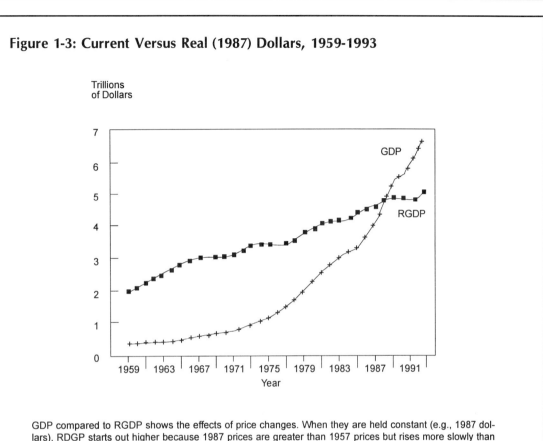

GDP compared to RGDP shows the effects of price changes. When they are held constant (e.g., 1987 dollars), RDGP starts out higher because 1987 prices are greater than 1957 prices but rises more slowly than GDP. The curves are equal in the year of common prices.

Consumers have an extremely important role to play in our economy. Dominance, stability, and change are all reflected in the data. Dominance refers to the share of overall economic activity used by consumers. Stability applies to the relatively constant shares of consumption with respect to the RDGP and RDInc. Change applies to the proportions spent on each of the major components of consumption. Consumers have been gradually reallocating their expenditures to durable goods and services and away from nondurables. This book develops the elementary economic tools that can be used to explain how people make purchase decisions which, when combined, result in the observed consumption patterns.

Figure 1-4: Consumption Components Versus RGDP and RDInc, 1959-1993

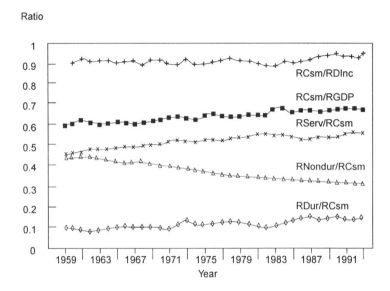

Consuption relative to the RGDP and RDInc are fairly constant ratios. However, there have been long-run changes in the components as shares of Rcsm.

STUDY QUESTIONS

One Measure of Consumer Power

3. Why are only final goods used in calculating the GDP?
4. Why is the GDP referred to as the flow of final goods and services?
5. Identify the three major groups of final users.
6. Define personal consumption expenditure, and discuss its relationship to the GDP.
7. Why does the GDP increase over time?
8. What evidence is there for concluding that consumption is not a random process?

● The Consumer Interest ●

What are the causes of consumers' frustrations with our economic system, especially since they comprise the largest segment? The issues associated with the question are complex and have evolved over time. Many subsequent chapters focus on specific aspects of the question in more detail, but an overview of the answer provides insights in to the relevance of consumer economics.

Prior to and during colonial times, consumers made most of their own goods and services. Very little was purchased through the marketplace. As the economy developed, consumers acquired more and more by means of exchange. Markets became more impersonal, and an individual consumer's purchases became a smaller and smaller share of retailers' revenues.

Not only have more goods and services become available, but they have also become more complex. Many have reached the point that special labels are required to provide the relevant information (e.g., nutrition and energy guide labeling). Consumers have readily accepted the new products and services prompting further growth. Marketing and advertising techniques have improved as well. Today, most people do not possess all the needed information about the broad spectrum of available consumer goods and services. Increasingly, it is necessary to turn to consumer groups to represent our interests in the exchange process and for advice on purchase decisions. The government has also found it necessary to intervene with regulations and standards.

The growth in sophistication and power of producers jeopardizes **consumer sovereignty**, or the assumption that consumers determine what goods and services are bought. Implicit in the discussion in the preceding section was the assumption that producers react to consumers. That is, the activity of producers is to satisfy the needs and wants of consumers. But the increased sophistication of advertising and marketing has enabled producers to manipulate consumers. This is reflected in the rising expectations consumers have regarding the "good life" and new products. When products do not live up to their advertisements, consumer dissatisfaction results.

Adverse economic conditions also are a source of consumer frustration and lead to increased awareness of the impact of purchase decisions. Inflation, rising taxes, job security, and expectations about the standard of living have intensified budgetary pressures for most people. A direct result is increased concern about spending limited funds in a more beneficial manner.

What about the future? Many of the forces identified above are going to be present in the coming years. Producers will continue to use techniques that generate increased sales. Goods and services will become even more complex. Concerns such as job security, retirement income, and quality of life will not go away. The struggle for balance between the roles of the various levels of governments and the rest of the economy is on-going.

Decisions, decisions, decisions typify everyone's long-term situation. The pressures and economic setting that characterize our recent history will always be present. Given limited resources, all consumers will continue to be confronted with the problem of choice. Because consumer economics focuses on guiding principles for selecting the best alternative, this area of study will continue to provide relevant help to people in the efforts to improve their quality of life.

The plan of the book is as follows. Part I outlines the basic economic problem, including some key economic concepts with which any economic system must wrestle. Part II describes how these concepts can be applied, first considering consumer management of resources and then applying economic principles to a long-term analysis of the demographic changes consumers have experienced in the United States. Part III presents the elements of the economic models of consumer choice. A consumer is viewed as trying to achieve the highest level of satisfaction possible given the constraints within which this can be accomplished. Part IV applies the analysis of consumer behavior to the decision to purchase under various types of competition. Decision-making over time is the common thread in Part V. Borrowing and saving are viewed in the intertemporal choice model as ways of changing consumption from one period to another.

STUDY QUESTIONS

The Consumer Interest

9. What forces have led to consumer frustrations within our market economy?
10. Is the economic environment likely to reduce consumer frustrations in the coming years?

● Summary ●

This book is an introduction to the economic analysis of consumer behavior. As such, it focuses on a description of the major economic pressures confronting individuals and how they react. Elementary economic principles are identified, and these become the foundation for understanding and evaluating consumer behavior. An individual consumer unit is defined as one or more persons who pool resources and income to acquire goods and services. Observed consumer behavior is considered to be the result of each consumer unit's efforts to maximize well-being subject to economic constraints.

Consumers comprise the major force in our economy. Evidence of this can be seen in the share of the GDP directly attributed to consumer expenditure. Data on consumer expenditure support the contention that observed consumer behavior is the result of systematic decision making, as opposed to a random process. Total consumption has retained a relatively constant share of the GDP, although the proportions spent on various consumption categories has changed gradually over time. The framework developed in this book serves as a structure for evaluating consumer behavior, as foundation for understanding consumer activism, and as a basis for identifying those areas where public intervention on behalf of consumers is appropriate.

● Key Terms ●

Consumer economics: the study of the forces of people in acquiring goods and services and managing their resources.

Consumer sovereignty: the assumption that consumers determine what goods and services are produced by an economy.

Consumer unit: one or more persons who act together to allocate the resources and use goods and services.

Consumption: expenditures by consumer units and nonprofit institutions for goods and services.

Economy: an organization for the production and distribution of goods and services.

Family: two or more persons related by blood, marriage, or adoption residing together.

Gross domestic product: the value of all final goods and services produced within the borders of an economy over a specified time period.

Household: one or more persons who reside in the same dwelling.

Real consumption: consumption expressed in constant dollars.

Real gross domestic product: the gross domestic product in constant dollars.

● Appendix Table 1.1: GDP and Demand Components, 1959-1993, Current and 1987 Dollars. ●

Year	GDP	C	I	G	X-M	RDGP	RCsm	RInv	RGov	RX-RM
1959	494.2	318.1	78.8	99.0	-1.7	1928.8	1178.9	296.4	475.3	-21.8
1960	513.4	332.4	78.7	99.8	2.4	1970.8	1210.8	290.8	476.9	-7.6
1961	531.8	343.5	77.9	107.8	3.4	2023.8	1238.4	289.4	501.5	-5.5
1962	571.6	364.4	87.9	116.8	2.4	2128.1	1293.3	321.2	524.2	-10.5
1963	603.1	384.2	93.4	122.3	3.3	2215.6	1341.9	343.1	536.3	-5.8
1964	648.0	412.5	101.7	128.3	5.5	2340.6	1417.2	371.8	549.1	2.5
1965	702.7	444.6	118.0	136.3	3.9	2470.5	1497.0	413.0	566.9	-6.4
1966	769.8	481.6	130.4	155.9	1.9	2616.2	1573.8	438.0	622.4	-18.0
1967	814.3	509.3	128.0	175.6	1.4	2685.2	1622.4	418.6	667.9	-23.7
1968	889.3	559.1	139.9	191.5	-1.3	2796.9	1707.5	440.1	686.8	-37.5
1969	959.5	603.7	155.2	201.8	-1.2	2873.0	1771.2	461.3	682.0	-41.5
1970	1010.7	646.5	150.3	212.7	1.2	2873.9	1813.5	429.7	665.8	-35.2
1971	1097.2	700.3	175.5	224.3	-3.0	2955.9	1873.7	475.7	652.4	-45.9
1972	2207.0	767.8	204.6	241.5	-8.0	3107.1	1978.4	532.2	653.0	-56.5
1973	1349.6	848.1	243.1	257.7	0.6	3268.6	2066.7	591.7	644.2	-34.1
1974	1458.6	927.7	245.8	288.3	-3.1	3248.1	2053.8	543.0	655.4	-4.1
1975	1585.9	1024.9	226.0	321.4	13.6	3221.7	2097.5	437.6	663.5	23.1
1976	1768.4	1143.1	286.4	341.3	-2.3	3380.8	2207.3	520.6	659.2	-6.4
1977	1974.1	1271.5	358.3	368.0	-23.7	3533.3	2296.6	602.4	664.1	-27.8
1978	2232.7	1421.2	434.0	403.6	-26.1	3703.5	2391.8	664.6	677.0	-29.9
1979	2488.6	1583.7	480.2	448.5	-23.8	3796.8	2448.4	669.7	689.3	-10.6
1980	2708.0	1748.1	467.6	507.1	-14.7	3776.3	2447.1	594.4	704.2	30.7
1981	3030.6	1926.2	558.0	561.1	-14.7	3843.1	2476.9	631.1	713.2	22.0
1982	3149.6	2059.2	503.4	607.6	-20.6	3760.3	2503.7	540.5	723.6	-7.4
1983	3405.0	2257.5	546.7	652.3	-51.4	3906.6	2619.4	599.5	743.8	-5.6
1984	3777.2	2460.3	718.9	700.8	-102.7	4158.5	2746.1	757.5	766.9	-122.0
1985	4038.7	2667.4	714.5	772.3	-115.6	4279.8	2865.8	545.9	813.4	-145.3
1986	4268.6	2850.6	717.9	833.0	-132.5	4404.5	2969.1	735.1	855.4	-155.1
1987	4539.9	3052.2	749.3	881.5	-143.1	4539.9	3052.2	749.3	881.5	-143.1
1988	4900.4	3296.1	793.6	918.7	-108.0	4718.6	3162.4	773.4	886.8	-104.0
1989	5244.0	3517.9	837.6	971.4	-82.9	4836.9	3223.1	789.2	900.4	-75.7
1990	5513.8	3742.6	802.6	1042.9	-74.4	4884.9	3263.6	744.5	929.1	-51.3
1991	5672.6	3889.1	726.7	1087.5	-30.7	4848.8	3259.0	673.7	937.1	-20.9
1992	6020.2	4136.9	788.3	1125.3	-30.3	4979.3	3349.5	725.3	936.9	-32.3
1993	6343.3	4378.2	822.0	1148.4	-65.3	5134.5	3458.7	819.9	929.8	-73.9

Source: U.S. Department of Commerce, *Survey of Current Busines*, selected issues.

Year	RDInc	RDur	RNon-dur	RServ	RCsm/RGDP	RCsm/RDInc	RDur/RCsm	RNond/RCsm	RServ/RCsm
1959	1284.9	114.4	518.5	546.0	0.61	0.92	0.10	0.44	0.46
1960	1313.0	115.4	526.9	568.5	0.61	0.92	0.10	0.44	0.47
1961	1356.4	109.4	537.7	591.3	0.61	0.91	0.09	0.43	0.48
1962	1414.8	120.2	553.0	620.0	0.61	0.91	0.09	0.43	0.48
1963	1461.1	130.3	563.6	648.0	0.61	0.92	0.10	0.42	0.48
1964	1562.2	140.7	588.2	688.3	0.61	0.91	0.10	0.42	0.49
1965	1653.5	156.2	616.7	724.1	0.61	0.91	0.10	0.41	0.48
1966	1734.3	166.0	647.6	760.2	0.60	0.91	0.11	0.41	0.48
1967	1811.4	167.2	659.0	796.2	0.60	0.90	0.10	0.41	0.49
1968	1886.8	184.5	686.0	837.0	0.61	0.90	0.11	0.40	0.49
1969	1947.4	190.8	703.2	877.2	0.62	0.91	0.11	0.40	0.50
1970	2025.3	183.7	717.2	912.5	0.63	0.90	0.10	0.40	0.50
1971	2099.9	201.4	725.6	946.7	0.63	0.89	0.11	0.39	0.51
1972	2186.2	255.2	755.8	997.4	0.64	0.90	0.13	0.38	0.50
1973	2334.1	246.6	777.9	1042.2	0.63	0.89	0.12	0.38	0.50
1974	2317.0	227.2	759.8	1066.8	0.63	0.89	0.11	0.37	0.52
1975	2355.4	226.8	767.1	1103.6	0.65	0.89	0.11	0.37	0.53
1976	2440.9	256.4	801.3	1149.5	0.65	0.90	0.12	0.36	0.52
1977	2512.6	280.0	819.8	1196.8	0.65	0.91	0.12	0.36	0.52
1978	2638.4	292.9	844.8	1254.1	0.65	0.91	0.12	0.35	0.52
1979	2710.0	289.0	862.8	1296.5	0.64	0.90	0.12	0.35	0.53
1980	2733.6	262.7	860.5	1323.9	0.65	0.90	0.11	0.35	0.54
1981	2795.8	246.6	867.9	1344.4	0.64	0.89	0.10	0.35	0.54
1982	2820.4	262.5	872.2	1368.9	0.67	0.89	0.10	0.35	0.55
1983	2893.6	297.7	900.3	1421.4	0.67	0.91	0.11	0.34	0.54
1984	3080.1	338.5	934.6	1473.0	0.66	0.89	0.12	0.34	0.54
1985	3162.1	370.1	958.7	1537.0	0.67	0.91	0.13	0.33	0.54
1986	3261.9	420.0	991.0	1576.1	0.67	0.91	0.14	0.33	0.53
1987	3289.5	403.7	1011.1	1637.4	0.67	0.93	0.13	0.33	0.54
1988	3404.3	428.7	1035.1	1698.5	0.67	0.93	0.14	0.33	0.54
1989	3471.2	440.8	1049.3	1732.9	0.67	0.93	0.14	0.33	0.54
1990	3538.3	438.9	1050.8	1773.0	0.67	0.92	0.13	0.32	0.54
1991	3534.9	412.5	1043.0	1803.4	0.67	0.92	0.13	0.32	0.55
1992	3648.1	452.6	1057.7	1839.1	0.67	0.92	0.14	0.32	0.55
1993	3704.1	489.9	1078.5	1890.3	0.67	0.93	0.14	0.31	0.55

Source: U.S. Department of Commerce, *Survey of Current Business*, selected issues.

Chapter 2

Too Few Resources for What We Want

Scarcity and choice are basic components of daily living. Unlimited wants are constrained by limited goods and services, resources to produce them, limited income, and limited time. Thus, the consumer is forced to make choices. If a person is to be as well off as possible, it is crucial that only the best alternatives, not just among goods and services to use today, but also, between borrowing and saving/investing. Goods and services should be made as efficiently as possible, which involves choosing the best technologies and capital for production. Time should be allocated carefully among income generating, consumption, and leisure activities.

Efficient use of limited resources is the fundamental economic concern. This chapter lays the foundation for applying economic tools to the analysis of consumer behavior. Economics is defined, and its relevance for consumer behavior is outlined. The ways in which consumers function in an economic system are discussed. Three ways of organizing production and exchange are identified, and the U.S. economy is described as one that relies primarily on buyers and sellers interacting through a free exchange process. Usually, these exchanges occur with the aid of money, so the chapter concludes with a brief discussion of the major features of money and prices.

● Scarcity ●

Economic analysis can be applied to a very wide variety of issues. Examples include taxation, employment, investment, family size, environmental protection, education, and demand analysis. How can one discipline provide insights for such a diverse set of issues? The answer lies in the basic definition of economics.

Three observations about the world comprise a starting point. First, human wants are virtually unlimited. No matter how much a person has, there always is a desire for more. Second, almost all of the things people want do not exist naturally. Rather, they must be produced. Third, **resources**, which are all the things used to produce goods and services, are limited in supply.

There are three major categories of resources: land, labor, and capital. **Land** includes not only the surface area for agriculture, housing, business, recreation, and government, but also the natural resources below the surface. **Capital** can be thought of generally as plant and equipment, although a more complete explanation of the economic perspective on capital is presented in Chapter 6. There is a limit to the amount of each resource available during a specified time period, such as a year. For example, there is a limit to the amount of electrical power that can be generated, a limit to the number of cars that can be produced, a limit to the labor available, etc.

Unlimited desires constrained by the limited resources that can be used to satisfy them cause the basic economic problem. **Economics** is the study of the efficient allocation of resources to produce goods and services. Concern focuses on doing the best that is possible given what is available. Scarcity is the starting point of economic analysis. The pervasiveness of the problem of scarcity is the reason why economic analysis can be applied to so many pressing issues.

While economics is concerned with the efficient allocation of any scarce resource, the emphasis in this book is on the role individuals have as consumers. Since economic activity is an attempt to provide goods and services to people, consumers are at the heart of the economic problem. Consumers are not only the cause of the activity but also a resource in the production process and the source of decisions about what to buy.

In their roles as producers, people are considered to be a scarce resource. But can labor be a limited resource when people are unemployed? For example, the unemployment rate for January, 1995 was 5.7 percent.[1] Does this mean that labor is not scarce?

To answer this question, we must define the labor force. The **labor force** is the number of people in the civilian population, age 16 and over, who are employed, plus those who are unemployed and actively looking for a job.[2] There are three basic causes of unemployment. First, some workers are simply between jobs. For example, a computer systems engineer may have quit one company and be in the process of choosing among several job offers. Such people have the skills to secure another job, and it is only a matter of time before they select one. This type of unemployment is called **frictional unemployment**. Second, some people do not have the skills to find another job when they lose one. Suppose a textile manufacturer closes a facility in the Southeast. What happens to the workers? Many are unable to find other jobs—especially older workers with low educational levels. These people may have to acquire other skills before they can get another job. This type of unemployment is called **structural unemployment**. Third, industries have cyclical patterns. These may be annual, as in the case of retail sales, or they may relate to other economic developments, as in the case of home construction. The cyclical patterns are a result of the normal operation of the economy. Unemployment fluctuates with these cyclical patterns. Therefore, some people are out of work because of the cyclical nature of business activity. This type of unemployment is called **cyclical unemployment.**

The existence of these three types of unemployment means that some people in our economic system are always unemployed and actively looking for jobs. Individuals frequently change jobs, creating frictional unemployment. Not everyone possesses needed skills for job openings, so structural unemployment arises.[3] Cyclical patterns and the resulting cyclical unemployment are normal parts of business activity. The **unemployment rate** is the number of people who are unemployed, expressed as a percent of the labor force. If some people are always unemployed, then the unemployment rate can never be zero.[4]

How close to zero can the unemployment rate be? In other words, if frictional, structural, and cyclical unemployment are at their minimums, what would the unemployment rate be? This is difficult to answer precisely because in a dynamic labor market as the age and educational distributions of the workers change the number of people who are structurally and frictionally unemployed changes. Economists have not been able to agree on a specific number. However, most feel that, given the current characteristics of the labor force, the minimum unemployment rate is somewhere between 5.5 and 6.5 percent. This minimum is called the **full employment unemployment rate.**

---

[1]   U.S. Bureau of Labor Statistics, *Monthly Labor Review*, April, 1995.

[2]   Let L be the labor force be the labor force, E represent those who are employed, U denote those who are unemployed, and t is the time period. Then $L_t = E_t + U_t$.

[3]   With respect to consumer units with more than one person, a key part of decision making is deciding who works in the marketplace, who works at home, and who can acquire new skills.

[4]   The unemployment rate in period t is $UR_t = U_t/L_t$. The only way U_t/L_t can be zero is if U_t is zero, and it has just been argued that this cannot occur.

Given this background information, the question becomes is there an economic rationale for the proposition that labor is a scarce resource even when the unemployment rate is greater than the full employment unemployment rate? The answer is yes, for in addition to the fact that labor is an essential factor in the operation of an economic system, there are four other reasons why labor is a central concern of economics.

First, Chapter 1 has shown that consumption is the major component of economic activity, and consumers can buy goods and services only if they have an income, which is derived primarily from working. Second, each consumer unit has a limited amount of labor available, which must be allocated in the most efficient way possible in order to maximize satisfaction. Even if people are unemployed, they would not work for an employer at a zero wage, since they could use the time at home to produce goods and services directly through activities such as sewing and household maintenance. The allocation of the consumer unit's labor at home is an economic problem. Given that time is spent at home, which home production activities should be undertaken? Third, since businesses must use a scarce resource, money, to hire labor, it follows that they have to be efficient in the use of labor if businesses are to be efficient managers of money. Finally, there is a relationship between employment and government programs aimed at helping the unemployed. As unemployment increases, the costs of transfer programs such as unemployment compensation, aid to families with dependent children, and food stamps increases. These costs are borne to a large extent by those who continue to be employed.

STUDY QUESTIONS

Scarcity

1. Explain why scarcity is an economic problem for developing nations as well as for industrialized nations.
2. How does scarcity enter into consumer unit decision making?
3. Why is the following statement false? "The unemployment rate can never equal zero because some people are lazy and do not look for a job."
4. Consider UR for different age groups and levels of educational attainment. How do you think the rates change with increasing age and education?
5. The office of the future for many people may be at home. How might the ability to work at home affect a family's resource allocation?

● Three Economic Questions ●

Three fundamental questions that any economic system must address are (1) what to produce, (2) how to produce, and (3) for whom to produce. Each question is discussed below, in turn.

● What to Produce?

There are two aspects of this question. The first concerns today. What should be made for today: hamburger, steak, shirts, winter coats, housing,...? Individuals acting alone or through society must decide. The second aspect pertains to tomorrow. Are the scarce resources to be used to make things just for today, or are they to be used to make more plant and equipment? Resources devoted to the generation of investment goods cannot be used for current consumption. However, the investment can be used to increase future consumption. For example, the plastic diverted from the production of automobile parts today and employed instead to make a robot can be used to make more cars (and other goods) tomorrow.

● How to Produce?

Deciding how to produce involves choosing the technology as well as the resources to be used in the production of goods and services. **Technology** is any method of combining resources to produce an output. In almost all instances, more than one technology could be used. Cooking provides an excellent illustration. Suppose the task is to make a white cake with chocolate frosting. A recipe for making this type of cake is the equivalent of a technology, and there are many such cake recipes from which to choose. A specific recipe must be chosen from among them, along with the associated ingredients.

How to produce also involves investment choices about today versus tomorrow. Firms must choose among research and development alternatives, and there are different ways of incorporating new products into business operations. For example, computer manufacturers must choose among various configurations of hardware and software (e.g., type of processor and operating system).

● For Whom to Produce?

The question of for whom goods are produced focuses on distribution. Once goods and services are available, the problem becomes one of allocating them among the various segments of the economy. Scarcity, in conjunction with unlimited wants, creates the need for devising some scheme for the distribution of goods and services.

Each consumer is in a situation analogous to that of the economy. Limited resources must be managed efficiently in order for the consumer to be as satisfied as possible. The consumer has to choose among consumer goods today because of limited purchasing power. Choices between today and tomorrow also must be made. For example, a decision to return to a university to earn an MBA degree entails sacrifices today in return for increased opportunities in the future. How to produce also must be addressed. Think of all the different ways of acquiring a steak dinner: restaurant, fast-food steak house, oven-broiled, stir-fry, grilled, etc. Distribution issues also confront the consumer unit. Whenever there is more than one person in the unit, the question of the distribution of goods and services within the unit needs to be answered. For example, a family has to decide not only whether to buy a home computer, but also when and by whom the computer can be used.

STUDY QUESTIONS

Three Economic Questions

6. Explain why each of the three economic questions is a consequence of scarcity.
7. How do the three economic questions apply to the consumer unit's decision making?
8. Consider a family of four living in a typical home in 1960 versus the same family today. In what ways do you think that the technology for producing goods and services in the home has changed?

● Types of Economies ●

Although any economic system has to answer the questions discussed above, the manner in which the answers are provided differs according to the type of economic system. Economies are distinguished theoretically on the basis of the form of ownership. **Capitalism** is characterized by private ownership of resources, production, income, and consumption. **Socialism** is characterized by public ownership of production, with everything else privately owned. The complete absence of private ownership of resources, production, income, and consumption is the basis of **communism**.

A capitalist system relies on a free exchange between buyers and sellers in order to function. Since everything is privately owned, there is no governmental intervention. Thus, the only way for exchange to take place is for buyers and sellers to get together. Under a socialist system, although the production side of the economy is publicly operated, buyers and sellers are permitted to interact—especially at the consumer level. A communist system does not rely on private exchange because complete public ownership means that the public is both buyer and seller. Other methods of ensuring interaction are required, such as the use of detailed national economic planning and coordination.

Comparisons of theoretical economic systems to those actually in existence in the world lead to the conclusion that no system in practice fits a specific theoretical model. Existing systems are mixes of the three types, with greater reliance on one particular form. The U.S. economy has both private and public sectors. Although constraints are often imposed on buyers and sellers by the government, the U.S. economy is primarily a capitalist system, relying on free exchanges, using the market mechanism except in those instances where it fails. Communist countries do not have complete public control—free exchange has been allowed to operate in some areas.

The predominant type of system can change for any economy. The fall, 1994 elections in the United States and the Republican Party's "Contract with America" represented an effort on the part of the electorate to reduce governments' intervention in the economy. The radical departure from communism in the former Soviet Union and Eastern Europe has necessitated a struggle to create smoothly operating markets in the absence of complete government control.

Types of Economies

9. How does the form of ownership allow us to distinguish among economic systems?
10. We have argued that there are three theoretical types of economic systems. Could elements of each be found within a consumer unit? Explain.

● The Dual Roles of Producers and Consumers ●

A better understanding of the economic forces associated with consumer decision making begins with an understanding of how consumers operate in a market system. **Markets** arise whenever buyers and sellers get together to have an exchange. Notice that buyers and sellers need not be located in the same physical place. Avenues of interaction include phone conversations, FAX exchanges, and the Internet.

There are two basic groups within a market system: consumers and producers. To keep the discussion to the bare minimum, it is assumed that there is no government (i.e., Gov of Chapter 1 = 0). Two fundamental types of markets exist in this model. One is the final goods market in which goods and services are bought for consumption. The other is the factor market in which the resources used to produce goods are exchanged.

Figure 2-1 shows how consumers and producers interact in the final goods and factor markets. The connecting arrows indicate the directions of the flows. Consumers, portrayed on the left-center of the figure, take their money to the final goods market and spend it. In exchange, they receive goods and services. The flow of consumer goods and services, measured in dollars, is the same as the value of the money flow. For example a consumer who spends $100 for food receives $100 worth of food from grocery stores. Consumers function in the factor market, shown in the bottom center of the figure, by selling their resources to producers. The major consumer resource is labor, but other resources consumers control include property and money in the form of savings. In exchange for these resources, they receive wages, rent, dividends, interest, and capital gains. These two flows also offset each other.

Producers, located in the right-center of the figure, operate in the two markets as well. Factors of production can be acquired only by paying the appropriate wage, or price. This means that as resources flow to the firm, there is an equal flow of money from the producers to the owners of the factors. Finished goods flow from the firm to the final goods market, and in exchange producers receive their sales revenue.

While this is a very simplified discussion of how a market economy operates, it nevertheless outlines the fundamental dual roles of consumers and producers. Both groups act as buyers and sellers. Consumers buy final goods, but they must also sell their resources in the factor market. Similarly, producers sell final goods, but they must also buy the resources to make the final goods and services. Figure 2-1 clearly illustrates that any analysis of consumer behavior cannot be limited to purchase decisions alone. Such a myopic approach only covers half of the consumers' role in a market system. A complete approach requires the analysis of resource allocation as well.

Figure 2-1: Circular Flow Diagram

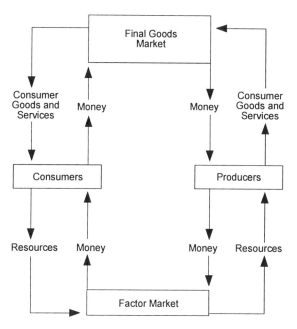

A circular flow diagram presents a simplified view of a market economy. There are only two economic groups: consumers and producers. The two groups interact in a final goods market and a factor market. Both groups have dual roles as buyers and sellers. Consumers receive goods and services in the final goods market by exchanging money. Consumers also sell their resources in the factor market, for which they receive an income.

STUDY QUESTIONS

The Dual Role of Producers and Consumers

11. Explain how a circular flow diagram can be used to represent the position of consumers in a market system.
12. What is a market? How can a consumer be both a buyer and a seller?
13. What are some of the consumer problems that have arisen in Eastern Europe and Russia as more capitalism is introduced?

● Money and Prices ●

Money is something near and dear to everyone. Why? Because it plays a pivotal role in a market system. Anything that serves the following three functions can be called **money**. First, it has to be an acceptable medium of exchange. People must be willing to use it to acquire goods and services. Second, it must be a store of value. This means that one must be able to hold on to the money for a period of time and then use it to purchase goods and services. Finally, money has to be a unit of account. That is, money must serve as a standard for the valuation of other goods and services.

Exchange takes place in most economies with the aid of money. If one is to understand how consumers operate in this setting, it is necessary to have an appreciation for the role of money. The best way to get a handle on this is to ask: how would an economy operate if there was no money? Direct exchange of goods and services would have to occur, and this is called a **barter** system. In a barter system, it is necessary to have a matched group for a mutual exchange. Money eliminated direct exchange by separating trade into two parts. A good can be sold for money, and the money can be used to buy other things. The separation allows different people and producers to be involved in the exchanges. The separation allows an economy to function much more efficiently.

Transaction costs are reduced considerably when money is introduced into the exchange process. Transactions costs are those that occur when buyers and sellers get together to agree upon voluntary exchanges; they include the costs of keeping records and negotiating agreements, as well as locating interested parties. In a barter system, since a direct exchange must occur, arranging for a matched group of traders, negotiating a trade, keeping track of agreements, and ensuring that contracts are fulfilled are more difficult. Another advantage when money is used is that negotiations and deliveries of goods and services can be recorded in a uniform, consistent manner.

Money also promotes efficiency by allowing increased specialization. With a barter system the best way to function is to make many goods so the probability of being able to trade is increased. By separating the direct exchange process, money enables people to specialize in areas in which they are most efficient because they no longer need to find matched groups.

A significant part of consumer behavior is directed toward acquiring money because of the control it represents over goods, services, and resources. Consequently, an understanding of consumer behavior can be enhanced by an appreciation of how money works in a market system. Consumers use money in several different forms. Examples are currency, coins, and checking accounts. A brief discussion of the evolution of modern monetary systems provides an excellent way to become familiar with the different forms of money and to develop an awareness of consumers' uses of money.

Current forms of money had their genesis in the Near East with the use of heavy precious metals. Three properties made these materials ideal as an early form of money. First, they are heavy so they can be divided into very small units on the basis of weight. Second, they are easily recognized. Third, they are durable.

Since precious metals were broken down by weight, a problem arose very early concerning whose scale to use. Buyers were reluctant to trust merchants' scales, and sellers felt the same way about using the buyers' scales. The solution was for the government to certify the weight by placing a stamp on the metal, and this led to coins. While coins provided an efficient system, it should be noted that governments acquired the ability to "control the scales." Governments can still alter the precious metal content of coins. Recent examples of this in the United States are changes in the composition of the quarter, dime, and penny.

Coins served as a satisfactory form of money until the end of the Middle Ages, when three factors in Western Europe combined to create a need to change the system. One was the accumulation of wealth by some families, resulting in the need for a safe place to store money. Another was the emergence of large financial transactions due to increased trade. Finally, more people were beginning to live in cities and to engage in production away from home, thereby creating the demand for more exchange with the aid of money.

Some enterprising people went into the business of filling the need for a safe, convenient place for storing money; thus early forms of banks began to appear. Anyone storing precious metal at a bank wanted a receipt. Before long, the receipts started to be exchanged rather than the precious metals. Because some banks were not managed very well, people needed a way to tell a good bank from a bad one. The problem was solved by having governments take over the management and/or regulation of banks. Governments stored the precious metals and had the responsibility of printing certificates for the amounts held. Paper currency began to serve the three functions of money.

Much more recently, checks have come to serve as money. Currency is convenient to carry, but many transactions are so large that the use of currency is somewhat awkward. Procedurally, it is much easier to write a large dollar amount on a check than to use the equivalent amount of coins and currency. Coins and currency also can be difficult to transport when buyers and sellers are geographically separated. Checks have the advantage of allowing the buyer to control who receives the money by specifying on the check to whom it is payable. Earlier forms of money did not have this feature, so checks have facilitated the exchange process.

The most recent developments are credit and debit cards. Buyers have the same control over designating who receives the money as with checks. Carrying these cards is much more convenient than carrying blank checks and writing then as needed. Another advantage is the record keeping that automatically comes with the monthly card statements.

What is a check or a credit/debit card transaction? It is simply a piece of paper or an electronic transaction involving a number. Notice that the use of money has evolved to the point where numbers are frequently exchanged, not currency, coins, or precious metals. What gives the checks and card transactions their value? Let's take a closer look at the U.S. money supply. Checking account balances equalled $1,155.4 billion and currency (including travelers checks) amounted to $361.5 billion in November, 1994.[5] Comparing the value of the U.S. money supply to estimates of the amount of precious metals that the government has stored shows that the money supply is much larger than the value of the precious metals. An implication is that the dollar's value is not based on precious metals. Another way of looking at this is to ask "What can be done with a precious metal such as gold?" Although it does have industrial uses, it cannot be eaten, and only a little of it can be worn. Gold can be purchased as an investment; but in this role, it is similar to a stock, a bond, or any other investment.

A dollar derives its basic value not from its worth in gold, but from what you can buy with it. Thus, $1.00 in a checking account, a dollar bill, or a card transaction can be used to buy $1.00's worth of goods, services, savings, or investments. Dollars, as the U.S. monetary unit, represent claims against U.S. production, or the ability to acquire goods, services, and other resources. Because so much is produced, dollars are very desirable. Consumers who receive money for the resources they supplied to the factor market accept these payments because the money can be used to buy a wide variety of goods and services.

Since the value of a dollar depends on what it can buy, let us now consider the definition of the price of a good. For example, if the price of a six-pack of 12-ounce cans of beer is $3.75, what exactly does this mean? Most people can readily answer this question, but it is useful to clarify the issue to

---

[5] Federal Reserve Board, *Federal Reserve Bulletin*, February, 1995.

set the stage for the consumer perspective on prices in later chapters. The **price** of a particular good is the amount of the monetary unit required to purchase a specific item. Thus, three and three-quarters of the dollar monetary unit are to be exchanged for the beer.

Notice that the discussion of the role of money has not included any reference to income. Income is a different, distinct concept. In Chapter 4 this discussion of money is used to develop a broader definition of the income of a consumer unit. This broader definition provides a basis for a better understanding of the economic pressures affecting consumers. The fact that the price just denotes the amount of money that has to be exchanged to acquire the good or service in a market is the basis for a discussion of how consumers react to prices in Chapter 7.

So far, the discussion of money has focused primarily on consumer aspects of money as a medium of exchange. A few remarks are in order with respect to a consumer viewpoint for the other two characteristics of money. The ability of money to serve as a store of value means that consumers do not have to spend all their money immediately. Rather, they can choose to hold on to this money and use it later. While the store of value property may not be perfect (holding on to money by itself does not generate interest), nevertheless, most consumers choose to hold on to some money for future use.

Because a price is the amount of a monetary unit required for a good or service to be purchased in the marketplace, monetary standards, such as the dollar, serve as measuring devices for goods and services when their values are expressed in terms of the standards. This is what permitted our analysis of the GDP, RGDP, and RCsm and its components in Chapter 1.

STUDY QUESTIONS

Money and Prices

14. Explain why money is more than an end in itself.
15. In the past, a consumer unit produced all is consumer goods directly. As economies developed, more and more production took place outside the home. How has the evolution of our monetary system helped to facilitate this development?
16. If the price of a 19-inch color cable-ready TV is $539, what does this price really mean?
17. How does the presence of money in an economic system help address the problem of scarcity?

● Summary ●

Economics is defined as the efficient allocation of scarce resources to produce goods and services. Because human wants are virtually unlimited, the goal is to do the best with what is available. The economic justification for being concerned about people stems from the fact that production activity is ultimately directed toward meeting human needs and that labor must be used in production. Just as an economy must deal with resource allocation questions, so too must a consumer unit. The U.S. economy is a mixed economic system, relying on free exchange whenever possible. Reliance on the market system means that consumers have dual roles to perform: buying and selling. Money streamlines the exchange process, allowing for a more efficient operation of an economy through increased specialization and decreased transaction costs. A price is the number of monetary units required to buy a good or service in a market.

● Key Words ●

Barter: direct exchange of goods and services.

Capitalism: complete private ownership and free exchange.

Communism: complete public ownership.

Cyclical unemployment: unemployment due to the cyclical behavior of business.

Economics: study of the efficient allocation of resources to produce goods and services.

Frictional unemployment: unemployment of workers who have skills to acquire another job.

Full employment unemployment rate: rate of unemployment associated minimum frictional, structural, and cyclical unemployment.

Labor force: civilians age 16 and over who are working or actively seeking employment.

Market: interaction of buyers and sellers.

Money: an acceptable medium of exchange, store of value, and unit of account.

Price: amount of money required to purchase an item in the marketplace.

Resource: anything used in the production process to make goods and services.

Socialism: an economic system in which there is public ownership of production but private ownership of income and consumption.

Structural unemployment: unemployed workers who do not have the skills to acquire another job.

Technology: a way of combining resources to produce a good or service.

Unemployment rate: percent of the labor force that is unemployed.

Chapter 3

Some Basic Economics

As buyers and sellers in a market system, consumers must constantly make choices. Decisions arise because limited resources used in one activity cannot be used simultaneously in another. Economics focuses on the efficiency aspects of the alternatives. A logical starting point to study resource allocation is the problem of how to produce. Once some important economic principles have been introduced, they provide the basis for developing a framework for understanding the economic pressures associated with consumer decision making in the next chapter.

● The Production Possibility Frontier ●

The problem of scarcity causes choices to be made about the way limited resources are allocated among their alternative uses. Economists have developed a diagrammatic tool to depict how these choices affect the production of goods and services. The pictorial tool presented here provides many useful insights and applications. One discussed in this chapter concerns resource allocation between the public and private sectors. Another problem covered here involves population growth and family size. Other applications appear in subsequent chapters.

What is the largest the RGDP could be for a specific year? That is, how much could be produced during a period, such as twelve months, if the economy was as efficient as possible and there was full employment? "Could be produced" is critical to the discussion because it specifies the maximum feasible production—not what is actually produced. The maximum should be distinguished clearly from the actual RGDP, which is a constant dollar measure of actual production that occurred during a period of time. Whenever there is less than full employment, the RGDP is less than the maximum.

Two aspects of the production problem are fixed during a specified period of time. One is the amount of resources available to the economy. Examples are the fixed amount of land available and the maximum amount of electricity that can be generated. Levels of resources can be altered only over an extended period of time, so a fixed period precludes changes in resources. The other fixed aspect is the level of technology. **Technology** refers to the ways of combining resources to produce goods and services. Fixed technology means that there is a fixed number of ways in which production can occur. No new production methods are assumed to arise during the period. Changes in technology require time for research and development, as well as time for introduction into manufacturing processes. For example, it takes several years for new processors to be developed for computers and addition time for them to be mass produced and for software to be written that can take advantage of the improvements. Consequently, the fixed technology assumption is not very unrealistic.

One other restriction is required to construct a diagram of the situation. It is that the economy produces only two goods. The reason for this limitation is to enable the construction of a two-dimensional diagram in which an axis measures units produced. Three goods would require a three-dimensional diagram. Extension beyond three goods must rely on mathematics. There is no need for this complication, because the two-goods case provides sufficient insight.

Resource allocation focuses on uses of scarce inputs into the production of goods and services. Consequently, discussion centers on the feasibility of producing, as opposed to preferences (likes-dislikes) for the resulting outputs. The representative goods are arbitrary and can even be a composite. For example, suppose that one axis is a composite of goods and services produced for consumers, called the consumer sector, and the other is a composite of the goods and services produced for all levels of government, called the public sector. These are the axes shown in Figure 3-1.

Figure 3-1: A Straight Line Production Possibility Frontier

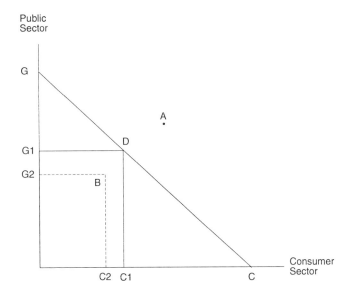

A production possibility frontier shows maximum combinations of goods and services an economy could produce, given fixed resources and fixed technology. It is a boundary between what is and is not feasible for an economy to produce. Unemployment occurs whenever actual production is represented by a point inside the frontier. The frontier GC has a negative slope. Whenever an economy is on its' frontier, more of one good can be obtained only at the expense of another. In other words, a trade-off must occur.

Scarce resources can be used to produce either public or consumer sector goods and services. Electricity, for example, can be used in the production of both types. The same is true for labor, wire, steel, paper, clothing (e.g., uniforms and civilian), and so on. The central problem of resource allocation is that as long as there are alternative uses for resources, decisions must be made about where these inputs will be used. Resources used in one production activity cannot be used in another at the same time. To illustrate, the clothing used to make uniforms cannot be used to make civilian apparel, and the labor used to build and repair our highway network cannot be used to build housing.

One possibility is to use all of the resources and technology to produce a maximum of a single good. All of the resources and technology could be used to produce public sector goods exclusively. Such a possibility is represented by point G in Figure 3-1. Notice that it lies on the vertical axis, which means that zero units of consumer sector goods are produced. It is also possible that all the resources and technology could be used just to produce consumer sector goods, shown as point C.

While the two either/or extremes are feasible, economic systems also can produce combinations of public and consumer sector goods that are maximums in the sense of efficiently using all resources and technology. That is, the either/or situations depicted by G and C do not represent all of the actual feasible resource allocation choices, assuming that resources can be shifted incrementally from one sector to another. For example, 80 percent of the labor force could be used to produce public sector goods, and the remaining 20 percent used to generate consumer sector goods.

The line connecting GC represents the maximum combinations that can be produced, given the shifting of fixed resources and technology within the economy. Such a line is called a **production possibility frontier**. Moving from G to C implies that resources that had been used entirely in the production of public sector goods are transferred gradually to the production of consumer sector goods. C represents the maximum that occurs when all the resources have been shifted.

Whenever two points are to be connected, the first inclination is to connect them with a straight line, as shown in Figure 3-1.[1] Every point on this straight line shows a maximum production combination, given the assumptions. Several important features of this line need to be identified. First, it represents a boundary, which is why it is called a frontier. The economy does not have the resources or technology to produce beyond the frontier, so a point such as A is not feasible. However, it is possible to be inside the frontier, as at point B. What can be said about the use of resources at B? This can be answered easily by comparing B to the feasible point D where more of both goods are produced. The only way that both B and D can be feasible is if some resources are idle at B. Any point, such as B inside the frontier, represents less than full employment combined production, or a recessionary period.

A production possibility frontier falls from left to right, or the line has a negative slope. This indicates that as long as the economy is on the frontier, production of public and consumer goods changes in opposite directions. What does this imply? If all of the resources are being used, along with the most efficient technologies, the only way to have more of one good is to have less of the other. That is, a **trade-off** must occur. The economy is faced with a problem of choice. However, a trade-off does not have to occur at a point like B, because more of both goods could be produced.

Another inference to be drawn stems from the manner in which the resources are transferred from one sector to the other. What is implied as resources are transferred from G to C? Figure 3-2 provides the analysis. Starting at the extreme of G, suppose the production of public sector goods decreases by the amount A. Resources can now be used to produce consumer sector goods. Point a shows the corresponding maximum combination of production that can result, and B on the horizontal scale measures the increase in consumer sector goods. Suppose the economy was operating at point b, and production of public sector goods is reduced again by the amount A. The release of resources allows the production of consumer sector goods to increase, so the maximum production point becomes c,

---

[1]   Other ways of connecting GC are discussed later in the chapter.

and B measures the increase. Finally, if the economy was at d, and production of public sector goods decreases by A, B measures the corresponding increase in consumer sector production.

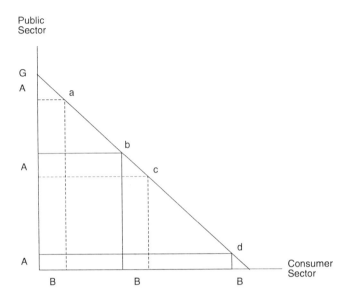

Figure 3-2: A Straight Line Production Possibility Frontier—Shifting Resources

An economy must decide where to use fixed resources. Although an economy can produce anywhere on its' frontier, points G, b, and d are considered. Let A denote the amount of the decrease in public sector production at each of the three points. The decreases release resources to be used in production by the consumer sector. Corresponding maximum increases lead to points a, c, and the horizontal intercept, and they are measured as B on the horizontal scale. Because the vertical changes are always the same, the horizontal changes can be compared directly. They all equal B. A straight line production possibility frontier implies that resources can be shifted in a uniform manner from one sector to another.

Because the changes in public sector production are always the same amount, A, the corresponding maximum changes in consumer sector production can be compared directly. The comparison reveals that all the increases, B, are identical. This is a direct consequence of the fact that the frontier was drawn as a straight line. Thus, resources can be shifted in a very uniform manner. In terms of production possibilities, production of one good can be transformed into production of another good at a uniform rate by shifting resources. The rate is constant everywhere on such a frontier.

Another way of connecting the either-or production extremes G and C is with the curve shown in Figure 3-3. This frontier is a more realistic representation of production possibilities. The economic interpretation of this alternative frontier can be outlined with the same analytical procedures used for the straight line case.[2]

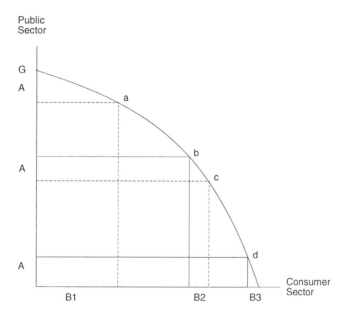

Figure 3-3: A Concave Production Possibility Frontier

As a frontier this curve also shows maximum combinations of goods and services that can be produced in the two sectors, given fixed resources and technology. It is a boundary line and reflects the trade-offs that must occur. This frontier implies that it becomes harder and harder to shift resources. As the economy moves down and to the right from point G, the same decrease in public sector goods, A, is associated with smaller and smaller increases in consumer sector goods (ie., B1>B2>B3).

The curve, which is concave to the origin, still is assumed to represent maximum combinations that can be produced given fixed technology and resources. Therefore, the curve depicts a boundary between what is and is not feasible. Unemployment occurs if actual production is inside the frontier. This frontier falls from left to right, so it is negatively sloped. A trade-off must occur when one moves along the frontier.

---

[2]   This is not a trivial point. Remarkably few tools are used to analyze choice, although they have wide applications. The key to understanding economics is to become familiar with these few tools and the ways in which they are used.

The important distinction between the concave and straight line frontiers has to do with the shifting of resources. Using the same approach as before, we derive a different result. Given the same change in production of public sector goods, A, the successive changes in the production of C become progressively smaller as one moves away from G (i.e., B1 > B2 > B3). Thus, it becomes harder and harder to move down and to the right along this frontier. Using the same procedure, but starting at the horizontal intercept, leads to the same conclusion that it becomes progressively harder to shift resources and technology from consumer production to public production.

Why should it become progressively harder to move in any direction along a concave production possibility frontier? The answer lies in a comparison of the most efficient input combinations. Suppose there are only two resources, capital and labor, and production in either sector uses both resources. However, the production of public sector goods is more labor intensive than for the consumer sector. That is, although capital (buildings, machinery, silicon chips, etc.) is used, labor is the relatively more important ingredient in the provision of public sector goods (e.g., police protection). Just the opposite holds for the consumer sector, or capital is relatively more important.

Return to G in Figure 3-3. If there is a decrease in the production by the amount A, some capital and labor can be shifted to produce consumer goods. What is the likely mix of capital and labor? Relatively more capital than labor would initially be available for the production of consumer goods. This means that consumer goods producers would obtain resources in a favorable proportion, so the increase , B1, is relatively large.

But what occurs if the economy is at d and the production of public sector goods decreases by the amount A? The last reduction also releases capital and labor to be used to produce consumer goods. But the mix contains relatively more labor than capital, as the public sector producers have tried to keep more of their relatively important input. This means that consumer sector producers receive the resources in a less favorable proportion, so the increase B3 is relatively small.

An argument that concave production possibility frontiers are better representations of technically feasible production than straight line frontiers can be developed. As long as different goods are to be produced, production technologies favor different mixes of the fixed resources. Otherwise, the same thing would be made. Frontiers that are concave to the origin reflect the difficulties in shifting resources. The difficulties are a direct consequence of the problem of obtaining resources in a desirable mix to produce different goods and services.

A change in the quantity of a resource has a very straightforward effect on the production possibility frontier. Increased resources allow the frontier to shift to the right, making it feasible to produce more. An increase in labor, for example, makes it possible to produce more goods in both sectors, but the effect is more pronounced for the production of public sector goods, assuming this sector is labor intensive. This is illustrated in Figure 3-4.

Changing technology also causes the frontier to shift. An increase in technology means that the same combination of inputs produces a larger output, so the frontier shifts away from the origin. Technological change can affect either capital or labor, For example, improved on-the-job training increases the efficiency of labor, so the same work force can produce more with the same capital. Figure 3-4 also reflects this type of change. Fixed resources and technology must be assumed in order to be able to draw a specific production possibility frontier.

Many economic problems can be understood with the aid of a production possibility frontier. The usefulness of the model stems from its representation of the economic problem of scarcity. Limited resources and technology impose limited production possibilities. If an economic system wants to be as efficient as possible and to provide as many goods and services as it can for its members, the objective is to stay on the frontier. Choices, or trade-offs, must be made concerning the mix of

Figure 3-4: A Production Possibility Frontier—Changing Resources & Technology

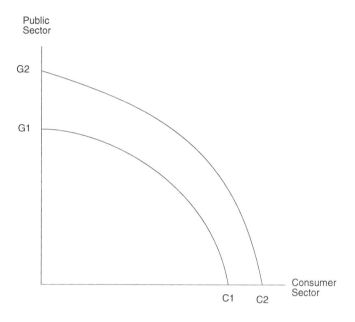

Changes in the amount of resources and technology available to an economy cause the frontier to shift. Consequently, in order to be able to draw any frontier, it is necessary to assume that resources and technology are fixed.

produced goods as long as the economy is on the frontier. The decision making includes policies that affect the position of the frontier. For example, the introduction of the information superhighway should enhance the productivity of capital and labor, thereby shifting the frontier further away from the origin.

Figure 3-5 portrays the choices associated with conservative views on the economic environment of the mid-1990s. The economy was operating fairly close to full employment, and an important debate was taking place regarding the extent of the influence of the government. The situation could be reduced to two composite goods: the public and private sectors. They are the axes in the figure. Conservatives argued the economy was over regulated, and decreasing governments' role would stimulate activity. Their contention was this would increase investment in new, more productive capital and increase technological change. These would shift the frontier outward to F2, and production would move toward b. Under this scenario, everyone would be better off.

Figure 3-5: An Application of the Production Possibility Frontier

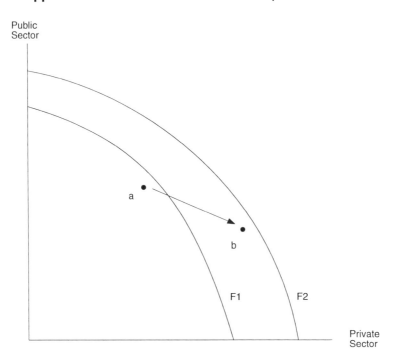

Suppose an economy's production is grouped into public and private sectors, and it is operating near full employment at point a on F1. If there is sufficient investment in productive plant and equipment, the labor force increases, and/or other resources become available, the curve shifts out to F2, allowing the economy to expand to b.

STUDY QUESTIONS

The Production Possibility Frontier

1. Why is it necessary to assume fixed resources and technology to construct a production possibility frontier?
2. How does a production possibility frontier reflect the problems of scarcity and choice facing an economy?
3. Why is the concave frontier in Figure 3-6 more realistic?
4. Regarding the analysis of the mid-1990s, how would you use the production possibility frontier to present a liberal perspective?
5. OPEC implemented an oil embargo in 1973. Use a production possibility frontier to outline the economic impact.

Figure 3-6

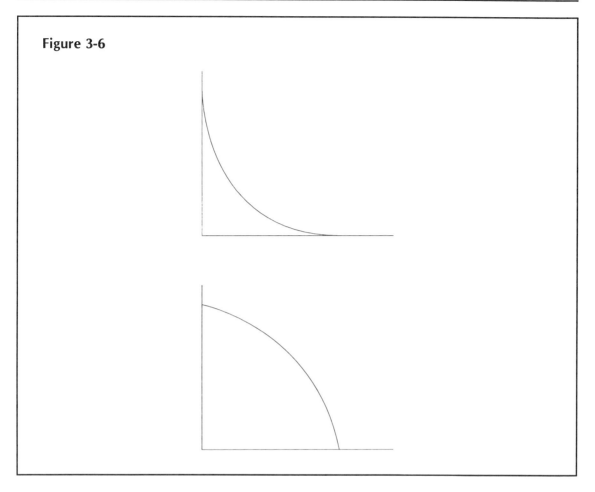

● Opportunity Cost ●

Unlimited wants constrained by scarce resources and technology create the basic economic concern for efficiency. Trade-offs, shown by the slope of the frontier, indicate that in order to have more of one good, there must be less of another, because resources have to be shifted. Alternative uses for scarce resources mean an economy must be concerned about the efficient utilization of the factors of production.

Economists have developed a concept to reflect the production opportunities foregone because of the current use of a resource. **Opportunity cost** is the value of a resource in its best alternative use. The cost stems from the loss in output that could have occurred from other production activities. A resource used in one sector could have been employed in many other areas. The concept of opportunity cost focuses on choosing the best, or most valued, of all the alternatives. If resources are being used in the most efficient way, then the value of the best alternative is less than or equal to the value in the current use. Otherwise, the resource should be transferred to where it is valued more highly.

Time allocation provides an excellent illustration of the opportunity cost concept. A college student is constantly confronted with choices in the uses of time. Studying for courses, attending classes, and fulfilling social and leisure needs are the major alternative uses of time. No matter how a student manages time, some opportunities are foregone. For example, the time spent studying cannot also be spent in recreational activity. The opportunity cost of the time spent in one activity, such as studying, is the value of that time in its best alternative use. If the student manages time efficiently, then this opportunity cost is less than or equal to the value of the time as allocated. Otherwise, the time should be reallocated to the better use.

Returning to the production possibility frontier, opportunity cost is reflected in the frontier's shape. A negative slope is interpreted as a trade-off among produced goods and services. In order to include opportunity cost, analysis centers on the resources themselves, as opposed to the resulting outputs. Straight line frontiers imply constant tradeoffs of produced goods. In terms of shifting resources, the opportunity cost never changes. A concave to the origin frontier on the other hand, implies that the trade-off becomes more difficult. This means that the opportunity cost rises as resources are transferred.

STUDY QUESTIONS

Opportunity Cost

6. Define opportunity cost. Distinguish between opportunity cost and the trade-off of a frontier. Also, identify the similarities.
7. Explain how opportunity cost enters into your allocation of time near the end of the quarter or semester versus during vacation.
8. What are some economic arguments for the government paying employers for the training of unskilled workers who receive public assistance?
9. Use the concept of opportunity cost to explain why presidential candidates spend so much of their time and energy in the big electoral states.

● The Law of Diminishing Returns ●

Production possibility frontiers focus on the effects of shifting all factors of production from one sector to another. Quite often in allocation decisions some of the inputs are varied while others remain fixed. For example, a common problem facing a manufacturer is that of determining how many people to employ in a factory of fixed size.

The **law of diminishing returns** states that as more of a variable factor of production is added to a fixed amount of another input, the changes in output must eventually get smaller, assuming no change in technology. A good way to understand the law is to use a numerical illustration. Suppose capital and labor are the factors of production. The amount of capital is assumed to be fixed at ten units, and the amount of labor can vary between zero and eight units.[3] Table 3-1 presents data

---

[3] The definition of a unit of capital or labor is arbitrary. It can vary from one situation to another. Examples for capital are the number of production lines, the number of hours of computer time, and so on. Examples for labor include hours, days, or weeks of work.

illustrating how various amounts of labor can be combined with the fixed amount of capital to produce the output. These changes are shown in columns 4 and 5. Labor always changes by one unit, but production changes vary. Since labor changes are constant, the changes in output can be compared directly.

Table 3-1: Illustration of the Law of Diminishing Returns

(1)	(2)	(3)	(4)	(5)	(6)
K	L	X	ΔK	ΔL	K/L
10	0	0			
10	1	10	1	10	10.00
10	2	40	1	30	5.00
10	3	80	1	40	3.33
10	4	115	1	35	2.50
10	5	145	1	30	2.00
10	6	170	1	25	1.80
10	7	190	1	20	1.43
10	8	205	1	15	1.25

K = capital, L = labor, X = production, and Δ = change.

The word "eventually" is a key part of the definition. It is not necessary that the changes in output decline from the outset. Rather, at some point the changes must decline. In Table 3-1, the decline begins when labor is increased beyond three units. This means that, in the illustration, the law of diminishing returns sets in with three units of labor.

Why is it reasonable to assume the existence of this law? The rationale is based on the changing proportions between a fixed input and a variable input. Initially, increasing the variable factor may cause one to approach a better combination. However, at some point the increases in the variable factor cause one to move away from a desirable combination. This is reflected in declining changes in output. Carried to the extreme, one can imagine that in the above illustration, labor could be increased to such an extent that, given fixed capital, output could fall because workers were getting in each others' way.

The argument for there being better combinations of a fixed and a variable factor is based on the amount of capital relative to the amount of labor. This is called the capital-labor ratio and is shown in column 6 of Table 3-1. At first the ratio is undefined, because labor has a value of zero. As the ten units of capital are spread over more and more labor, K/L falls from 10 to 1.25. Initially, the spreading out may be productive, but at some point continued dilution brings on diminishing returns.

STUDY QUESTIONS

The Law of Diminishing Returns

10. What is the law of diminishing returns?
11. Is the law realistic?
12. Why is the word "eventually" used in the definition of the law?
13. Given your response to question 9, how can the law be used to explain why presidential candidates do not spend all of their efforts in the few large states?

● Population Growth: An Application ●

One of the more interesting applications of the law of diminishing returns has to do with the economic analysis of population growth. A crucial determinant of population growth is food. Because land is essentially fixed, the law of diminishing returns should apply to food production. Thomas Malthus studied population growth and the ability of the population to feed itself during the early stages of the Industrial Revolution.[4] Data used in the analysis were provided by Benjamin Franklin. Malthus argued that although agricultural production tended to grow, the population tended to grow at a much more rapid rate.[5] Table 3-2 presents estimates of the world's population which illustrate how rapidly the population can grow.

Given the difference in growth potentials for the population and for food, how could a population feed itself? Malthus described an adjustment mechanism. It was based on the notion of a **subsistence wage**, which is defined as the minimum amount labor can be paid and still survive. Population growth was assumed to be a function of the wage, and the relationship was considered to be very straightforward. If wages were above the subsistence level, people had a good time and the population grew. A short period of time elapsed between the increase in the population and an increase in the labor force. Children at very young ages worked in mines, farms, and factories. The increase in the labor force tended to cause the wage rate to fall. When the wage rate fell below the subsistence level, then the population and the labor force declined. A decline in the labor force would cause the wage rate to rise, and the cycle would continue. In the long run, the best the population could expect would be to merely survive. This presented a very bleak picture for the future. The adjustment process was termed the **iron law of wages**.

An illustration of the iron law of wages is shown in Figure 3-7. Wage rates are measured on the vertical scale, and time is measured on the horizontal scale. The subsistence wage, ws, is a horizontal line, because it does not vary over time. According to the adjustment process, actual wages, wa, fluctuate around the subsistence wage, making a wave-like pattern centered on ws. On average, in the long run, the best labor can expect is to receive the subsistence wage.

---

[4]   Thomas R. Malthus, *An Essay on the Principle of Population and Summary View of the Principle of Population* (Baltimore: Penguin, 1970), originally published in 1798.

[5]   More precisely, Malthus argued that agricultural production increased at an arithmetic rate, whereas the population tended to grow at a geometric rate.

Table 3-2: History of Population Growth

Year	Estimated Population	Approximate Time (years) Required for the Population to Double
8000 B.C.		
1 A.D.	8 million	1500
1750 A.D.	300 million	1240
1800 A.D.	800 million	155
1850 A.D.	1.3 billion	132
1900 A.D.	1.7 billion	129
1950 A.D.	2.5 billion	90
1974 A.D.	3.9 billion	79
2000 A.D.	6.4 billion	36

Source: Ansley J. Coale, "The History of the Human Population," *Scientific American*, Vol. 231, No. 3(September, 1974), pp. 41-51.

Was Malthus right or wrong? Has the population remained at the subsistence level since 1798? Certainly, the developed countries have experienced dramatic increases in their standards of living, but the developing nations have not. Whether Malthus was right must be determined initially in reference to the law of diminishing returns. As long as technological change occurs, the condition for the imposition of the law does not hold. What has permitted the rise in the standard of living in the developed countries has been the dramatic change in the technology of agricultural production over time. Changes in the way food is grown, processed, and distributed have permitted such large increases in agricultural production that resources have been reallocated to production of other goods and services resulting in the rising standard of living. An indication of this is the fact that 73.7 percent of the U.S. Labor force was in agriculture in 1800 versus 2.7 percent in 1992.[6]

---

[6]   U.S. Bureau of the Census, *Historical Statistics of the United States: Colonial Times to 1970* (Washington, D. C.: Government Printing Office, 1975) and U.S. Bureau of Labor Statistics, *Monthly Labor Review* (February, 1995).

Figure 3-7: The Iron Law of Wages

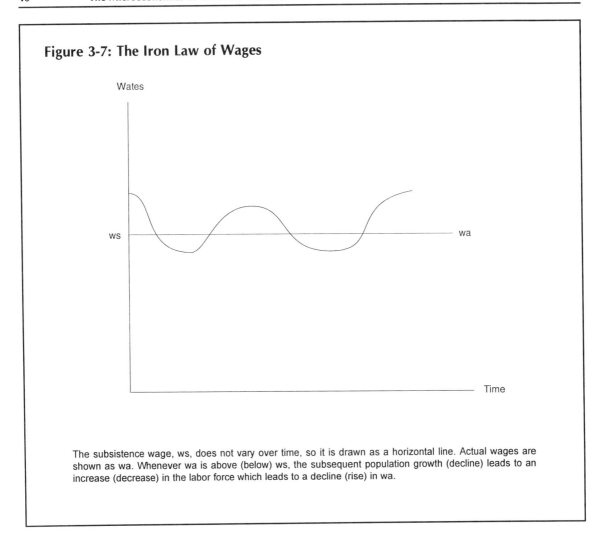

The subsistence wage, ws, does not vary over time, so it is drawn as a horizontal line. Actual wages are shown as wa. Whenever wa is above (below) ws, the subsequent population growth (decline) leads to an increase (decrease) in the labor force which leads to a decline (rise) in wa.

Figure 3-8 presents estimates of populations of developed and less developed countries. The less developed nations have experienced much more explosive growth. Typically, these countries have low standards of living, and their farming technologies have not kept pace with those of the rest of the world. The iron law of wages would seem to be applicable. Any increases in agricultural production generate increases in the population of less developed countries, so on a per-person basis there is no rise in the standard of living.

Figure 3-8 reveals a deficiency in the Malthusian theory. The theory does not explain why developed countries have experienced relatively low population growth along with a rising standard of living. A theory of population growth that is consistent with this phenomenon is outlined in Chapter 6. This alternative theory is based on a more complete evaluation of the economic pressures confronting consumer units.

Figure 3-8: Actual and Projected Population of Developing and Developed Countries, 1950-2020

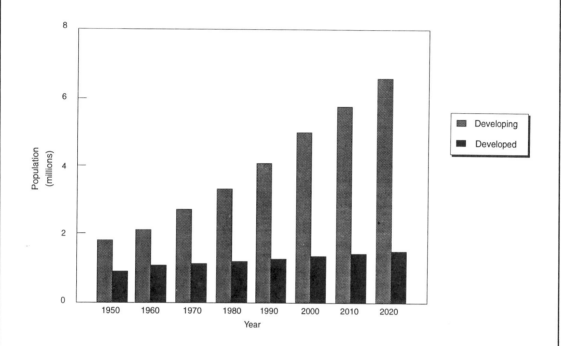

This figure shows the explosive potential of population growth. Developing countries, in particular, have experienced large increases in population, but their standards of living have remained very low. This is consistent with Malthus' iron law of wages. Developing countries, on the other hand, have experienced relatively small increases in their populations.

Source: U.S. Bureau of the Census, *World population Profile*: 1994. GPO, 1994.

STUDY QUESTIONS

Population Growth: An Application

14. Draw a production possibility frontier for agricultural production versus production of all other goods. What has happened to the frontier over time?
15. What is the iron law of wages?
16. Suppose the United States experiences no further increases in agricultural technology. What does Malthus's theory indicate the outcome would be in the long run?

● Summary ●

A production possibility frontier shows that there are limits to the production capability of an economy because resources and technology are fixed during a set period of time. As long as an economy is on the frontier, the problem of how to use resources arises. If actual production is inside the frontier, there is less than full employment. The straight line frontier implies that resources can be shifted uniformly from one sector to another, whereas the concave frontier implies that it becomes progressively harder to transfer resources. Changes in the level of resources and technology available to an economy cause a given production possibility frontier to shift.

Opportunity cost is the value of a resource in its best alternative use. Efficient use of resources requires the opportunity cost of a resource to be less than or equal to the value of that resource in its current use.

The law of diminishing returns asserts that changes in production must eventually decline whenever there is a least one fixed factor, there is no change in technology, and other factors of production are increased. Malthus's iron law of wages is an application of the law of diminishing returns.

● Key Words ●

Iron law of wages: Malthus's adjustment process through which population growth is constrained by food production.

Law of diminishing returns: adding more of a variable factor to fixed factors must eventually cause the change in output to decline, assuming there is no change in technology.

Opportunity cost: the value of a resource in its best alternative use.

Production possibility frontier: maximum combinations of goods and services that can be produced with fixed technology and resources.

Subsistence wage: the minimum amount labor can be paid and still survive.

Technology: a method for combining factors of production to produce goods and services.

Trade-off: a negative relationship in which more of one item can be acquired only if the amount of another is reduced.

Chapter 4

Basic Economics Applied to Consumer Units

Scarcity, trade-offs, opportunity cost, and money, introduced in the preceding chapters, comprise the economic foundation for analyzing consumer behavior. In this chapter we apply them to an examination of the activities of consumers in a market system. A closer look is given to the dual roles of buying and selling. The economic interpretation of money is used to develop a general definition of consumer satisfaction, and opportunity cost is found to play a pivotal role in the acquisition of income. Resource allocation decisions are related to the production possibility frontier and opportunity cost.

● Dual Roles of a Consumer Unit: Buyer and Seller ●

The circular flow diagram, presented in Chapter 2, indicates how the two basic groups, consumers and producers, interact in a market system. The diagram clearly portrays the dual economic functions of buying and selling. The relationship between the final goods market and the consumer is only one of the elements in the consumer half of that diagram. Granted, a large part of consumer activity is directed toward purchase decisions. But what determines the ability to purchase in the final goods market? The answer, of course, is that, in an economy with a monetary system, money must be earned in the factor market. That is, the consumer unit must make decisions about the allocation of resources, such as time and labor, as well as decisions about how to spend.

Consumer decisions are assumed to be guided by one primary objective—to be as well off as possible given constraints on the ability to operate in a market system. The circular flow diagram identifies the general setting in which a consumer unit operates. Behavior affecting the allocation of resources and income generation in the factor market is related to expenditures in the final goods market and the unit's well being. Purposeful, rational decision making is assumed to be reflected in all economic behavior of a consumer unit.

On the one hand, the circular flow diagram presents a simplified overview of the economic roles of households. On the other hand, the diagram points out the complexity of decision making. The activities of a consumer unit mirror those of a business. Resource allocation decisions are not independent of purchase decisions. Both are considered as a consumer unit attempts to make itself as well off as possible.

Traditionally, economists have emphasized the expenditure role of consumer activity. Attention focused on the consumers' decisions to spend limited incomes on various market goods. These market goods were assumed to have a direct effect on the well-being of the household. The decision to work (i.e., supply of labor) tended to be viewed on an aggregate basis, rather than as a collection of individual consumer units' decisions to allocate members' time to work in the factor market. During the 1960s, economists began to focus attention on the economic decision making within the household.[1] Theoretical models and data bases for their empirical testing started to emerge. Consumer

---

[1] The seminal paper is by Gary S. Becker, "A Theory of the Allocation of Time," *Economic Journal* LXXV(1965): 493-517.

economics evolved as a separate field of study within economics, focusing on the entire spectrum of the dual roles.

The various aspects of consumer economic behavior are discussed throughout the remainder of this book. When you study these topics, it is helpful to remember the dual economic roles and to identify which aspect is being examined. This enables you to see how the various parts are related. Initially, this book focuses on the ways in which consumers operate in the two markets, in order to provide the basis for understanding how decisions to maximize well-being ought to be made. Comparison of actual market situations with the optimal conditions points out those areas where consumers need assistance and permits an evaluation of proposed remedies.

An added insight of the circular flow diagram is it shows consumer issues or problems have implications for other aspects of the economic behavior of households. For example, there are economic reasons for setting product standards for consumer goods and for requiring product labels.[2] If higher standards or product labels raise prices, however, then economic evaluations should include the effects these price increases would have on purchase decisions in the final goods market and secondary impacts in the factor market.

STUDY QUESTIONS

Dual Roles of a Consumer Unit: Buyer and Seller

1. Identify the resource allocation decisions you can recall while growing up.
2. How have your resource allocation decisions changed while in college versus when in high school?
3. Why is it important to have an overview of the dual roles of consumer units?

● Utility and Income ●

The economic problem of scarcity coupled with unlimited wants results in opportunity cost playing a central role in decision making. Observed consumer behavior (actual purchase and resource allocation decisions) is considered to be the result of systematic selection among alternatives. What is the basic motivation of the consumer? A consumer attempts to maximize **utility**, which is defined as the satisfaction derived by a consumer through the use of goods and services.

A consumer's problem is more involved than just maximizing utility. The consumer must also deal with constraints. For example, the acquisition of market goods and services is limited by the household's purchasing power. Time is also a limiting factor. Current services derived from durables are determined to a large extent by past purchases. Market imperfections and inertia limit consumer choice. Legal and social considerations also limit the range of options. Each of these constraints is recognized at various places in the text. For instance, Chapter 7 covers the limited purchasing power of a consumer. Time is introduced in Chapter 11 and Part V.

---

[2]   · Chapter 11 covers one reason.

Before utility maximizing behavior can be discussed, it is necessary to distinguish among money, income, and utility. An understanding of the interrelationships among these three factors enhances one's appreciation of the economic pressures on the consumer. A clear conceptual distinction exists between money and utility. Money is anything that meets the three conditions identified in Chapter 2. Consumers value money because it serves as a means of acquiring the things desired in the marketplace. Utility, on the other hand, is defined as a consumer's satisfaction. Money is used by consumers to buy goods and services, but the goods and services produce utility, not money.

The way in which a monetary system facilitates the exchange process sometimes blurs the distinctions between income and utility. Many people equate utility with a consumer's income, or salary plus interest, dividends, and rent. Such a definition of utility is incorrect because it is not consistent with the function of money. Utility is not measured in dollars. Income is related to utility by the flow of satisfaction a consumer receives from the use of marketplace goods and services bought with money.

This is a subtle but key point. Anyone would undoubtedly conclude that a consumer is better off with a $40,000 after-tax income than with a $35,000 after-tax income. But why is the family better off? The extra $5,000 itself does not increase utility, but it does represent control over $5,000 more goods and services. Thus, a consumer's income provides a means of using the goods and services that generate utility.

Utility can be divided into five specific areas. This separation leads to a more complete description of the economic environment in which consumers operate. Once the types have been identified, the trade-offs involved in consumer resource allocation can be understood, and the opportunity costs of the alternatives can be examined.

Market utility is the utility derived from goods and services purchased in the final goods market. How does the household obtain this utility? The only legitimate way is to purchase the goods and services with money. How is the money obtained? A consumer unit must sell its resources in the factor market and, in turn, receive payment in the form of money. The total of the market income from sources such as wages, dividends, royalties, rent, and borrowing comprises the consumer's market income which can be used to buy goods and services that generate satisfaction. It is very useful to keep in mind the distinction among money, income, and market utility.

Home production utility is the satisfaction derived from the use of commodities produced directly by the consumer unit. Examples are meal preparation, cleaning, yardwork, and transportation. Historically, home production utility has been the largest component of total utility. However, as the economy has developed, more and more consumer goods have become available in the marketplace, replacing much of the home production.

Leisure-recreational utility is the utility derived from leisure time. Everyone enjoys weekends, holidays, and time away from the marketplace and home production work. The time allocated to such activities can contribute significantly to one's utility. Leisure-recreational utility is becoming an increasingly important component of total utility as the work week shortens and less time is required for home production activities.

External utility is the satisfaction derived from goods and services provided indirectly to the consumer. These are goods and services that a consumer can use without being required to purchase them directly or to produce them at home. Many are provided by the public sector, which uses its resources for goods and services such as parks, police and fire protection, and cultural activities. However, external utility may have negative features, as in the case of pollution. The production activities of businesses and households, for example, can have detrimental effects on air and water quality. The use of fireplaces and wood stoves for heat has resulted in a decline in air quality in many areas during the winter—even for those residents who do not use this fuel.

The fifth type of utility is called **nonresource allocation utility**. All of the preceding sources of consumer satisfaction involved the allocation of scarce resources in order to generate utility. But there are ways of generating utility that do not necessarily entail resource allocation. Two examples are health and friendship. Both can be enjoyed with or without the allocation of resources.

Consumer decision making, within the context of a mixed market system can be viewed much more clearly given this division of utility. The objective is to maximize utility subject to constraints imposed on consumer behavior. The dual roles of consumers focus on decisions pertaining to the generation of market utility. But time spent in market work cannot be used to produce other types of utility. Consequently, trade-offs are involved, and the consumer must choose among them. Limited resources, such as money and time, have alternative uses with respect to the various avenues for generating utility. Opportunity cost plays a pivotal role in the decision making, as the consumer unit attempts to answer the three economic questions to maximize utility.

STUDY QUESTIONS

Utility and Income

4.   Distinguish between money and income and income and utility.
5.   Referring back to question 1 in this chapter, categorize the resource allocation decisions your family has had according to the five-part division of utility.
6.   How is opportunity cost related to money, income, and utility?
7.   Identify some social and legal constraints on consumer economic behavior.
8.   Data from consumer expenditure surveys indicate that the share of disposable income spent on food at home declined from 16 percent in 1960 to 8.6 percent in 1991. How can opportunity cost and the types of utility be used to explain this trend?

● A Production Possibility Frontier for Consumers ●

Now that the key economic principles and the basic economic objectives of a household have been covered, let us apply this knowledge to an analysis of the economic behavior of consumers in a market system. A consumer unit has a limited amount of labor that can be used to generate the various types of utility. Skills of the unit's members, their market wages, and the time spent working in the factor market determine the earned income of the unit. Because these limited resources have alternative uses, people must consider the opportunity costs of various courses of action. The economic problem of scarcity means that a household needs to answer the three economic questions.

What to produce? Consumers must be concerned with the allocation of time among the activities to generate the types of income. For example, should a wife engage in production at home or should a she work in the factor market? The latter would permit the household to have a higher market utility, but less home-produced utility. Hence, opportunity cost is involved. What to produce? The question also involves decisions about today versus tomorrow. Not spending all of the money income permits saving and investing for tomorrow. Consumer units could decide to improve the marketable skills of members through more education, which would involve using some of the money income and certainly would reduce the time available for producing other types of utility.

How to produce? After a household has determined what it wants, decisions must be made about how to produce the desired items. If the household wants transportation service from a new automobile, this item must be acquired in the final goods market, and a key part of the choice centers on alternatives for having the money to acquire the vehicle. A consumer unit may decide to have one of its members repair and maintain the automobile, as opposed to having the work done at a garage. The latter primarily entails spending money, whereas the former involves spending less money but using more time. Which alternative is chosen depends on the opportunity costs. Another example is if the consumer unit wants to obtain a college education for one of its members, how is the education to be financed and which higher educational institution will be attended?

Who uses the goods and services? The question of distribution within a consumer unit involves more than just market goods. Home-produced commodities must be distributed among household members as well. Within-household distribution has been studied primarily by behavior-oriented researchers rather than economists. The reason why economists have not devoted much attention to it is that the traditional economic tools are not well suited for this analysis. Once a consumer unit has determined the goods it wants, has decided how to produce them, and has acquired them, most of the economic decision making has occurred. Distribution is very difficult to analyze. It involves motivations of individuals within groups and considers the trade-offs associated with the gains and losses of continuing as a unit. Analysis is complicated further by these decisions having long-run impacts and by the unobservable (nonmarket) nature of the outcomes.[3]

Home production decisions are determined, in part, by the technology available to the consumer unit. Depending on the appliances and other market goods that have been acquired, different methods of production are available to different households. Microwave ovens provide one technology for meal production, convection ovens another. Over time, there is technological change in household production. New appliances and consumer goods are developed that alter the manner in which home production occurs. But during a fixed period of time, it is reasonable to assume that the technologies available to the consumer unit are limited. The technology for preparing evening meals is fixed. However, over the longer run, the technology has changed dramatically. Schur estimates that 65 years ago it took approximately two and one-half hours to prepare dinner, 45 years ago one hour, 25 years ago 30 minutes, and 5 years ago 15 minutes.[4]

Constrained by fixed resources and fixed technology during a period of time, a household must decide how to maximize utility given the feasible alternatives. The situation is analogous to that of the economy as a whole. In Chapter 3, a production possibility frontier was used to depict the problem of choice that an economy must address. Every point on a frontier represents a maximum combination of goods that an economy could produce. A similar situation applies to the consumer unit. There are many ways in which utility could be produced, and the production possibility frontier is a convenient way of conceptualizing the consumer unit's production choices.

The setting for a consumer unit's production possibility frontier is presented below, and a more complete analysis is found in Chapter 10. Assume there are two goods that the consumer unit can produce: food and clothing. All of the unit's fixed resources and technology could be directed toward

---

3   A recent survey of this literature is found in Robert A. Pollak, "A Transaction Cost Approach to Families and Households," *Journal of Economic Literature* 23(June, 1985):581-608.

4   Sylvia Schur, "Revolution in the Kitchen," *Marketing Insights* (September, 1989).

producing a maximum amount of either commodity alone. These are shown as the intercepts F1 and C1 in Figure 4-1. A concave production possibility frontier is drawn, showing maximum combinations of food and clothing that could be produced. Limited resources and technology establish the boundary between what the unit can and cannot produce. The negatively sloped curve shows that trade-offs are involved, and the concavity implies increased difficulty in shifting resources. If actual production is a point inside the frontier, the family is not using its resources efficiently and/or the best production technology.

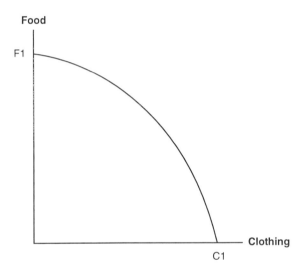

Figure 4-1: A Household Production Possibility Frontier

For a given period of time, a consumer unit is constrained by limited resources with alternative uses (e.g., labor) and fixed technologies (e.g., type of oven). Assume food, F, and clothing, C, are the two home produced goods. F1 and C1 represent the maximum amounts of each good that can be produced by the unit. The production possibility frontier involves reallocating resources from one activity to another. The negative slope implies a trade-off occurs, and the concavity indicates that it becomes harder and harder to shift resources.

A good example of the economic approach to the study of consumer units is provided by Lazear and Michael.[5] Their research centers on the decision of a family to be a **dual working family**, in which both spouses generate income. There are trade-offs involved with this choice. While a larger market

---

[5]   Edward P. Lazear and Robert t. Michael, "Real Income Equivalence Among One-Earner and Two-Earner Families," *American Economic Review* 70(May, 1980):203-8.

utility is obtained, the opportunity cost is the loss in home production utility. Consequently, the mix of market consumption and home production is different for a dual working family and a single-earner family.

Three differences in the generation of utility are identified for the two types of families. They are income taxes paid, employment costs, and household production. The 1972-73 Consumer Expenditure Survey was used to compare single- and dual-earner couples with no children. Some of the differences found are as follows. Two-earner couples on average had a 35 percent higher before-tax income, though the after-tax difference was reduced to 25 percent. As an indication of employment cost differences, women's clothing expenditure was 60 percent higher for two-earner couples, and this type of family spent 51 percent more on transportation vehicles. Home production differences were indicated by the fact that single-earner couples spent 15 percent more on food at home and dual earners spent 55 percent more on restaurants and 42 percent more on dry cleaning.

These comparisons reveal that one- and two-earner couples have chosen different paths for utility maximization. The two-earner couple has less time for the generation of home production but a higher income to acquire marketplace utility. In single-earner situations, one spouse can prepare meals at home, has fewer clothing needs, and can spend more time doing the laundry. These results support the contention that dual-earner households must substitute market utility for home production utility. Thus although two-earner families have higher incomes, they also incur higher expenses. Lazear and Michael estimate that for the 1972-73 period every $100 spent by a two-earner couple was the equivalent of $77 for the single-earner couple.

STUDY QUESTIONS

A Production Possibility Frontier for Consumers

9. Identify some common economic factors between an economy and a consumer unit in terms of how to produce.
10. How does technological change, such as development of the microwave oven, affect household production possibilities?
11. What is the effect on a production possibility frontier of increases in family size, especially the addition of older children and adults?

● Summary ●

Economic principles outlined in the first three chapters have been applied to consumer behavior. The dual roles of a consumer unit involve the allocation of resources to the factor market to generate income and the use of the income in the final goods market to acquire desired goods and services. The unit can generate utility via avenues other than market goods. Consumer decision making involves utility maximization subject to constraints such as income and time. Limited resources must be allocated among the alternative ways of producing utility; the opportunity costs of these allocation decisions are crucial. If resources and technology during a specified period of time are fixed, a consumer's resource allocation choices can be represented by a production possibility frontier.

● Key Words ●

Dual working family: a family in which more than one person generates marketplace income.
External utility: utility derived from activity external to the consumer.
Home production utility: utility from commodities that are produced by the consumer.
Leisure-recreational utility: utility from leisure and recreational activities.
Market utility: utility from marketplace goods and services.
Nonresource allocation utility: utility from activities that do not always require resource allocation.
Utility: the satisfaction derived by a consumer.

Chapter 5

An Overview of the Recent History of U.S. Consumer Units

Recent demographic changes in households and families (the major components of consumer units) have received a great deal of attention in the media. An example is the perceived decline in family values which some people argue is reflected in the rise in the divorce rate and the rise in mothers working outside the home. However, the media tends to emphasize changes that can be dramatized easily. More importantly, are the changes temporary and do they reflect choices that make consumers as well off as possible? Answers to the questions can be provided in two parts. The first is to realize how consumer units have changed. The second is to construct a decision making framework that is explains the observed behavior.

This chapter is a descriptive one intended to familiarize readers with what has happened over an extended period to the typical consumer unit. The focus is not on the life cycle changes of a single unit as it goes through the aging process, but rather, on the long-term changes in the typical consumer unit. Some of the information is well known, and some of it is more arcane. Do not become lost in the data as they are presented just to show what, in fact, has taken place. There is no need to memorize any numbers or exact patterns of the various series. Instead, attention should be directed toward ways in which households and families have changed over time.

One important point at the heart of an economic analysis of the consumer unit is the fact that decisions about marriage, divorce, procreation, division of labor, as well as what to buy are all primarily voluntary decisions. Economic concepts, such as the separation of total utility into its components and opportunity cost, can be used to examine the decision making, and thereby provide an explanation of the observed trends.

● Some Characteristics of the Population ●

Gloom and doom analyses of families have received a great deal of coverage in the media. While there is cause to be concerned about the viability of the U.S. Family, Table 5-1 presents some interesting data on family formation and dissolution over time. Notice that the percentages of males and females married rose between 1950 and 1970 and then declined slightly through 1990. On a percentage basis, more males are married because there are fewer males than females in the population. Marriage rates also have remained relatively constant over this extended period.

Much of the adverse publicity about the future of the U.S. Family is based on an analysis of divorce. Table 5-1 shows that since 1920, the divorce rate has risen nearly three fold. The rise was most pronounced during the 1970s. Altogether, the data in the table suggest people are trying out marriage as much as ever, but they are also giving up on marriage more frequently today than in past decades, although a plateau may have been reached. With respect to marriage dissolution, Hernandez found that the proportion of families with children maintained by a single parent more than doubled between 1970 and 1990, rising from 11 to 24 percent.[1]

Table 5-1: Some Family Formation Data, 1920 to 1990, Selected Years

Year	Marriage Rate	Divorce Rate	Percent Males Married	Percent Females Married	Median Age at First Marriage	
					Male	Female
1920	12.0	8.0	NA	NA	24.6	21.2
1930	9.8	7.5	NA	NA	24.3	21.3
1940	12.1	8.8	NA	NA	24.3	21.5
1950	11.1	10.3	68.0	66.1	22.8	20.3
1960	8.5	9.2	69.1	65.6	22.8	20.3
1970	10.6	14.9	75.3	68.5	23.2	20.8
1989	10.6	22.8	69.2	63.5	24.6	22.1
1990	9.8	20.7	64.3	59.7	26.1	23.9

NA = not available. Marriage rates are per 1,000 population. Divorce rates are per 1,000 females. Percents married are for the respective population subgroup over 18 years old.

Source: U.S. Bureau of the Census, *Historical Statistics of the United States: Colonial Times to 1970*, Part I (GPO, 1975) and U.S. Bureau of the Census, *Statistical Abstract of the United States, 1992* (GPO, 1992).

Data for the median age at first marriage have a U-shaped pattern. From 1920 to 1960, the age fell for both sexes. By 1970 men and women typically married at a slightly older age. Since 1970 the tendency to postpone marriage has increased for men and women, as indicated by the rising median age at first marriage.

Fertility rate data over an extended period of time establish a basis for arguing that birth control had been practiced well before the advent of "the pill." Inspection of the series provides some indication that economic considerations have had an important role to play. Figure 5-1 displays birth and death rates for the period 1860-1990. Both declined by more than 50 percent of their 1860 levels. The death rate fell from 18.7 in 1860 to 8.6 in 1990, and the birth rate declined from 44.3 in 1860 to 16.8 in 1990. The former is an indication of increased longevity and improved health care. The decline in fertility may be more surprising to some readers. Notice that not only has the there been a long-run decline in the birth rate, but there is a visible dip for 1930 when the last great depression was underway. Following World War II, fertility rates increased until the late 1950s, then they

---

[1]   Donald J. Hernandez, *When Households Continue, Discontinue, and Form*, U.S. Bureau of the Census, Current Population Reports, Series P23-179, (GPO, 1992).

declined to 1980 and rose slightly to 1990. Detailed studies of birth records in Western Europe from medieval times to 1700 have produced results that are consistent with the pattern shown here.[2]

These data are compatible with Malthus's iron law of wages, outlined in Chapter 3. During periods of rising real wages, the population tends to grow. During periods of poor economic performance, when real wages fall, so does the birth rate.

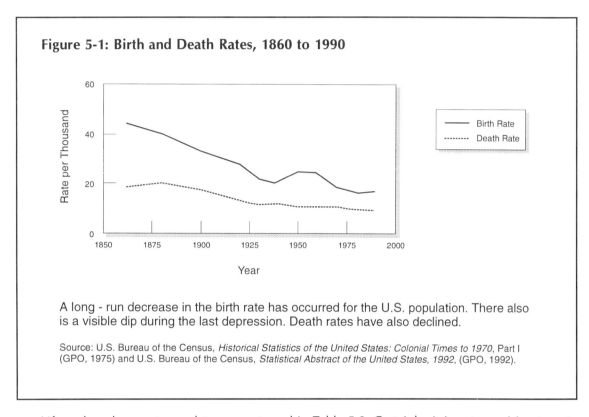

Figure 5-1: Birth and Death Rates, 1860 to 1990

A long - run decrease in the birth rate has occurred for the U.S. population. There also is a visible dip during the last depression. Death rates have also declined.

Source: U.S. Bureau of the Census, *Historical Statistics of the United States: Colonial Times to 1970*, Part I (GPO, 1975) and U.S. Bureau of the Census, *Statistical Abstract of the United States, 1992*, (GPO, 1992).

Life and work expectancy data are portrayed in Table 5-2. Certainly, it is not surprising to note that both have increased since 1900 for males and females. The increased life expectancy has permitted an increase in the nonwork life as well as the work life of both sexes. Of particular note is the increase in women's work life as a percentage of men's, shown in the bottom row of the table. Not only are women living longer and having more time for both market and home production activities, but they are also increasing their market work activities relative to men.

Educational attainment, shown in Figure 5-2, has been rising over time. Males and females are staying in school longer. On a percentage basis more females graduated from high school, but proportionately more males have graduated from college. Since 1960 the proportions completing college have risen more rapidly than during earlier decades.

A very important relationship exists between market employment and education. The higher the educational attainment, the more likely it is that the person is employed. As discussed in Chapter 2,

---

[2]   T. Paul Schultz, *Economics of Population* (Reading, MA: Addison-Wesley, 1981).

Table 5-2: Life and Work Expectancy at Birth by Sex, 1990 to 1970, Selected Years

Men	1900	1940	1950	1970	1990
Life Expectancy	48.2	61.2	65.5	67.1	72.7
Work Expectancy	32.1	38.1	41.5	40.1	44.4
Nonwork Expectancy	16.1	23.1	24.0	27.0	28.3
Women					
Life Expectancy	50.7	65.7	71.0	74.8	79.4
Work Expectancy	6.3	12.1	15.1	22.9	30.0
Nonwork Expectancy	44.4	53.6	55.9	51.9	49.4
Women's Worklife as a Percentage of Men's	19.6	31.6	36.3	57.1	67.6

Note: 1990 work and nonwork data are estimates.

Source: U.S. National Center for Health Statistics, *Vital Statistics of the United States*, selected issues.

Figure 5-2: Educational Attainment of Men and Women, 1910 to 1990

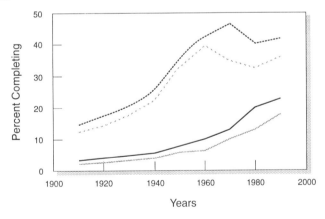
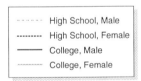

Educational attainment of both sexes is rising. Proportionately more men and women are going on to college and graduating.

Source: John K. Folger and Charles B. Nam, *Education of the American Population*, U.S. Bureau of the Census 1960 monograph (GPO 1967) Table V-5; U.S. Bureau of the Census, *Statistical Abstract of the United States*, 1981, (GPO, 1981); and Robert Kominski and Andrea Adams, *Educational Attainment in the United States: March 1993 and 1992*, U.S. Bureau of the Census Current Population Reports P20 - 476, (GPO, 1994).

the labor force is defined as those who are 16 and older and are working or actively looking for a job. The labor force, consequently, is a subset of the population over 16 years of age. A **labor force participation rate** is the ratio of the labor force to the population, usually the civilian population. Labor force participation rates can be computed for any group within the population (e.g., women who are 25 and older). All that is required is that the labor force and the population data reflect the common demographic unit.

Figure 5-3a presents the labor force participation rates of people who are at least 25 years old by age, sex, and educational attainment for the last two decades. For both sexes, labor force participation increases with education. Notice that for those with less than four years of high school, the participation rates have declined, and that men's declined by larger percents. The other three levels of educational attainment show opposite trends for men versus women: men's decreased while women's increased.

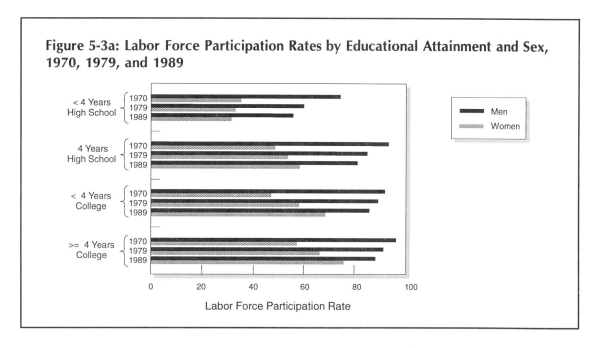

Figure 5-3a: Labor Force Participation Rates by Educational Attainment and Sex, 1970, 1979, and 1989

Inspection of unemployment rate data by sex and educational attainment (Figure 5-3b) provides additional evidence of relationships among employment, education, and sex. Since the labor force contains the unemployed as well as the employed, a complete analysis should include the patterns of unemployment rates on the basis of education and sex. The importance of education in finding and holding a job is seen in the unemployment rates. Not only do the rates fall with higher education, but comparing the rates for the three years reveals a differential impact of the basis of education. People with lower educational attainment fared worse in each successive year.

Not only are women staying in school longer, but the types of degrees earned beyond high school have changed substantially. Figures 5-4 provide some documentation in this regard. Panel a shows that aside from the education, foreign language, and health sciences, where women earned more than half the bachelor's degrees awarded, there have been very large increases in the shares going to women. This pattern also holds for masters degrees, panel b, Doctoral degrees, panel c, and

Figure 5-3b: Unemployment Rates by Educational Attainment and Sex, 1970, 1979, and 1989.

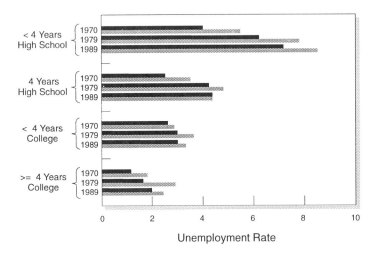

Labor force participation rates increased with educational attainment. Over the period men's rates declined slightly within each level of education, whereas women's increased with the exception of not completing high school.

Source: U.S. Bureau of Labor Statistics, Educational Attainment of Workers, March 1979, Special Labor Report 240 (January 1981) and U.S. Department of Labor, *1993 Handbook on Women Workers: Trends and Issues,(GPO 1994)*.

professional degrees, panel d. These data suggest that women are seeking educations that have greater marketplace employment opportunities than in the past.

STUDY QUESTIONS

Some Characteristics of the Population

1.   Can you think of any explanations for the observed pattern of birth rates?
2.   Why should the iron law of wages apply to the period from roughly 1200 to 1700 A. D. in Western Europe?
3.   What explanations can you give for education and employment being related?
4.   What does Figure 5-3 indicate about the importance of education with respect to market work?

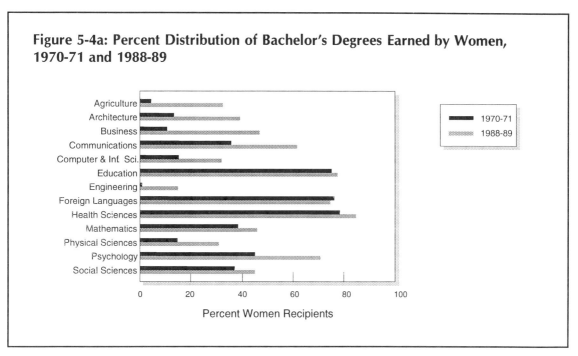

Figure 5-4a: Percent Distribution of Bachelor's Degrees Earned by Women, 1970-71 and 1988-89

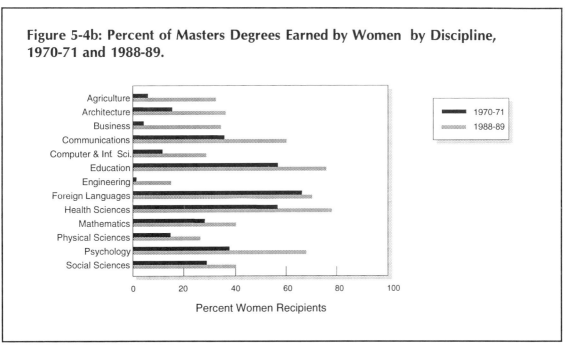

Figure 5-4b: Percent of Masters Degrees Earned by Women by Discipline, 1970-71 and 1988-89.

Figure 5-4c: Percent Distribution of Doctoral Degrees Earned by Women, 1970-71 and 1988-89.

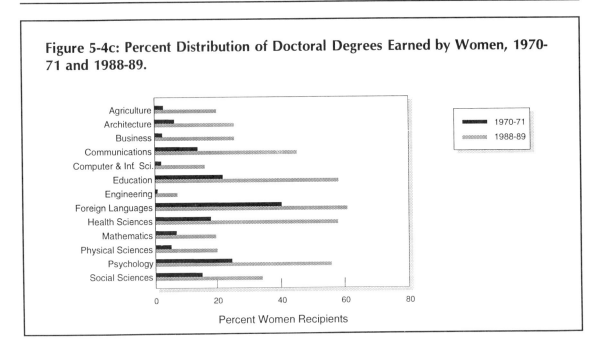

Percent Women Recipients

Figure 5-4d: Percent Distribution of Professional Degrees Earned by Women, 1970-71 and 1988-89.

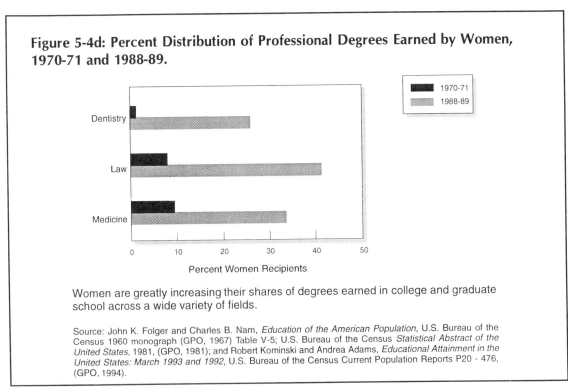

Percent Women Recipients

Women are greatly increasing their shares of degrees earned in college and graduate school across a wide variety of fields.

Source: John K. Folger and Charles B. Nam, *Education of the American Population*, U.S. Bureau of the Census 1960 monograph (GPO, 1967) Table V-5; U.S. Bureau of the Census *Statistical Abstract of the United States, 1981*, (GPO, 1981); and Robert Kominski and Andrea Adams, *Educational Attainment in the United States: March 1993 and 1992*, U.S. Bureau of the Census Current Population Reports P20 - 476, (GPO, 1994).

● Family Characteristics ●

The decline in family formation is reflected in Table 5-3. The percents of males and females never marrying during the 20-34 age span has risen dramatically. Another way of expressing this trend is to consider the percentages of all men and all women, regardless of age, who had never married. In 1970, 18.9 percent of males aged 18 and over had never married and the percent for females was13.7. These percents had risen to 23.6 and 18.6, respectively, in 1993.[3] This indicates that relatively more people are not marrying, but at the same time approximately four out of five people try marriage at least once during their lifetimes.

What can be said about the typical marriage? Demographers, sociologists, and family studies of researchers have identified the following traits.[4] Most marriages are between partners of the same race. Spouses tend to be of the same socioeconomic standing. Such observations are consistent with the notion that people marry persons they have met in the course of educational, business, and social activities. In the next chapter an economic view of the decision to marry is presented. That approach

Table 5-3: Percent Never Married by Age and Sex, 1960-1993, Selected Years

Women	1960	1970	1980	1993
20-24	28.4	35.8	50.2	66.8
25-29	10.5	10.5	20.9	33.1
30-34	6.9	6.2	9.5	19.3
Men				
20-24	53.1	54.7	68.0	81.0
25-29	20.8	19.1	33.1	48.4
30-34	11.9	9.4	15.9	30.1

Source: Arlene F.Saluter, *Marital Status and Living Arrangements, March 1993.* U.S. Bureau of the Census Current Population Reports, Series P20-478, (GPO, 1994).

assumes that marriage is primarily a voluntary act. Potential spouses marry within the context of a utility maximizing framework. But before this is developed, it is useful to become acquainted with some additional characteristics of families.

As the population has grown, so has the number of households and the number of families. But the size of the typical household and family has declined, causing a change in the distribution of

---

[3]   Arlene Saluter, *Marital Status and Living Arrangements, March, 1993,* U.S. Bureau of the Census, Current Population Reports, series P20-478, (GPO, 1994).

[4]   For example, Alan Kerchoff, "Patterns of Marriage and Family Formation and Dissolution," *Selected Aspects of Consumer Behavior,* prepared for the National Science Foundation Directorate for Research Applications (GPO: 1977).

household size. Table 5-4 provides these data. Since 1790, the average size of a household has fallen by more than half, from 5.79 to 2.63. The most pronounced changes were at the extremes. Households having seven or more members comprised 35.8 percent of all households in 1790, but only 1.3 percent in 1990. One-person and two-person households, on the other hand, have increased their proportions of the distribution during this period. The proportion of children living with a lone parent doubled between 1970 and 1990, reaching 25 percent (not shown in the table).[5]

Table 5-4: Household and Family Size 1790 to 1990, Selected Years

Year	Number of Households	Average Size	Percent Distribution by Household Size							Average Size of Family
			1	2	3	4	5	6	7	
1790	558	5.79	3.7	7.8	11.7	13.8	13.9	23.0	35.8	NA
1890	12960	4.93	3.6	13.2	16.7	16.8	15.1	11.6	23.8	NA
1900	15964	4.76	5.1	15.0	17.6	16.9	14.2	10.9	20.4	NA
1930	29905	4.11	7.9	23.4	20.8	17.5	12.0	7.6	10.9	NA
1940	34949	3.67	7.1	24.8	22.4	18.1	11.5	6.8	9.3	3.67
1950	43468	3.37	10.9	28.8	22.6	17.8	10.0	5.1	4.9	3.54
1960	52610	3.33	13.1	27.8	18.9	17.6	11.5	5.7	5.4	3.67
1970	62874	3.14	17.0	28.8	17.3	15.8	10.4	5.6	5.1	3.58
1980	79108	2.75	22.5	31.3	17.5	18.8	7.6	3.2	2.2	3.28
1990	93347	2.63	24.5	32.3	17.5	15.5	6.6	2.3	1.3	3.16

NA = not available.   Households are in thousands.

Source: U.S. Bureau of the Census, *Historical Statistics of the United States: Colonial Times to 1970*, Part I (GPO,1975); and U.S. Bureau of the Census, *Statistical Abstract of the United States, 1994* (GPO, 1994).

There are several noneconomic reasons for the changes. One is the decline in the extended family. Generations of the same family typically do not live together as they did in the past. A closely related factor is the increased mobility of the population, which has tended to split up generations of the same family. Another is the increased social acceptance of divorce. Other factors are a rise in the single life-style, an increase in single parenting, longer life span, and an increase in childless marriages.

More data on family size are displayed in Table 5-5. We have seen that birth rates tend to be compatible with long cycles of economic activity and that family size has been declining for an extended period. The distribution of births on the basis of the mother's age has been changing over time as well. Of particular interest are the birth rates of women during their primary market working years. Notice that for the four age groups between 20 and 39, the birth rates rose from 1940 to 1960 and then declined thereafter. The data also show that women are waiting longer to have their first child and are having their last child at an earlier age.

---

[5]   Terry Ligaila, *Households, Families, and Children: A 30 Year Perspective*. U.S. Bureau of the Census Current Population Reports, P23-181, (GPO:1992).

Table 5-5: Birth Rates by Age of Mother, 1940-1990, Selected Years

			Age of Mother				
Year	10-14	15-19	20-24	25-29	30-34	35-39	40-44
1940	0.7	54.1	135.6	122.8	83.4	46.3	15.6
1950	1.0	81.6	196.6	166.1	103.7	52.9	15.1
1960	0.8	89.1	258.1	197.4	112.7	56.2	15.5
1970	1.2	68.3	167.8	145.1	73.3	31.7	8.1
1980	1.1	53.0	115.1	112.9	61.9	19.8	3.9
1990	1.4	59.9	116.5	120.2	80.8	31.7	5.5

Number of births per 1,000 women of the age group.

Source: U.S. Bureau of the Census, *Statistical Abstract of the United States*, Selected Years, (GPO).

The distribution of birth rates by the age of the mother may change to some extent in future years. Recent data suggest that married women who have career marketplace employment are waiting even longer to have their first child. These are women who generally expect to have small families. In the next chapter, economic considerations associated with this pattern of births are outlined; these economic forces suggest that the trend will continue.

STUDY QUESTIONS

Family Characteristics

5. Identify those factors that contribute to choosing marriage as a lifestyle.
6. How would you characterize a successful marriage, and what factors contribute to the likelihood of success?
7. How has the emergence of modern birth control methods contributed to the increased importance of economic factors in the decision of whether or not to have children?

● Work Patterns ●

The consumer unit maximizes total utility by allocating resources—especially time—among various alternatives. A crucial aspect of the decision making involves the choice between work in the marketplace and work in household production. This section focuses on the observed results of decisions about whether the wife will generate market utility.

Table 5-6 presents labor force participation rates of males and females by age. Since 1890, men have had a fairly constant marketplace work pattern. The data are somewhat affected by the state of the economy during the different years, but the consistency of the data over varied economic conditions provides a clear indication that the primary activity of men has been to generate market utility. Social Security and pension systems have enabled proportionately more males aged 65 and over to drop out of the labor force.

Surely no one is surprised to see the rise in the labor force participation rates of women across life span. A closer examination of the pattern of increase sheds some interesting light on the composition of the changes. While the overall increase has been dramatic, it is primarily women between 20 and 64 who have been entering the labor force in record proportions. Teenage women have increased their participation, but not to the same extent as those in the primary working age groups. There has been little overall change for women 65 and older.

Table 5-6: Labor Force Participation Rates by Age and Sex, 1890 to 1990, Selected Years

		Male						Female				
Year	Total	16-19	20-24	25-44	45-64	≥65	Total	16-19	20-24	25-44	45-64	≥65
1890	**84.3**	50.0	90.9	96.0	92.0	68.3	**18.2**	24.5	30.2	15.1	12.1	7.6
1900	**85.7**	62.0	90.6	94.7	90.3	63.1	**20.0**	26.8	31.7	17.5	13.6	8.3
1920	**84.6**	51.5	89.9	95.6	90.7	55.6	**22.7**	28.4	37.5	21.7	16.5	7.3
1930	**82.1**	40.1	88.8	95.8	91.0	54.0	**23.6**	22.8	41.8	24.6	18.0	7.3
1940	**79.1**	34.7	88.1	94.9	88.7	41.8	**25.8**	18.9	45.6	30.5	20.2	6.1
1950	**81.6**	51.7	81.9	93.3	88.2	41.4	**29.9**	31.1	42.9	33.3	28.8	7.8
1960	**80.4**	50.0	86.2	95.3	89.0	30.5	**35.7**	32.6	44.8	39.1	41.6	10.3
1970	**76.6**	47.2	80.9	94.3	87.2	24.8	**41.4**	34.9	56.1	47.5	47.8	10.0
1980	**77.4**	60.7	86.0	95.4	83.0	19.1	**51.6**	53.1	69.0	65.4	52.5	8.1
1990	**76.1**	55.7	84.3	92.3	81.0	19.0	**57.5**	51.8	71.6	75.5	60.0	8.7

Source: U.S. Bureau of the Census, *Historical Statistics of the United States: Colonial Times to 1970*, Part I (GPO,1975) and U.S. Bureau of Labor Statistics, *Monthly Labor Review*, selected issues.

More information about the rise of the working woman is found in Table 5-7. Labor force participation rates are shown for the period 1890 through 1990, with marital status used to separate women into groups. Single women underwent a 50 percent increase in their labor force participation rate during this period, as did widowed or divorced women. Married women experienced an even more pronounced increase, as their rate increased 400 percent. The increase for married women, husband present, appears to be even larger. This rate started out below the total rate in 1940, and by 1990 they were almost the same. Today, nearly 6 out of every 10 married women with husbands present are members of the labor force at some time during the year. An implication is the rise of the working women could be characterized as being primarily due to the rise of the married working woman.

Table 5-8 further defines the source of the rise of the working woman. It focuses on the labor force participation rates of married women who have husbands present and children in the family. Overall, these females more than doubled their rate since 1950. The increase for those having no children under 18 is just over 50 percent. Those with school-aged children more than doubled their

Table 5-7: Labor Force Participation Rates of Women by Marital Status, 1890 to 1990, Selected Years

| | | MARRIED | | |
Year	Single	Total	Husband Present	Widowed/ Divorced
1890	40.5	4.6	NA	29.9
1900	43.5	5.6	NA	32.5
1920	46.4	9.0	NA	NA
1930	50.5	11.7	NA	34.4
1940	45.5	15.6	13.8	30.2
1950	46.3	23.0	21.6	32.7
1960	42.9	31.7	30.6	36.1
1970	50.9	40.2	39.6	36.8
1980	61.2	49.9	50.2	44.1
1990	66.9	58.5	58.2	44.1

NA = not available. Persons 16 and over after 1940; persons 14 and over for 1940 and earlier.

Source: U.S. Bureau of the Census, *Historical Statistics of the United States: Colonial Times to 1970*, Part I (GPO, 1975); U.S. Office of the President, *Employment and Training Report,1981*, (GPO, 1981); and U.S. Department of Labor, *1993 Handbook on Women Workers: Trends and Issues* (GPO, 1994).

rate, and those with young children had a five-fold increase. These data lead to the conclusion that since 1950 most of the increase in the labor force participation rate of women has been due to the rise of the working mother in a family where the husband is present and there are children. This table also shows that over the last decade the increases were very small, suggesting that a plateau has been reached.

Much of what has been covered regarding the labor force participation rates of women is summarized in Figure 5-5. For each year shown in the diagram, the labor force participation rate of women by age is displayed. Every age is associated with a higher labor force participation rate over time. The shapes of the curves are revealing. Each year by itself has important characteristics. In 1890, when women were in their middle twenties, the participation rate began to decline and did so across the older age groups. This is attributed to their getting married, working at home, and tending not to re-enter the labor force. For 1960, women still dropped out in their early twenties, but those in the older age groups gradually returned to the labor force. The 1992 curve shows that women joined the labor force by their early twenties, and they tended not to drop out of the labor force for the remainder of the work life years.

Table 5-8: Labor Force Participation Rates of Married Women with Children, Husband Present, 1950-1990, Selected Years

Year	Total	With no Children Under 18	With Children 6 to 17 Years, None Younger	With Children Under 6
1950	23.8	30.3	28.3	11.9
1960	30.5	34.7	39.0	18.6
1970	40.8	42.2	49.2	30.3
1980	50.2	46.1	61.8	45.0
1990	58.2	46.3	62.5	58.9

Source: U.S. Office of the President, *Employment and Training Report, 1981* (GPO,1981) and U.S. Department of Labor, *1993 Handbook on Women Workers: Trends and Issues* (GPO, 1994).

Figure 5-5: Labor Force Participation Rates of Women by Age, 1890, 1960, and 1992

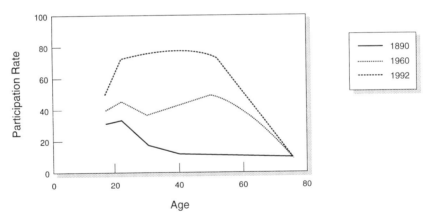

Patterns of the labor force participation by women of different ages have altered remarkably over the years. The trend is toward greater participation for all ages.

Source: U.S. Office of the President, *Employment and Training Report, 1976,* (GPO, 1976) and U.S. Bureau of the Census, *Statistical Abstract of the United States, 1992,* (GPO, 1992).

The type of employment women have sought has been changing as well. Figure 5-6 presents data on the percentage changes in employment by industry and sex for the 1964-1990 period. In every industry group, the percentage changes for women are much greater than those for men. These data

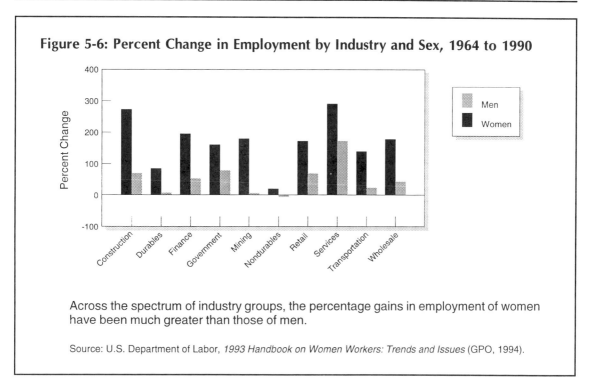

Figure 5-6: Percent Change in Employment by Industry and Sex, 1964 to 1990

Across the spectrum of industry groups, the percentage gains in employment of women have been much greater than those of men.

Source: U.S. Department of Labor, *1993 Handbook on Women Workers: Trends and Issues* (GPO, 1994).

do not mean that there is no sex discrimination in the workplace. Rather, they show that during this period relatively more women are using their increased educational training to obtain market utility.

Hayghe and Bianchi characterize recent changes in the typical family as follows.[6] Mothers in 1993 are twice as likely to work full time versus mothers 20 years ago. In 1992, two-thirds of all married mothers were members of the labor force, including more than half of those with children under six. Nearly three-quarters of married mothers worked at some time during 1992, and approximately four out of ten worked year round full time. With respect to two parent families, 70 percent had both spouses working either full or part-time.

---

[6]   Howard Hayghe and Suzanne Bianchi, "Married Mothers' Work Patterns: The Job-Family Compromise," *Monthly Labor Review*, (January, 1994):24-30.

STUDY QUESTIONS

Work Patterns

8. Explain the basis for arguing that the rise of the working woman is the rise of the married working woman who has a husband present and children in the family.

9. The notion of sex role stereotypes is that the roles taken on by men and women are related to their sex, as opposed to other criteria. How to the data presented in this chapter illustrate the argument that sex role stereotyping may be declining?

10. From a purely economic perspective, what arguments could you provide to support the argument that sex role stereotyping is not desirable?

● Summary ●

Over time, the typical U.S. Consumer unit has experienced significant changes indicating that the outcomes of resource allocation decisions within the household have changed. These changes are not just recent phenomena, but have occurred over an extended period. Among the important changes are higher educational attainment and smaller families. Birth rates have fluctuated, in part, because of changes in economic activity. Women are having their first child at a later age and their youngest at an earlier age. The rise of the working woman has been found to be the rise of the working mother with husband present. Examination of occupations revealed that women are seeking careers across the spectrum of industries. As recently as 1950, the typical U.S. Family could be characterized as one in which there were three children, the mother was engaged in home production exclusively, and the husband generated market income. Today, the average U.S. Family has fewer than two children, both parents generate market income, and the mother's employment is likely to be career oriented.

● Key term ●

Labor force participation rate: ratio of the labor force to the population.

Chapter 6

The Economics of Consumer Units

The typical U.S. consumer unit is a dynamic entity. Significant changes in the two major groups of units (households and families) have occurred since colonial times. Observed changes in marriage, divorce, family size, market employment opportunities, and time allocation are the results of people's decisions. All choices in these areas are considered to reflect attempts to maximize utility subject to constraints. The scarcity and opportunity costs of consumer resources are at the heart of the decision making.

This chapter provides an overview of the ways in which two economic forces have contributed to the observed changes in consumer units. Essentially, the chapter uses the economic principles outlined in Chapters 1-4 to explain why the changes identified in Chapter 5 have taken place. Opportunity cost and the production possibility frontier provide a partial explanation of the changes in resource allocation that have occurred within consumer units. The objective is to stimulate your thinking about the application of these tools to decision making. At various points in the rest of the book, additional tools are developed and related to the changes described in Chapter 5.

Although the economic environment is dynamic, it is important to realize that the economic logic and decision making criteria used by consumers have not changed. The consumer has always been motivated by the desire to be as well off as possible, and the problem continues to be one of selecting the best alternative. Changes in the economic environment have caused the economic logic to point to different alternatives as optimal. For example, the decision process for the allocation of a mother's labor has always centered on choosing the most efficient alternative. However, since the economic setting changes over time, the most efficient alternative is not the same today as it was during earlier periods. The optimal choice has been changing from home production to marketplace production, although the process for making the choice has remained the same.

● Human Capital and the Size of Consumer Units ●

Capital, as defined by economists, is anything that satisfies the following three criteria. First, it must be produced by people and be used, in turn, in the production process. Second, it must have a longer service life. Third, investment is required in order to generate, maintain, and improve it. Many things are made by people and used to produce other goods. However, not all are capital. For example, the information exchange that occurs on Internet is not capital, but the equipment and transmission lines used to make the exchange are capital.

Investment, as defined in Chapter 1, is the addition to or the replacement of capital. By definition, then, capital grows through investment. Furthermore, investment is the way of replacing older and technologically obsolete capital with new and improved capital. A crucial part of business decision making focuses on determining how much capital a firm should have given the problems of scarcity and the opportunity costs of the resources used. A business invests as long as it feels investment is profitable. That is, investment occurs whenever a firm concludes that the cost of the investment is more than offset by the returns. A retailer will switch to the bar code and scanner technology, for example, when the returns from the new capital are expected to be greater than the costs.

The discussion may seem to have gone far afield, but in reality, it has not. Because capital and investment have conventionally been associated with the business sector, the best way of outlining their essential economic features is from the producer's perspective. These features can be extended to individuals and their effects on consumer units.

The circular flow diagram in Chapter 2 illustrated the fundamental principle that both a business and a consumer have dual roles. Just as a business must manage its resources as efficiently as possible, so too must a consumer unit. This includes decisions about members of the unit. In fact, people can be considered as a form of capital, because the three criteria that define capital apply to people. Certainly people are made by people and are used in the production process at home and in the marketplace. People also have long working lives. Investment is required in order to create people and to increase their productivity—resources must be allocated to the raising of children, and through investments in education and better medical care, individuals can become more productive. **Human capital** is a phrase used to associate the properties of capital with people.

The size of the consumer unit can be considered a result of investment decisions. The profitability of children is determined by two factors. One is the cost. Parents must allocate resources, such as their time to raising children and money for food, clothing, and education. These resources could be used in different ways by a consumer unit if there were no children. The other factor affecting the profitability is the return of children, or the contributions of children over their life spans to the well-being of the unit. Returns are in the forms of direct satisfaction, contributions to home production, and old age security for the parents. When the returns are felt to be greater (less) than the costs, family size increases (decreases).

A human capital perspective provides a good explanation of the decline in the number of children per family since colonial times. The profitability of children has declined, because the cost of raising children has risen, and the returns have fallen. During colonial times, investment costs were relatively low. Educational costs were minimal, and the children were watched by spouses who were nearby or by older siblings. At a very early age children could begin to provide home production returns by carrying out various chores. In addition, the extended family was common, so the long working lives embodied in children represented very long periods of returns to parents. A couple's children and potential grandchildren represented long-run home production utility. The profitability of children led to large families.

The migration of families from farms to urban areas occurred as changes in agricultural production reduced the number of workers needed to produce food and fiber for the economy and as jobs became available during the early stages of the Industrial Revolution. Machinery in use at this time in factories did not require strength and was relatively easy to operate. Factories served as places of employment for young children. Consequently, children continued to be profitable, although their returns were in the form of earned income instead of home production.

Two factors in the economic environment began to affect family size. These were the implementation of child labor laws and the introduction of mandatory education for children. After 1850, all of the states passed laws prohibiting child labor in factories and requiring children between certain ages to attend school. Compulsory schooling increased the investment costs for the family by having to feed, clothe, and care for children for a longer period of time. Mandatory education also curtailed the time children could spend working at home or in the marketplace. Thus, child labor laws, by prohibiting full-time employment of children, made it necessary for the family to support children longer, while at the same time the returns from children were reduced. By the time children were able to leave school and legally work full-time, they were almost ready to start their own families. Children had become considerably less profitable.

The reduction in the profitability of children has continued during this century. Occupational opportunities to a large extent depend on educational attainment. Expanding employment has centered on white collar jobs such as management, administration, clerical work, and services. Today a high school education is barely enough to qualify one for entry positions in these fields. As shown in the previous chapter, children are staying in school at least through high school, and many go on to college. By the time a family is finished with the investment, the children generally are ready to be on their own. Increased mobility, due to marketplace employment, has further decreased the return by decreasing the likelihood that parents will be able to count on the proximity of children during retirement years.

An alternative way of viewing the situation focuses on the quality as well as the quantity of children. The typical family wants to produce higher quality children. That is, consumer units generally want to provide more educational opportunities and more medical care and other amenities for children. Such motivation raises the investment costs of a child, thereby decreasing profitability. The increased cost of quality children has led the typical family to conclude that it can afford fewer offspring. An estimate of this relationship is provided by Joerding who concluded that a 1 percent increase in the cost of raising a child leads to more than a 2 percent decline in the number of children per family.[1]

Data generated by the U.S. Department of Agriculture (USDA) provide some indication of the rising cost of investment in children. Based on periodic surveys of consumer expenditure, out-of-pocket costs of raising a child from birth through age 17 are estimated for three budget levels. The highest cost estimates are for a "moderate" income level. For a child born in 1960 in the urban North Central region, the current dollar cost was estimated to be $34,274. The corresponding forecast for a child born in 1979 was estimated to be $134,414, assuming an 8 percent annual rate of inflation through 1996.[2] Lino has estimated similar costs for a second child born to a family in 1993 and raised through age 17. This cost for a middle income family ($32,000 to $54,100 before tax income) is an estimated $231,140.[3] While the estimates for the three birth dates are not strictly comparable, they serve to illustrate the point that the costs of children have been rising over time. Also bear in mind that these costs do not include the cost of a college education, and to the extent that families feel a responsibility to educate their children through college, the costs are not only much larger, but college costs have been rising faster than incomes, so the real cost to families of a college education is rising.

Another way to apply the human capital approach to the analysis of family size is to consider farm versus nonfarm families. Children are somewhat more profitable to farm families. Even though these children must attend school, they can still help on the farm. With respect to investment costs, USDA estimates show a slight cost disadvantage for urban families. The cost of raising a child from birth through age 17 in constant 1980 dollars at the thrifty level is $36,500 for a farm family, while for an urban family it ranges from $33,100 to $37,900, depending on the region, and for a child born in 1993 the urban family constant dollar cost ranged from $131,400 to $142,680 depending on the region versus $128,760 for a rural family.[4] The human capital approach suggests that a farm family

---

[1]   Wayne Joerding, "Lifetime Consumption, Labor Supply, and Fertility: A Complete Demand System," *Economic Inquiry*, 20(1982):255-276.
[2]   Carolyn S. Edwards, *USDA Estimates of the Cost of Raising a Child: A Guide to Their Use and Interpretation*, U.S. Department of Agriculture, Miscellaneous Publication 1411 (1981).
[3]   Mark Lino, "Expenditures on a Child by Families, 1993," *Family Economics Review*, 7,3(1994):3-19.
[4]   Edwards, *op. cit.*, and Lino, *op. cit.*

should be somewhat larger than an urban family because of the greater profitability of farm children stemming from their higher return and lower cost.

This hypothesis is supported by data in Table 6-1. Altogether, family size declined between 1970 and 1989, as measured by the number of persons per family and the mean number of own children per family. The declines occurred for both farm and nonfarm families, reflecting the continued reduction in the profitability of children. However, farm families, on average, have been larger and tended to have had more own children than nonfarm families.

Table 6-1: Farm and Nonfarm Family Size, 1970 to 1989, Selected Years.

	1970		1980		1989	
Number of persons per family	3.77	3.61	3.35	3.27	3.20	3.16
Mean number of own children	2.61	2.32	2.00	1.89	2.02	1.82

Source: U.S. Bureau of the Census, *Statistical Abstract of the United States*, selected issues (GPO).

The human capital approach to the study of family size may seem to be a cold-hearted, uncaring point of view. However, this is an incorrect appraisal. Procreation is considered to be a voluntary choice involving the opportunity costs of family resources. Investment costs and returns of children have had pronounced impacts on family size. They have been changing over time, and the typical family is concluding that fewer children can be afforded. Investment costs have risen dramatically, and the productive rewards have become very small. The returns today stem primarily from the personal satisfaction of parenting.

In fact, human capital considerations are becoming more relevant. Part of the current policy debate on welfare programs draws upon the economic analysis of family size. Conservatives point to data on family size that indicate consumer units receiving public assistance are larger than other units and draw the inference that these programs encourage more children in order to increase payments. For example, the estimated average size of a family below the poverty level in 1991 is 3.52, which is considerably above the average of 3.18 for all families for the same year.[5] Their argument suggests the assistance lowers the parents' investment costs of children. To the extent there is no expectation of being able to pay for higher education on the part of lower income families, the economics are further directed toward larger families.

Counter arguments abound. Program advocates point out the assistance does not come close to covering the costs of children. Parents receiving assistance may have higher education aspirations for their children. Other considerations include a need to help all consumers, especially children who are in situations they did not create. In addition, everyone is better off through providing necessities

---

[5]   U.S. Bureau of the Census, *Statistical Abstract of the United States, 1994* (GPO, 1994).

so children can become productive members of society. In fact, many of the progressive changes in public assistance are directed toward not only helping the children but also helping the parents acquire the marketplace skills that can enable them to function independently.

STUDY QUESTIONS

Human Capital and the Size of Consumer Units

1. Distinguish between money and capital.
2. What are the justifications for viewing children as an investment?
3. Identify some of the investment costs your family has paid for you.
4. What returns have you provided to your family?
5. How would your answers to questions 3 and 4 differ if you had lived 150 years ago?

● Opportunity Cost and Resource Allocation Within Consumer Units ●

Chapter 5 identified married women with children as the part of the female labor force that underwent the most pronounced change during the last 150 years. Men have not altered their labor force participation significantly. Single, widowed, and divorced women's participation has increased, but not to the degree that married women's has. An understanding of the economic forces that have fostered the changing work patterns of married women begins with two economic principles: opportunity costs and total utility. Among the key economic decisions that must be made by consumer units are those relating the allocation of time to the generation of the various types of utility. The scarce labor available to the unit has alternative uses, so opportunity cost must be considered. Since colonial times, more and more mothers have been changing their time allocation from home production to marketplace production.

Home production activities were the primary types of work for men and women when this country was settled. Families were nearly self-sufficient, living off the land. Men were expected to hunt and to do most of the heavier agricultural production. Women also helped with farm tasks, but primarily, they managed the home and transformed the crops and other commodities into needed household goods. Only a very small proportion of married women worked outside the home in restricted occupations such as the needle trades, primary school teaching, and shopkeeping.

Leaving the farm became a viable alternative as the expansion of manufacturing employment in the cities attracted potential workers and as the increase in agricultural production kept food prices relatively low, permitting the movement of labor out of agriculture. The machinery that enabled children to work in a factory also made it possible for women to do so. But such employment was not considered acceptable for married women.

The rise in the proportion of working women during this time resulted primarily from the entrance into the labor force of single, widowed, and divorced women. Social attitudes toward working women, especially married women, were reflected in the attitudes of the legal system and the medical profession. As late as 1875 courts ruled against working women, and doctors argued that women should not work in the marketplace.[6] A husband was considered to be inadequate if the wife worked outside the home. Even as recently as the 1930s, adverse economic conditions were associated with the notion that women were taking jobs away from men.

The transition to the city changed the way the typical family could generate utility. Fewer needs could be accommodated by home production. More and more goods, such as food and clothing, had to be acquired through the final goods market or the public sector. Consequently, the need for an earned income increased with the move to the city. Since employment opportunities outside the home were not generally available to married women, the solution was for the housewife to undertake activities within the home that could produce some earned income. Sewing, laundering, taking in boarders, and providing homemade foods are examples of such activities. Many of these endeavors expanded into major businesses in subsequent years.

Pressure for additional earned income increased during the early 1900s with the emergence of consumer durables. Consumers readily accepted the new durables as part of a rising standard of living. Having these durables became part and parcel of the American way of life. Two characteristics of durables caused them to increase the money needs of the household. One was their relatively high purchase price. The other was the nature of the service flows associated with the durables. Consumer units, in general, could not acquire the service flows of durables through home production. A radio, for example, had to be purchased in the final goods market. It was not possible for most consumers to make such items on their own.

How was the typical household to afford durables? By the end of the nineteenth century, the employment opportunities for women had expanded with the emergence of clerical, teaching, and service occupations. Initially, these positions were filled primarily by single, divorced, and widowed women. But many of the jobs were suitable for part-time and temporary workers and thus appealed to married women with children.

The increased pressure on working class families to acquire market goods, coupled with the availability of temporary, part-time employment, helped to create the economic environment for a change in resource allocation within families. Married women began to work on a supplemental basis. Of course, such work had to become socially acceptable. It was justified on the basis the employment was not full-time and the income was only being used to purchase a new durable or a home.

Much of the continued economic growth in this century has centered on white collar, service-oriented occupations. These jobs can be filled by men or women; and since the educational attainment of both males and females has continued to rise, both sexes have acquired the educational background to qualify for entry level positions. The availability of jobs and the increased educational attainment have changed the opportunity cost of having the mother remain exclusively in home production. It has become more and more costly in terms of foregone employment opportunities.

Further evidence of the changing allocation of the wife's time during this century is found in Chadwick and Bradford.[7] Their study compared statistics for 1920-1924 and 1973-1977 on two random samples of married women with at least one child between 6 and 18 years of age in a Midwestern town. The proportion of working class wives who worked outside the home was approximately the same in both periods. However, there was a significant increase in the proportion

6   Robert W. Smuts, *Women and Work in America*, New York: Columbia University Press, 1959.
7   Bruce A. Chadwick and Chappell C. Bradford, "The Two Income Family in Middletown," in *Economics and the Family*, Stephen Bahr, ed., Lexington, Massachusetts: Lexington Books, 1979.

of business class wives in marketplace work in the later period. During 1920-1924, a working wife on average increased the earned income of the family by 20 percent. Data for 1977 indicated that a working wife increased family income by 36 percent for working class families and 38 percent for business class families.

More recent empirical work shows the trends are continuing. Hayghe characterizes the current situation as follows.[8] In 1991 wives' earnings comprised approximately 31 percent of family income, which was an increase of 4 percent over the 1970 level. Managerial/professional occupations accounted for 17 percent of the employed women in 1970, and this increased to 27 percent in 1991. Fifty-four percent of the married women worked year-round in 1991, and their marketplace work contributed 41 percent of family income. The employment opportunities for wives have been extended to career-oriented positions. The dual working family is becoming the **dual career family**.

Family size has been affected by the increased opportunity cost of having women work at home. Bearing and raising children is a very time-consuming investment on the part of the family. Time devoted to the birth and care of infants adversely affects employment possibilities, including those of a supplemental nature. Marketplace employment opportunities have the effect of increasing the investment costs of children and result in the lower profitability of children, thereby leading to smaller families.

Changes in the work opportunities for women have been facilitated by the legal system. Starting with President Roosevelt's first Executive Order, signed in 1941, federal contractors have been required to be "equal opportunity employers." The Equal Pay Act of 1963 was the first federal law against sex discrimination, and Title VII of the Civil Rights Act of 1964 prohibited wage discrimination based on sex, as well as race. The Civil Rights Act of 1991 allowed successful sex discrimination plaintiffs to recover compensatory and punitive damages.

These laws have served several beneficial purposes. The obvious opportunity to seek redress through the legal system is an important right and has helped to open employment opportunities. Consumer units that were able to reallocate time to take advantage of the opportunities benefitted. Society as a whole also benefitted because the labor market has been opened to a larger group of potential workers. The cost of final market goods can be kept as low as possible through the work of the most productive people. Eliminating discrimination (sex discrimination in the context of this chapter) means that businesses have a bigger pool from which to select their employees, and costs can be held down by using more productive workers.

● The Effect of New Consumer Goods ●

The emergence of durables and convenience goods has had an effect on consumer decision making beyond increasing the demand for money.[9] They have had a significant impact on the production of goods and services within the consumer unit. Home production technologies have changed. New products have altered the ways in which households can combine resources to produce commodities. For example, meal preparation has changed dramatically. New appliances, along with new food products, have made it considerably less time consuming. The reduction in household time required for food-related activities beyond meal preparation also has been significant.

---

[8]   Howard Hayghe, "Working Wives' Contributions to Family Incomes," *Monthly Labor Review*, (August, 1993):39-43.
[9]   A decision making framework is presented in Chapter 10.

STUDY QUESTIONS

Opportunity Cost and Resource Allocation within Consumer Units

6.   How can opportunity cost be used to explain the rising proportion of dual working families in the United States?

7.   Distinguish between a dual working family and a dual career family.

8.   How can opportunity cost be used to explain why the labor force participation rate of single women rose from 46.3 percent in 1950 to 66.9 percent in 1990, whereas the rate for married women with children under age 6 rose from 11.9 percent to 58.9 percent in 1990?

9.   What is the effect in economic terms of married women having their first child at an older age and their youngest child at an earlier age?

No longer is it necessary to spend large amounts of time in fruit and vegetable preservation. Modern freezing techniques have made it easier to store meat and fish. Less appliance maintenance is required because of such advances as self-cleaning ovens and frost free refrigerators and freezers. These changes have enabled families to reallocate time to other activities without changing the quantity and quality of meals. In addition, just about any type of meal is available in urban areas in fast-food/take-out form.

Virtually every phase of home production has been affected by technological change. The same amount of household resources can now produce more commodities. These changes have enabled consumers to increase their living standards in the long run. One way of showing the effects of new consumer goods is with a production possibility frontier. Production possibility frontier AB in Figure 6-1 portrays the choices facing a consumer unit regarding the transformation of one household good, food, into another, clothing, by transferring resources. Fixed levels of technology and fixed levels of resources are assumed so a specific frontier can be drawn. The emergence of durable goods has changed the technologies of home production. Appliances such as washing machines, driers, and stoves have enabled a household to produce a larger output with the same amount of labor. This is shown in the shift in the frontier to CD in the figure.

Alternatively, because of changes in household production technology, the typical consumer unit can produce the same output (for example, the same number of meals) in less time. During this century consumer units have elected to use the savings in home production time to generate an earned income. Until recently, the time savings were especially conducive to part-time employment, because the savings were not sufficient to permit full-time work outside the home. But now, new types of durables, which expanded labor-saving technologies to additional areas of home production, have released even more time for other activities.

Stoves provide an illustration. Wood stoves were an improvement over fireplaces for cooking. They were replaced subsequently by oil, gas, and electric stoves. Timed bake features were a desirable option, because they allowed cooking to begin with no one at home. Self-cleaning ovens eliminated a very undesirable chore. Most recently, microwave and convection ovens have reduced the cooking

Figure 6-1: Technological Change and the Production Possibility Frontier

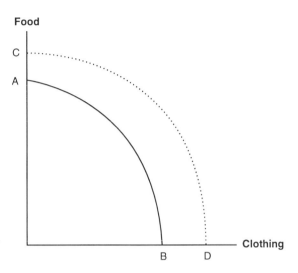

A representative consumer unit's production possibility frontier for food and clothing is shown as curve AB. During this century, the emergence of durables and convenience goods has changed production technologies so that in the same amount of time more production can occur. This means that over time a representative consumer unit has experienced a shift in the production possibility frontier away from the origin, as shown by CD.

time required for meal preparation. These changes in the technology of meal production have given women more time to produce utility via other avenues. Many married women have chosen marketplace employment as the best alternative.

Convenience goods have also affected the opportunity cost of women in the home. **Convenience goods** are nondurables that have been processed to such an extent that they are almost ready to generate utility. These goods have decreased the time required to achieve the same level of home production. For example, permanent press clothing has reduced the time needed for ironing, which is labor intensive. Just about any type of food has been processed to such an extent that it can be purchased in a grocery store virtually ready to eat. Precut fresh produce is one example of a new more highly processed food product that has gained widespread consumer acceptance.

Family size has been affected by the availability of new consumer goods. The reduction in time required for household production activities, except for child care, has contributed to the decline in family size. As long as the housewife's time could be spread over many activities, the opportunity cost of not working could be distributed among several tasks. New consumer goods have led to a redistribution of this opportunity cost, so the cost rests more heavily on children.

STUDY QUESTIONS

The Effect of New Consumer Goods

10. How has the emergence of new consumer durables affected home production?
11. Explain the manner in which new convenience goods have affected the opportunity cost of being a housewife.
12. Identify some new labor-saving appliances, and explain how they have affected home production.
13. Identify some new convenience goods, and explain how they have affected home production.

● Which Consumer Units Do Best Over Time? ●

The question of which families do best has been fairly difficult to answer until recently. The ideal method for studying this issue is to track the same group of families over time. Changes in their economic and social status could be followed and inferences drawn regarding the factors associated with family success or failure. Most studies of families have not done this, but instead, have examined a cross section of families at one point in time. Inferences in these situations must be based on comparisons across families, as opposed to an examination of the evolution of a single family.

The Survey Research Center at the University of Michigan is one source of relevant data. Beginning in 1967, the same families and the newly formed families of their offspring have formed a longitudinal survey. Major results of the research include the following.[10] Significant decreases in the economic well-being of a family are associated with disruptions in family life. Disruptions include retirement, divorce, and the creation of new families by children who have grown up. The family that remains intact has the best chance of improving its well-being over time. Most poor families are not below the poverty level all of the time. Rather, in a given year they may be above or below the poverty level depending on their employment. Families with higher educational attainment tend to fare better over time.

These results are consistent with other data on the economic status of consumer units. Initially, married women tended to enter the factor market to obtain supplemental income, which was socially acceptable, as it enabled families to acquire consumer durables. These wives tended to be from lower income families. Research by Chadwick and Bradford support this view.[11] During the 1920-1924 period, 44 percent of working class wives had marketplace employment, whereas only 3 percent of business class wives did. Between 1973 and 1977 they found that 48 percent of working class wives had been employed, and 42 percent of business class wives worked outside the home. The proportion of two parent families in which both spouses worked expanded by 50 percent between 1970 and

---

[10]   Greg J. Duncan, et al., Years of Poverty, Years of Plenty — The Changing Economic Fortunes of American Workers and Families, Ann Arbor: Institute for Social Research, University of Michigan, 1984.

[11]   Chadwick and Bradford, op. cit.

1990, rising from 40 to 60 percent.[12] The poverty rate of married couple families with children was 7.8 percent in 1990 compared to 44.5 percent for female headed households.[13]

The rise of the dual career family is leading to a two-tier structure of consumer units. Those families that have been able to increase their standards of living tend to have more highly educated and employed spouses. The lower tier is those families who have difficulty making ends meet, and the other is those consumer units that have rising real income. The latter group is composed primarily of dual career households. Difficulties for the former group tend to be long term as the children of single parents are less likely to complete high school, more likely to have low earnings, and more likely to experience periods of unemployment.[14]

A final point needs to be made regarding the decline in family size and the increased opportunity cost of women remaining in home production. It has to do with the availability of child day care. Until recently, social attitudes toward children favored having infants stay in the home under parental care. Spouses were considered to be uncaring if arrangements were made for others outside the family to take care of young children. It is now acceptable for parents to place their children in day care settings. Many educators feel that such environments help in the social development of the child. More employers are providing day care facilities.

Part of the rise in the divorce rate can be attributed to the rise of the dual career family. Much more coordination and cooperation is required of the spouses in this type of consumer unit. Household tasks still need to be performed, and determining just how they are to be accomplished can be a source of marital stress. Spouses can develop different social networks which cause them to drift apart. Job related interests also can cause conflict. What happens if one spouse has an opportunity for advancement, but it requires a move, and there are no jobs for the other spouse in the new location? Such additional pressure can have adverse effects on marital relationships.

Marriage and divorce, viewed as voluntary choices, can be analyzed from an economic perspective. A family provided a very efficient division of labor. The colonial household had well defined tasks to be performed, allowing men, women, and children to specialize. Consequently, marriage was viewed as a rational utility maximizing choice. The migration to urban areas did not alter the attractiveness of marriage. Household production responsibilities were very time intensive, leaving the typical housewife with little time for other activities. The evolution of new consumer goods increased the demand for money income and decreased the need for home production time, so a reallocation of the wife's time occurred. Continued technological change has enabled some couples to function as dual career families. On the other hand, the decline in household production time for most tasks has led some spouses to conclude that the gains from specialization through marriage no longer are as pronounced. Consequently, divorce is more likely, and some individuals choose not to marry.

---

[12]   Arthur Norton and Louisa Miller, *Marriage, Divorce, and Remarriage in the 1990's*, U.S. Bureau of the Census Current Population Reports, P23-180 (GPO, 1992).
[13]   U.S. Bureau of the Census, *Current Population Reports*, selected series.
[14]   McGraw-Hill, *Business Week*, June 29, 1992, p. 91. Haveman, Robert and Barbara Wolfe, *Succeeding Generations: On the Effects of Investments in Children*, New York: Russell Sage, 1994.

STUDY QUESTIONS

Which Consumer Units Do Best Over Time?

14. How do you expect the labor force participation rates of women by age to change in 2000 compared to the curves shown in Figure 5-5?
15. Recent studies of dual working families have revealed they tend to save less than single earner families with similar total earned income. Can you think of reasons why?
16. Use an economic view of families to explain why divorce rates will remain high.

● Population Growth and Opportunity Cost ●

Was Malthus right or wrong about population growth? Malthus conceived the iron law of wages as an adjustment mechanism to reconcile the tendency of population growth to exceed agricultural production. In the long run, there would be an ever present problem of starvation. Developing countries seem to fit this model fairly well. Agricultural production, at best, has barely kept ahead of population growth, and the standard of living has remained at or near the subsistence level.

Developed countries have not followed the Malthusian model. Technological change in agricultural production has enabled these countries to avoid the law of diminishing returns. This has permitted a rise in the standard of living. According to the iron law of wages, the result should have been very large population increases. However, this has not been the case—population growth of the developed countries has been considerably below that of the developing nations (see Figure 3-8). Something needs to be corrected in the Malthusian model.

At the heart of the issue is an implicit assumption associated with the iron law of wages. The argument that population growth depends only on the relationship between the market wage and the subsistence wage assumes that any other costs associated with having children either have not changed or do not affect birth rates. The human capital approach to the analysis of population growth argues that it is the profitability of children that matters, not the wage rate by itself. In determining whether or not to have children, a family considers the opportunity cost of the children.

The human capital approach to the study of family size and population growth produces a model that can explain the observed demographic changes in a developed country such as the United States and at the same time accommodates the experience of developing nations. This chapter presented the economic factors that have increased the investment costs of children and decreased the returns in the United States over an extended period. Developing countries, however, are in a different situation. Virtually no change in the profitability of children has occurred in these countries. Most families remain tied to agricultural production. There has been little change in available household technology. Offspring continue to be productive, and very little investment is required. Furthermore, the opportunity cost of women remaining in household production has not changed very much because of limited marketplace employment opportunities.

An implication is that many policies directed toward controlling population growth in less developed countries may be inappropriate. Rather than relying on birth control education, a more effective approach would be to improve the educational attainment of everyone, particularly women, and to work on economic development to provide marketplace employment opportunities.

STUDY QUESTIONS

Population Growth and Opportunity Cost

17. Is an expanding agricultural sector enough to ensure that a country will experience a rising standard of living?
18. What two modifications must be made in the Malthusian model in order to explain the different population growth experiences of developed versus developing countries?

● Summary ●

The economic view of the size of a consumer unit is based on a human capital perspective. People are considered to be a form of capital, having been made by people and used in production, having a long service life, and requiring investment. Spouses determine family size by considering the quantity and quality of children they can afford. The rise of the working mother is the result of the change in the opportunity cost of remaining in home production. Those consumer units that have done the best financially over time are those that have remained together. The concept of human capital can be used to explain the difference in population growth between developing and developed countries.

● Key Terms ●

Capital: an input to production that is made by people, has a long service life, and requires investment.

Convenience good: a nondurable that has been processed to such an extent that it is virtually ready to generate utility.

Dual career family: a family in which more than one person has employment that is career oriented.

Human capital: a person viewed as a form of capital.

Chapter 7

Elements of Consumer Choice

A person starts to learn at a very early age about the problem of constrained decision making. Young children are often seen looking at toys or candy, trying to decide how to spend a limited amount of money. Part of growing up is taking on expanded decision-making responsibilities. Money spent for one good or service cannot be used for another. If housing expenses rise, consumers have to cut back elsewhere. Time is another limited resource having alternative uses. Time allocated for one activity cannot be used for another. For example, the time spent studying for one course cannot be used to study for another or to enjoy leisure.

Opportunity cost is at the heart of consumer decision making. Because unlimited desires are constrained by scarce resources having several uses, a person must choose among alternatives. The economic view that has emerged in Parts I and II is that consumers function in a manner similar to the way businesses function. Every consumer unit must manage resources as efficiently as possible in order to achieve the highest possible well-being. This is accomplished by maximizing utility subject to various constraints. A **rational consumer** is one whose behavior is guided by this objective.

Elements of the consumer's choice problem are covered in this chapter. Market utility is maximized subject to a limited ability to purchase. This situation forms the basic environment in which a consumer operates. Rules are identified for determining the optimal purchase of market goods. These rules are equivalent to asking "Is the good worth the price?" Subsequent chapters show how the rules can be used to analyze consumer demand. Later chapters also use these rules as the structure for showing the need for public policies on behalf of consumers.

Take a moment to think about how you make choices to spend your money or time. Try to identify the recurrent criteria that are used. The real problem in decision making centers on balancing what the market allows you to do with what you would like to do. There are two crucial trade-offs associated with consumer decision making: market trade offs (prices) and the consumer's willingness to substitute one good for another (preferences). For example, if the price of steak is $2.00 per pound, and the price of chicken is $1.25 per pound, the market has set the trade-off at which steak and chicken can be substituted. A consumer has likes and dislikes for these two goods. The purchase decision is a function of each consumer's preferences in relation to the market cost—in the illustration, one's taste for chicken and steak and the prices. This chapter first looks at the market trade-offs and preference trade-offs separately. Then they are combined to construct an economic model of consumer decision making.

● The Ability to Buy—The Budget Constraint ●

In order to simplify the representation of what a consumer is able to do in the marketplace, borrowing and saving are ignored, effectively reducing the situation to a one-period time horizon called the budget period. The length of the period depends on the problem setting. It would be two weeks if the consumer budgets biweekly, a month for a monthly budget, and so on. While this produces an abstraction from the real-world, it simplifies the analysis and focuses attention on the essentials. Once these have been presented, the results can be extended to many other settings.

Only two goods are assumed to be purchased by the consumer. This keeps the choice as basic as possible. It also permits the construction of a two-dimensional diagram in which the axes represent units of the respective goods. While the two-goods model appears to be quite artificial at first, the results can be extended easily to the purchase of many goods and services. Furthermore, the goods can be arbitrarily defined to represent varied settings. If one is analyzing the purchase of chicken versus steak, then the goods are defined clearly. But is possible to deal with other situations, such as clothing versus all other goods. This flexibility allows the diagrammatic treatment to be extended to many situations.

The ability to purchase goods and services in the market depends on the money budgeted and prices. Obviously, expenditure on the two goods is limited by the budget, which determines the most that can be spent. Let M represent the money the consumer has budgeted for two goods, and X_S and X_C represent the quantities of steak and chicken, respectively. P_S and P_C are the respective prices per unit of quantity. Multiplying X_S by P_S yields the expenditure for steak, and the same can be done for chicken. Adding these two products together yields the combined expenditure. Total expenditure equals the amount budgeted if all of the money is spent. This can be easily shown as an equation.

money budgeted = expenditure on steak + expenditure on chicken, or

(7-1) $M = P_S(X_S) + P_C(X_C)$.

Suppose a consumer unit has budgeted $50 per month for steak and chicken. Given prices of $P_S = \$2.00$ per pound and $P_C = \$1.25$ per pound, there are many combinations of steak and chicken that the family could purchase. For example, they could purchase 40 pounds of chicken and no steak, no chicken and 25 pounds of steak, 24 pounds of chicken and 10 pounds of steak, and so on. Table 7-1 lists these and some additional combinations that the family could purchase. There are many more combinations than those provided in the table.

Table 7-1: Expenditure Combinations Equaling a Budget.

X_S	X_C	$[P_S(X_S)$	$+$ $P_C(X_C)$	$= M$]
0	40	0	50	50
5	32	10	40	50
10	24	20	30	50
15	16	30	20	50
20	8	40	10	50
25	0	50	0	50

X_S = quantity of steak, in pounds; X_C = quantity of chicken, in pounds; P_S = price of steak ($2.00/lb); P_C = price of chicken ($1.25/lb); M = money budgeted for steak and chicken($50).

This table points out the role of opportunity cost - the money spent on steak cannot be spent on chicken. A glance down the first two columns of Table 7-1 indicates that X_S rises while X_C falls. This must be the case as long as there is a fixed budget and all the money budgeted is spent.

The information contained in Table 7-1 can be shown in a diagram. Given prices and a budget, the units's decisions focus on how much X_S and X_C to purchase, so these variables comprise the axes in Figure 7-1. X_C is measured on the vertical scale, and X_S is measured on the horizontal scale. All of the pairs of quantities in the first two columns of Table 7-1 are points on line b in panel (a).

Figure 7-1a, b, & c: Illustration of a Budget Constraint

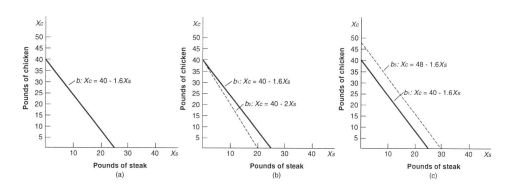

A budget constraint shows what a consumer is able to buy in the market, given a budget and prices. In panel (a) the budget is $50, and the per-pound prices of steak and chicken are $2.00 and $1.25, respectively. The slope of the budget constraint is the relative price, or the market trade-off of steak for chicken. Changes in the relative price change the slope of the budget constraint. Panel (b) shows the effect of an increase in the price of steak to $2.50, which changes the relative price to 2. Budget changes alone cause parallel shifts in the budget constraint. This is illustrated in panel (c), where the budget increases to $60. Notice that the two constraints are parallel, which implies that the relative price of 1.6 has not changed.

Equation 7-1 can be rearranged to conform to Figure 7-1. That is, since X_C is measured on the vertical scale, equation 7-1 can be expressed with X_C by itself on the left-hand side.[1] This is equation 7-2.

(7-2) $X_C = (M/P_C) - (P_s/P_C)X_S.$

Although equation 7-2 is just a restatement of equation 7-1, the second equation provides several useful insights regarding a consumer's ability to purchase in the final goods market. Substituting the price and budget values given previously into equation 7-2 yields:

$X_C = 40 - 1.6(X_S),$

which is line b in panel (a).[2] Notice that further substitution of any X_S value from Table 7-1 into this equation yields the corresponding X_C value.

---

[1] $P_C(X_C) = M - P_S(X_S)$, so $X_C = M/(P_C) - (P_s/P_C)X_S.$
[2] $X_C = 50/1.25 - (2/1.25)X_S$, so $X_C = 40 - 1.6(X_S).$

Where equation 7-1 (or 7-2) crosses the axes can be determined by alternately setting X_S and X_C equal to zero to obtain the maximum purchase of the other good. Without any X_S, the most X_C can be is 40 pounds; and without any X_C, the most X_S can be is 25 pounds. The intermediate purchases form the line in Figure 7-1a.

Equations 7-1 and 7-2 are both representations of what a consumer can purchase in the market with given prices and income. They are referred to as the **budget constraint**, because they represent the maximum quantities of X_S and X_C that can be purchased. The line depicts the budget constraint for the specific illustration.

There are six important properties of budget constraints that need to be understood because of their roles in consumer decision making. First, notice that the line in Figure 7-1a is negatively sloped. This simply means that a trade-off is occurring. If a consumer is spending the amount budgeted, the only way to have more of one good is to have less of the other.

Second, market prices determine the market trade-off. In the illustration, every pound of X_S that is not purchased releases $2.00 which can be used to purchase 1.6 pounds of X_C. This is the same as the coefficient of X_S in equation 7-2. In general, the trade-off is $-(P_S/P_C)$ which is called a **relative price**. The relative price is the slope of the budget constraint.

Third, a consumer's **ability to trade**, or market exchange of units of one good for another, is determined by the relative price, not the price of each good alone. A relative price indicates how a unit of one good can be transformed into another at market prices. For example, suppose the price for a six-pack of 12-ounce cans of beer is $4.00. Is the beer expensive? Most readers can readily answer the question. But suppose the same question is asked about a price of 25 francs. Most readers would find this a difficult question to answer. Why? A franc is a monetary unit, just like a dollar, so the difficulty cannot be attributed to the franc. Suppose you are given the additional information that the price of a 1-liter bottle of good wine is 20 francs. The additional price enables you to determine the market trade-off between the two goods, so the original question can be answered in the affirmative. The point of the exercise is to show that relative prices are what matter to the consumer. This fact tends to be overlooked when prices are stated in dollars, because a U. S. consumer knows how much a dollar can buy.

Since prices change frequently, it is useful to be able to identify the effect of such changes on the budget constraint. Returning to the budget problem, suppose P_S increases to $2.50 per pound. The maximum amount of X_C that can be bought remains fixed at 40 pounds, but the maximum amount of X_S is reduced to 20 pounds. When these two points are connected, as in Figure 7-1b, the slope changes. Substituting $P_S = \$2.50$ into equation 7-2 yields:

$$X_C = 40 - 2(X_S).$$

That is, the relative price has changed to 2, or one pound of steak in the market can be exchanged for two pounds of chicken. Increasing the relative price of X_S has made the budget constraint steeper.

The fourth property of budget constraints is that changes in the slope are changes in the relative price. The steeper the budget constraint, the higher the relative price of X_S in our example.

Changes in income can be represented easily. Returning to the original budget constraint, let the amount budgeted for chicken and steak increase to $60. The new constraint crosses the X_S and X_C axes at 30 and 48, respectively, as shown in Figure 7-1c. Notice the two budget constraints are parallel. Using $M = \$60$ in equation 7-2 yields:

$$X_C = 48 - 1.6(X_S).$$

That is, the slopes are the same, or the same relative price prevails in the market. The market trade-off for changing from X_S to X_C is still 1.6.

Thus, the fifth property is that parallel shifts in a budget constraint represent changes in income without any change in the relative price.

Equation 7-2 has a sixth property which should be noted. This equation, as a rearrangement of equation 7-1, shows how units of X_S are transformed into units X_C in the marketplace. Income is divided by P_C. An implication is that the relationship between the money budgeted and the prices of goods is very important. The concept of **real income**, or money income relative to the prices of goods and services, is consistent with the idea that money is desirable to the extent that it represents control over goods and services.

STUDY QUESTIONS

The Ability to Buy—The Budget Constraint

1. How is the ability to trade measured in a budget constraint?
2. What is a relative price, and why is the relative price important to consumers?
3. Define real income and explain how this definition is consistent with the definition of money.
4. How are changes in relative prices and changes in income shown in a budget constraint diagram?
5. Discuss how opportunity cost is involved in the budget constraint.
6. Assume that a family has budgeted $60 per week to spend on electricity (E) and water (W). Let the price of electricity, Pe, be $.30 per kilowatt hour, and let the price of water, Pw, be $.50 per cubic foot.
   a. What is the equation of the budget constraint?
   b. What is the trade-off between E and W?
   c. Use a diagram to show what happens if Pe rises to $.40 per kilowatt hour.
   d. Use a diagram to show what happens to the original budget constraint if the budget rises to $75.
7. A consumer unit has budgeted $140 this month for utilities (U) and gasoline (G). Suppose Pu = $1.00 and Pg = $1.25.
   a. Draw the budget constraint in a diagram. Then show in a diagram what happens to the constraint if the amount budgeted rises to $180 and Pg rises to $1.50.
   b. What has happened to the trade-off between U and G in part (a)?
8. Referring to problem 7, suppose prices and the amount budgeted in the initial budget constraint increase 20 percent. What happens to the budget constraint? What is the meaning of this result?

● The Willingness to Trade—The Indifference Curve ●

The market trade-off for goods and services, the relative price, is only half the picture. Purchases are also the result of a consumer unit's preferences for goods and services. A consumer's preferences determine the **willingness to trade**. This section develops a set of assumptions about the way an individual's preferences are formed. They are used to construct a diagrammatic representation of a consumer's willingness to trade.

As in the case of the budget constraint, borrowing and saving are ruled out, and only two goods are considered (that is, preferences are restricted to the use of two goods or services during the current time period.) These two conditions are relaxed later on, after the elements of the consumer model have been covered.

There are five assumptions that really form the basis of the analysis of the willingness to trade. These can be discussed in relation to Figure 7-2a. Quantities of two goods (X_i and X_j) are measured on the axes.[3] Any point in the diagram represents a combination of the two goods, which is referred to as a **bundle**. The first assumption is that a consumer can compare any two points, or bundles, in the figure. A second assumption is that both goods are desirable, so more is preferred to less. The third assumption is that only three types of choice are possible when two bundles, A and B, are compared. They are (1) A is preferred to B, (2) B is preferred to A, or (3) A is just as good as B. Notice that the third alternative is the boundary between the two other choice possibilities. The fourth assumption is that an individual's preferences are transitive. Suppose a consumer indicates that bundle A is preferred to B, and B is preferred to C, another bundle. Transitivity requires that A be preferred to C, or that preference orderings hold across pairs. The final assumption is that of consistency, which means that if a consumer prefers bundle A to B, then B can never be preferred to A.

Since X_i and X_j both produce utility for the consumer, it stands to reason that one of these goods can be substituted for the other in such a manner as to leave the level of utility unchanged. This is the type of substitution that is of interest, and there is an easy way to identify it. Draw a horizontal and vertical line through bundle A, as in Figure 7-2a. Four regions are created. Any point in region I is preferred to bundle A, because any point in this region has more of both goods than A. In like fashion, A is preferred to every point in region III.

Even-numbered regions require a little more analysis, because they are characterized by more of one good and less of the other. What follows is a description of a logical process that can be employed to find other bundles in the figure with the same level of utility as bundle A. Moving to the left of bundle A along the horizontal line decreases X_i while leaving X_j unchanged, so the consumer is worse off at bundle B than at bundle A. Suppose this consumer is compensated by an increase in the amount of X_j until the utility is the same as at bundle A. Call this bundle A' This approach can be used for any horizontal move to the left from A. The same procedure can also be employed for region IV by first moving down the vertical line and then compensating by moving to the right. If this were done many times, all of the corresponding bundles would form a curve such as the one shown in Figure 7-2b.

Because of the way the curve is constructed, every point (or bundle) located on it provides the same level of utility. Such a locus of points is called an **indifference curve**, because there is no change in utility. The consumer should be indifferent as to which bundle is received. There are several important properties of indifference curves. First, a consumer's willingness to trade is represented by the slope of the indifference curve. Since there is no change in utility, the consumer should be willing to move along a given indifference curve. Second, indifference curves are negatively sloped, because as long as a consumer prefers more to less, the only way to hold utility constant is to have a trade-off.

Third, indifference curves are convex to the origin. The convexity implies that it becomes progressively harder to substitute one good for another. This can be seen by examination of Figure 7-2c. Suppose the consumer is at bundle C. If X_j is decreased by $\Delta X_{j,c}$, the compensating change in X_i must be $\Delta X_{i,c}$, in order to maintain the same level of utility. If the consumer is at bundle E, then the

---

[3]   Subscripts i and j are just short-hand ways of noting that there are two arbitrary but distinct goods or services.

same decrease in X_j, $\Delta x_{j,c}$, requires a much larger compensating increase in X_i, $\Delta X_{i,E}$. to remain on the indifference curve I. Thus, the convexity implies that it becomes harder and harder to substitute one good for the other.

Figure 7-2a, b, & c: The Willingness to Trade

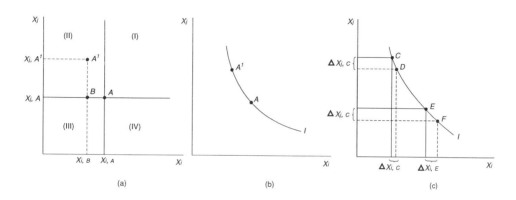

The five assumptions about consumer preferences generate the two points on the indifference curve found in panel (a). Bundles A and A' are equal in terms of utility to the consumer. The locus of all bundles having the same utility forms the indifference curve shown in panel (b). Indifference curves generally are represented as negatively sloped and convex to the origin. The negative slope occurs because more of one good must be associated with less of another in order to hold utility constant. A convex indifference curve shows, as indicated in panel (c), that it becomes harder and harder to substitute one good for another while holding utility constant.

There are two reasons for the convexity. One is that consumers value variety, and as the consumer moves down and to the right (or up and to the left) along an indifference curve, one good is becoming relatively scarce and the other relatively plentiful. Second, it is assumed that successive increments of a good add less and less to total utility. As one good becomes relatively scarce and the other relatively plentiful, the loss in utility from further decreases in the scarce good can be compensated only by increased changes in the relatively plentiful good.

In Figure 7-2a derivation of the indifference curve I is based on starting with bundle A. If another point were chosen, clearly the same logical process could be employed. If this other point lay on the indifference curve initially derived, then the same curve would be traced out. If the starting point were elsewhere, then another indifference curve would be derived. This suggests that each consumer has more than one indifference curve. In fact, an indifference curve, based on the same set of assumptions about comparing bundles and the types of choices, passes through every point in a diagram. Consequently, notation in diagrams and equations needs to be flexible enough to distinguish one indifference curve from another. Every indifference curve has the properties outlined above. In addition, preferring more to less means that, as a consumer moves away from the origin, successively higher levels of utility must be attained, or higher and higher indifference curves are crossed.

Given there is a set of indifference curves, we need to add one final property—indifference curves cannot cross. Inspection of Figure 7-3 reveals why. Bundles A and B lie on the curve I_1 and A and C lie on I_2. The inference to be drawn is that the consumer should be indifferent to a choice between B and C. However, C has more of both goods versus B, so the consumer must prefer C to B. Transitivity and consistency preclude the crossing of indifference curves.

Figure 7-3: Indifference Curves Crossing

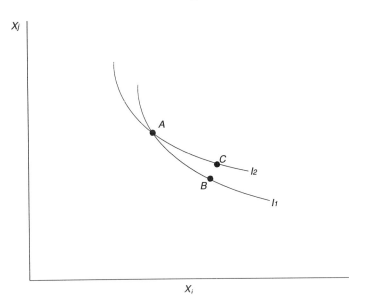

Indifference curves cannot cross. A comparison of bundles *A, B,* and *C* reveals why. Since *A* and *B* lie on *I₁*, they have the same utility. This applies also to bundles *A* and *C*. The implication is that the consumer should be indifferent in a choice between *B* and *C*. But *C* has more of both goods. The only way to avoid the problem is for the indifference curves not to cross.

STUDY QUESTIONS

The Willingness to Trade—The Indifference Curve

9. Why does the slope of an indifference curve represent the willingness to trade?
10. What are the properties of indifference curves, and how are they related to assumptions about consumer preferences?
11. Explain why indifference curves are convex to the origin.
12. Consider two individuals and their preferences for casual-informal clothing versus dress-business clothing. One is a college student, and the other is a middle-aged, middle-management professional. Representative indifference curves for the two individuals are presented in Figure 7-4. Which curve is more likely to be associated with each individual? Explain.
13. Imagine a family at two points in its life-cycle. One point is when the family has been newly formed, and the other is when it is nearing retirement. Preferences between savings and all other goods are shown in Figure 7-5 by representative indifference curves. Which curve is more likely to be associated with the life-cycle stages?
14. If indifference curves are not supposed to cross, explain why it is permissible for them to do so in the diagrams of questions 12 and 13.

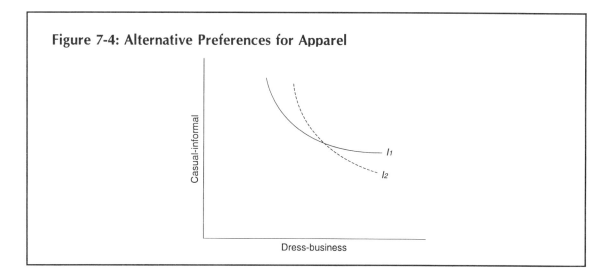

Figure 7-4: Alternative Preferences for Apparel

● The Optimal Purchase ●

Indifference curves and budget constraints can be presented in one diagram. Procedurally, there is no problem because quantities o X_i and X_j are measured on the axes. Conceptually, it is reasonable because each consumer must reconcile preferences for alternative combinations of goods and services with the allowable market purchases. Figure 7-6 is such a presentation. The budget constraint, b, has

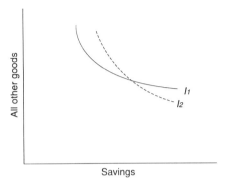

Figure 7-5: Alternative Preferences for All Other Goods and Savings

the general shape discussed previously, as does the set of indifference curves, of which three are drawn: I_1, I_2, and I_3.

Inspection if Figure 7-6 reveals the **optimal bundle**, which maximizes utility subject to the budget constraint. Given budget constraint b, the optimal bundle is found where an indifference curve just touches budget constraint b. This is bundle E in Figure 7-6. Anywhere an indifference curve crosses line b, a consumer can change purchases so as to reach higher indifference curves.

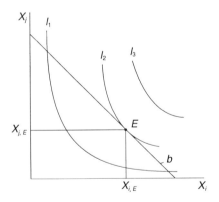

Figure 7-6: The Willingness and Ability to Trade

Combining the consumer's preferences for goods with the ability to purchase them in the market completes the model of consumer choice. The consumer reaches the highest utility by moving along the budget constraint to a point of tangency with the set of indifference curves. This is shown as point *E*. At point *E* the market trade-off (the slope of the budget constraint) is the same as the consumer's willingness to trade (the slope of the indifference curve).

How does a consumer know where this optimal position is? Suppose the consumer happens to be on the budget constraint at the position labeled "a" in Figure 7-7. Given prices and income, the consumer could make this purchase. The implication is that the consumer's willingness to trade (the slope of an indifference curve) is not the same as the ability to trade (the slope of b). Whenever this occurs, the consumer could increase utility by changing the consumption bundle.

Why should the consumer move from bundle "a"? Suppose the amount of X_j the consumer has is decreased to $X_{j,a'}$. How much X_i does the consumer require to remain indifferent? The answer is that X_i must increase to $X_{i,a'}$ because that keeps the consumer on I_1. But how much X_i can be purchased in the marketplace? By moving along b, the consumer can reach $X_{i,a*}$. Since $\Delta X_{ia} > \Delta X_{ia'}$, the consumer will become better off by moving down the budget constraint. The same logic can be used to show that if an indifference curve crosses the budget constraint from below, the consumer can become better off by moving up the budget constraint.

Further insight into the consumer decision-making process can be gained by returning to bundle E in Figure 7-6. The **marginal utility** of any good (i), MU_i, is defined as the change in utility due to consuming one unit more or less of the good. There is a general relationship for the slope of any indifference curve at any point. The slope of any curve at a specific point on it is the ratio of the vertical change to the horizontal change, and for indifference curves this can be shown to be the ratio of the marginal utilities. The slope is MU_i/MU_j in Figures 7-6 and 7-7.

Figure 7-7: Reaching the Optimal Bundle

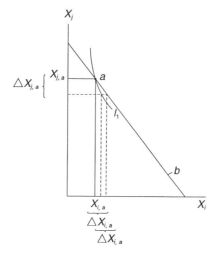

The manner in which a consumer reaches the optimal bundle is shown through an examination of bundle a. Whenever an indifference curve crosses the budget constraint, the consumer can gain by changing purchases. For example, if X_j is decreased by the amount $\Delta X_{j,a}$, the consumer needs $\Delta X_{i,a}$ in order to maintain utility. But by trading in the market-that is, using the money not spent for X_j to purchase X_i-the consumer can buy $\Delta X_{i,a}$. Since $\Delta X_{i,a} > \Delta X_{i,a}$, the consumer becomes better off in this case by moving down the budget constraint.

This definition of the slope has intuitive appeal. The negative sign implies a trade-off, which was noted as a property of indifference curves. A consumer's willingness to trade should be based on the change in utility due to an incremental change in the quantity of a good used. One's disposition to trade more of one good for less of another must depend on one's valuation of the trade-off. The ratio of the marginal utilities is the representation of such an assessment.

Graphically, the slope of any curve is a straight line that just touches but does not cross a curve. Such a line is called a tangent line. Notice that at point E the tangent line to I_2 is the same as the budget constraint b. Both slopes are negative. The slope of the budget constraint is $-P_i/P_j$, and the slope of the indifference curve is $-MU_i/MU_j$. The implication is that the slope of an indifference curve is the same as the slope of the budget constraint at E, or the willingness to trade is the same as the ability to trade $-P_i/P_j = -MU_i/MU_j$.

Table 7-2 shows how the equality of the two slopes at point E can be manipulated to obtain a relationship that is the key to consumer behavior. The ratio of the marginal utility of each good to its price relates the change in utility associated with an incremental change in quantity used by a consumer to the market cost of the incremental unit, so the ratio is called the **value of the last dollar spent**. Such a ratio relates how an incremental unit more or less of the good changes the utility for a consumer unit relative to the market price per unit. It is the equivalent of asking "Is it worth the price I have to pay?"

At any point other than E on the budget constraint in Figure 7-6, the slope of the indifference curve is not equal to the slope of the budget constraint.[4] The right-hand column of Table 7-2 shows that anywhere else the value of the last dollar spent is not the same for both goods. Movement along a budget constraint involves a trade-off based on relative prices. But any change in the quantities of goods also affects utility. More of one good and less of another causes a gain and a loss in utility. If the consumer is to move toward the optimal bundle, then the consumer should acquire more of the good that has the higher value of the last dollar spent and less of the other good.

Returning to point "a" of Figure 7-7, you can see that I_1 is steeper than b. Since the slopes are negative, it follows that $-MU_i/MU_j < -P_i/P_j$. Multiplying by -1 and rearranging leads to $MU_i/P_i > MU_j/P_j$. The consumer should increase purchases of X_i and decrease purchases of X_j to move toward the optimum.

Table 7-2: Analysis of Consumer Trade-offs.

At E in Figure 7-6			Elsewhere on b in Figure 7-6		
Slope of b		**Slope of I_2**	**Slope of b**		**Slope of I**
$-(P_i/P_j)$	=	$-(MU_i/MU_j)$	$-(P_i/P_j)$	> or <	$-(MU_i/MU_j)$
(P_i/P_j)	=	(MU_i/MU_j)	(P_i/P_j)	> or <	(MU_i/MU_j)
(MU_j/P_j)	=	(MU_i/P_i)	(MU_j/P_j)	> or <	(MU_i/P_i)

---

[4]   A mathematical analysis of the utility maximization problem indicates, among other things, that there can be only one point of tangency along a budget constraint.

Applying this logic to bundle E in Figure 7-6, one can see why the consumer would not move from this point. The value of the last dollar spent on both goods is the same. Regardless of which direction the consumer moved incrementally along b, there would be an off-setting change, so there would be no net gain.

Equations 7-3 and 7-4 summarize and extend the discussion. Whenever equation 7-3 holds, the consumer is making the optimal purchase. Notice that if more goods are introduced, the equality must hold for all of the pairs. Whenever there is an inequality, the consumer purchases more of the good that provides a larger satisfaction per dollar. Let n represent the number of goods.

Optimal consumption:

(7-3) $MU_i/P_i = MU_j/P_j$ for i,j = 1,...,n.

Change consumption:

(7-4) $MU_i/P_i \neq MU_j/P_j$ for i,j = 1,...,n.

The following numerical example is used for illustrative purposes only, to clarify the analysis. Such numbers are not required to develop the consumer decision-making rule, and the use of numbers for marginal utility necessitates imposition of some very restrictive assumptions about utility, which are beyond the scope of this introductory text. This point will be reconsidered shortly.

A consumer unit has budgeted $50 for steak and chicken. Suppose it purchases 12.5 pounds of steak and 20 pounds of chicken. This bundle is on the budget constraint, so the first part of the analysis has been completed. It is necessary to determine if the indifference curve passing through this point crosses or is tangent to the budget constraint. Figure 7-8 illustrates the possibilities. If I_1 represents the unit's preferences, then more steak and less chicken should be purchased. Just the opposite would hold if I_2 were the correct curve. Optimal consumption would occur if I_3 were the appropriate representation.

In order to distinguish among the possibilities, the marginal utilities of the family for the two goods must be known. This information permits the determination of the slope of the indifference curve for bundle A. Assume that $MU_S = 30$ and $MU_C = 25$. Given this information, equation 7-4 yields:

$$MU_S/P_S = 30/2 \text{ and } MU_C/P_C = 25/1.25$$
$$15 \quad < \quad 20$$

The unit should purchase more chicken and less steak in order to be better off. Given our numbers, indifference curve I_2 turns out to be the appropriate graphical representation. Notice that in this example the marginal utility of X_S is greater than that of X_C, but the consumer unit should purchase more X_C and less X_S. The reason is that steak costs more per unit, so the difference in marginal utilities is not enough to overcome the difference in prices.

Assume the unit changes its purchases to 10 pounds of steak and 24 pounds of chicken. The respective marginal utilities are 32 and 20. You should be able to verify that this is another bundle on the budget constraint and that the values of the last dollar spent on both goods are the same. Hence, this must be an optimal bundle.

Figure 7-8: Determination of the Optimal Choice

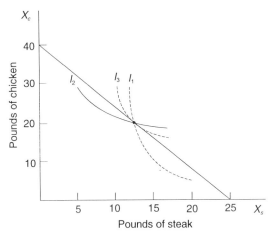

Given a budget and prices, a consumer might be anywhere on a budget constraint. The first assumption about preferences means that an indifference curve passes through every point on a budget constraint. Whether a point on the budget constraint is the optimal bundle depends on whether the indifference curve going through the point also crosses the budget constraint. Curves I_1, I_2, and I_3 show the possibilities, and Table 7-2 identifies the values of the last dollar spent for the three cases. I_3 depicts the optimal situation, as it is tangent to the budget constraint. Or, the values of the last dollar spent are equated as shown in the left-hand side of Table 7-2.

● This Is All Very Nice, But ... ●

What is the use of this theory? Is all of this necessary? What is the real-world relevance? These are some of the initial reactions one might have after preliminary exposure to the theory of consumer behavior. All such reservations about this approach should diminish as you reflect on the material. Working through the exercises and considering your own behavior should help you see how the model can be applied.

The consumer's situation is seen to be a constrained maximization problem, in which the objective is to attain the highest level of utility subject to the budget constraint. The optimal consumption bundle for a given set of market prices and income is at a point of tangency between the set of indifference curves and the budget constraint. At such a point, the consumer's willingness to trade is the same as the market's trade-off. The values of the last dollar spent for all goods and services are the same. Essentially, the consumer must ask whether the good or service is worth the price that has to be paid. Answers in the affirmative result in the commodity being purchased.

No unusual conditions are imposed by this analytical framework. The budget simply represents one-period market opportunities. Assumptions about a consumer's preferences are very reasonable—they do not inhibit the manner in which consumers form opinions. These assumptions do not indicate how preferences are formed; rather, they just establish the basis from which indifference curves can be constructed.

STUDY QUESTIONS

The Optimal Bundle

15. What are the justifications for combining indifference curves and the budget constraint into one diagram?
16. Explain the economic interpretation of the value of the last dollar spent.
17. Why is the following statement false? "The consumer has reached the optimal consumption bundle whenever the marginal utilities of the goods consumed are equal."
18. Show how changes in income, prices, and tastes would affect the optimal consumption bundle.
19. A family has a budget of $20 per month for potatoes and fresh vegetables. Let the price of potatoes be $1.00 per pound and the price of fresh vegetables be $1.25 per pound. The family purchases 10 pounds of potatoes and 8 pounds of fresh vegetables, and the respective marginal utilities are $MU_p = 30$ and $MU_{fv} = 35$.
    a. Since $MU_{fv} > MU_p$, why can't you just use this information to say that more fresh vegetables should be bought?
    b. Is the combination an optimal bundle? If not, in what direction should the family move?
20. A consumer unit has budgeted $45 per month for poultry and fish. Let the price of poultry be $2.00 per pound and that of fish be $1.50 per pound. Determine whether each combination described below is an optimal bundle. If not, in what direction should the family move?
    a. The unit purchases 18 pounds of poultry and 6 pounds of fish. The marginal utilities are $MU_p = 50$ and $MU_f = 45$.
    b. The unit purchases 13 pounds of poultry and 10 pounds of fish; $MU_p = 64$, and $MU_f = 48$.

In the above illustration numbers were used for marginal utility. It must be stressed that this was for illustrative purposes only. Indifference curves can be constructed and the optimizing rule developed without any recourse to exact numbers with respect to utility. All that is required is that consumers react to market prices for commodities and make determinations as to whether or not to purchase. It is not necessary that a consumer give a numerical value for the marginal utility of a particular good. A consumer need only relate the market price to the incremental utility in order to determine whether one unit more or less is worth the opportunity cost of the money used to buy the good or service.

This chapter outlined the elements of consumer decision making with respect to purchase decisions. Notice that the model referred to individual consumer choice. Although everyone faces the same market prices, each consumer reaches different conclusions about what to buy. These differences arise, in part, from differences in income. The individual variation also is a result of different preferences. Preferences determine the shape of indifference curves, and therefore, the points of tangency.

In previous chapters it was argued that consumer expenditure decisions were not the result of a random process. The model presented here shows that consumer purchases are the end result of consumers' efforts to maximize utility, subject to their budget constraints. Purchases are the consequence of systematic behavior. Optimal consumption bundles change as prices, income, and preferences change. To the extent that these determinants change gradually, consumer purchases also do so. The consumption data presented in Chapter 1 suggest that the economic setting has been changing gradually over time.

The objective behind the construction of any theoretical model is to develop a framework with which one can analyze all of the forces at work and derive optimizing conditions. Certainly this model serves as a useful basis for understanding consumer behavior in a market system. Consider the following data, which illustrate how the model can be applied. During 1980 per capita real disposable income remained virtually unchanged. The Consumer Price Index for poultry increased 5.1 percent, and the price increase for beef and veal was 5.7 percent.[5] Assuming that the representative consumer's budget for beef and veal and poultry did not change, what happened to the budget constraint? Figure 7-9 illustrates the situation where b_{1979} and b_{1980} are the respective budget constraints. Since the prices of both food groups rose faster than income, b_{1980} is inside b_{1979}. Because beef and veal prices increased more than poultry prices, b_{1980} must be flatter than b_{1979}. The maximum amount of beef and veal that could be purchased declined (vertical intercept) more than the maximum amount of poultry the consumer was able to buy (horizontal intercept). That is, assuming no change in the money budgeted, b_{1980} must also lie inside b_{1979}.

What is the anticipated effect on the representative consumer? Assuming that consumers' preferences did not change, it must be concluded that the consumers' situation with respect to these commodities worsened. Data on the per capita pounds of poultry and beef and veal consumed are consistent with the inference. The number of pounds of poultry consumed per capita during 1980 was 61.6, whereas for 1979 it was 62.2. Corresponding data for beef and veal were 79.6 for 1980 and 81.2 for 1979. Thus, less was consumed in 1980 in both categories. This is illustrated in Figure 7-9. Indifference curve I_1 is associated with a higher level of utility than is I_2. While the quantities of both goods declined, the absolute and percentage declines for beef and veal were greater than those for poultry. This suggests that the representative consumer substituted some poultry for beef and veal.[6] Notice that this analysis was conducted without quantifying utility.

Depending on the interests of the researcher, this economic analysis could be extended in several ways. Marketing specialists can use this type of analysis to determine the effect of price changes on the quantities consumed. Such research includes not only the effect of price changes in each commodity on the quantities of the respective good purchased (called own-price effects), but also the effects of price changes across categories (called cross-price effects). This introductory analysis suggests that consumers may be sensitive to cross-price effects, so these effects should be included in the analysis of consumer purchases.

The economic model also can be used to identify consumer trends, forecast expenditure, and locate sales opportunities. Public policy implications include the impact of inflation on consumer expenditure and the impact of pricing policies on the consumer. The next few chapters discuss how

---

[5]   Judith Putnam and Jane Allshouse, *Food Consumption, Prices, and Expenditures, 1970-90*. U. S. Department of Agriculture, Economic Research Service Statistical Bulletin 840 (1992).

[6]   The inference must remain tentative because a complete analysis of consumer expenditure in 1980 is beyond present interest.

such extensions can be accomplished. Not only can the model help businesses be responsive to consumers, but it can identify those areas where the market system does not work in the consumer's interest. Equations 7-3 and 7-4 represent the decision-making rule. Consumer activists and policy makers can use this model to identify those situations in which the consumer cannot properly assess the marginal utility of specific goods and services and to identify instances where the market price does not properly reflect the cost per unit. Whenever such situations can be shown to exist, this model can be used as the justification for intervention.

Figure 7-9: Poultry vs. Beef and Veal

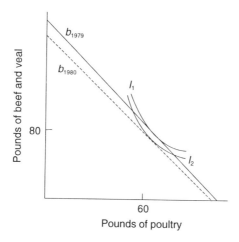

The consumer decision-making model can be applied to U.S. data on per capita consumer income, prices, and pounds of poultry and beef and veal purchased for 1979 and 1980. Between 1979 and 1980 there was no change in real consumer income, but the relative price of beef and veal increased, thereby creating the b_{1979} and b_{1980} constraints. Indifference curves I_1 and I_2 are associated with the actual consumption that occurred.

● Summary ●

This chapter has presented a simplified model of consumer choice. A consumer has a fixed budget to be allocated within one period. The goal is to spend the budget as wisely as possible. More of one good can be acquired only at the expense of another, so opportunity cost is involved. A budget constraint shows what a consumer is able to do in the marketplace. The slope of the budget constraint, the relative price, is the ability of the consumer unit to trade one good for another. Indifference curves represent the consumer's preferences for the goods. The slope of an indifference curve measures the willingness to trade, because movement along a given curve does not change the level of utility.

Optimal consumption occurs where the consumer attains the highest level of utility. It is shown as the point of tangency between the indifference curves and the budget constraint, where the ability to trade is the same as the willingness to trade. A consumer moves toward the optimal purchase by comparing the market trade-off to the willingness to trade. A consumer moves toward the optimal purchase by comparing the values of the last dollar spent on the goods. It is the same as asking "Is it worth the price I have to pay?"

STUDY QUESTIONS

This Is All Very Nice, But ...

21. Compare situations (a) and (b) of question 20 to determine what has been assumed about the marginal utility of each good.
22. Use the model of consumer choice (indifference curves and budget constraints) to analyze the situation described by the following data.

	Share of Food Budget	
	1950	1978
Food at home	80.2%	75.7%
Food away from home	19.8%	24.3%

Average annual percentage increase in the food budget = 9%.
Average annual percentage price change in food at home = 5%.
Average annual percentage price change in food away = 7%.

23. How has opportunity cost been used in the discussion of the optimal position of the consumer?

● Key Terms ●

Ability to trade: how units of one good may be exchanged for another at market prices.
Budget constraint: the set of maximum quantities that can be purchased given market prices and the consumer's available money income.
Bundle: a combination of goods.
Indifference curve: locus of bundles that provide the same level of utility.
Marginal utility: a change in utility due to an incremental change in the quantity of a good used by a consumer.
Optimal bundle: the bundle that maximizes utility subject to a budget constraint.
Rational consumer: a consumer who maximizes utility subject to constraints.
Real income: money income relative to the prices of goods and services.
Relative price: the price of one good relative to the price of another.
Value of the last dollar spent: the marginal utility of a good relative to its price.
Willingness to trade: how units of one good can be exchanged for another with utility held constant.

Chapter 8

Consumer Demand, Market Supply, and Price Adjustment

Understanding how buyers and sellers interact is the cornerstone of consumer economics. As we saw in Chapter 2, consumers interface with the economy primarily through the factor and final goods markets. Every day consumers acquire goods and services in the final goods market, so the way this exchange process works has a direct impact on consumer well-being. Similarly, buying and selling productive resources involves the same basics, although the roles of consumers and business are reversed.

The model of consumer choice, outlined in the previous chapter, is used to describe the quantity of a good or service the consumer unit is able and willing to buy. This information becomes the market demand when aggregated over all consumers. Determinants of the quantity supplied by producers are identified. Markets, in the absence of controls, are shown to operate through reactions of buyers and sellers to prices. This chapter ends by focusing on three applications of demand and supply analysis: rent control, seasonal gasoline prices, and a food safety scare.

● From Consumer Choice to Consumer Demand ●

The **demand** for a good is defined as the quantity a consumer is able and willing to purchase. $X_{j,E}$ and $X_{i,E}$ in Figure 7-6 are the quantities demanded in a fixed situation, defined by the given budget constraint and set of preferences. Any point of tangency, then, must be associated with the quantities of goods or services demanded. These optimal quantities are a consumer's purchases per time period, because the budget constraint incorporates market prices and the amount budgeted per time period and the indifference curves represent preferences for that period.

Although these situations do not remain fixed for long, the traditional consumer choice model can be used as the structure for identifying the effects of changes in the economic environment on the quantities purchased. Each budget constraint has an optimal level of consumption of X_i and X_j associated with it, determined by the point of tangency with the indifference curves, as Figure 8-1 illustrates.

A change in income, by itself, causes a parallel shift in the budget constraint. Figure 8-1a displays two parallel budget constraints, b_1 and b_2, and the optimal consumption bundles associated with each, E_1 and E_2. Since income is the element that is changing in the economic setting, this panel shows how income affects the demand for X_i and X_j.

Similarly, a price change alone causes the slope of the budget constraint to change, thereby causing the point of tangency to change. Consequently, changes in prices cause changes in the optimal consumption bundles. This is illustrated in Figure 8-1b. A change in consumer preferences alters the shape of the set of indifference curves, so the point of tangency on a given budget constraint changes, as indicated in Figure 8-1c. Changes in preferences therefore also lead to changes in the optimal consumption bundles.

Figure 8-1: Changing the Optimal Purchase

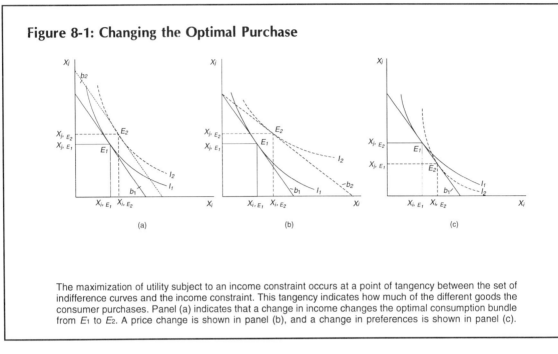

The maximization of utility subject to an income constraint occurs at a point of tangency between the set of indifference curves and the income constraint. This tangency indicates how much of the different goods the consumer purchases. Panel (a) indicates that a change in income changes the optimal consumption bundle from E_1 to E_2. A price change is shown in panel (b), and a change in preferences is shown in panel (c).

Thus, the optimal consumption bundle changes as the consumer's economic environment changes. Conceptually, a consumer moves to any point of tangency by evaluating the values of the last dollar spent of goods and services. The quantity demanded of a good or service per time period is determined by prices, income, and preferences.

In order to learn more about demand relationships which can be used to describe consumer behavior in final goods markets, we must be able to summarize the relationships in a short-hand manner. The way to do this is with functional notation. **Functional notation** is just a way of stating that values of one variable, termed the **dependent variable**, are the result of values of other variables, termed **independent variables**. Consider the simple algebraic equations shown below. Suppose the dependent variable is represented by DEP, and the independent variable is represented by IND. Each equation can be viewed as an alternative statement of exactly how DEP and IND are related, or a representation of the variables' **explicit relationship**. That is, for a given value of IND, each equation is a statement about the manner in which IND determines DEP.

$$DEP = -5 + 2(IND)$$
$$DEP = 20.3 + 0.9(1/IND)$$
$$DEP = 4.7(IND)^2$$

Each of the equations indicates an exact (but different) way in which an independent variable determines the value of the dependent variable. That is, the causal relationship is presented explicitly. Functional notation provides a handy way of stating that a causal relationship exists among variables without indicating exactly how. The equations above can be summarized by functional notation DEP = f(IND). This shows that DEP is determined by IND, but the symbol f replaces as an explicit statement of the relationship.

A functional equation is more general than an explicit equation, because it is consistent with any explicit equation relating the variables represented. However, a functional equation does not contain as much information, because it does not indicate how the variables are related, except to identify the dependent and independent variables(s).

Often it is not necessary to create explicit equations. One reason is that the model being developed may not have a precise enough theoretical base to generate an explicit relationship. Another is that there may be no need to be more specific than to recognize that a causal relationship exists. It is the latter case that is relevant here. Because this is as an introduction to the theory of consumer decision making, only those variables that are determinants of the quantity demanded need be identified. Functional notation is ideally suited for this objective.

According to the traditional model of consumer choice, the demand for a market good or service is determined by prices, income, and preferences. The explicit form of the demand relationship depends to a large extent on the slope of the indifference curves, or the preferences of a consumer. Because attention is directed toward identifying the causality in demand relationships, it is not necessary to specify an explicit mathematical representation of preferences. Rather, only functional notation is needed, where f encompasses all of the various ways in which preferences enter into the decision making. The two-goods/one-period model for chicken and steak demand (see Chapter 7) now can be presented in the form of **demand equations**, which associate the quantities of X_C and X_S the consumer is able and willing to buy as functions of several determinants. These are equations 8-1. Subscripts for the functional notation indicate that the explicit form of the demand equation for X_C does not have to be identical to that of X_S.

The quantity demanded for steak is a function of the price of steak, the price of chicken, and income.

The quantity demanded for chicken is a function of the price of steak, the price of chicken, and income.

Or:

$$X_S = f_s(P_s, P_c, M), \text{ and}$$
(8-1) $$X_C = f_c(P_s, P_c, M).$$

Extension of the model to include more than two goods precludes the use of a diagrammatic approach. A three-goods model requires a three-dimensional diagram, and more than three goods cannot be drawn. Mathematical tools beyond the scope of this book are required for the incorporation of many goods. However, the solution of the more general problem is consistent with, and can be related easily to, the two-goods model. This is fortunate, because the many-goods model is more appropriate for analyzing real-world consumer market behavior. Furthermore, the logic that has been developed in the two-goods model also applies in the more general setting. The consumer's problem remains one of utility maximization, subject to a budget constraint. A consumer attains the optimal bundle by comparing the values of the last dollar spent for every good. Opportunity cost plays a pivotal role, money spent for one good cannot be spent for another.

The general setting of a consumer's demand for many goods can be represented with functional notation. Quantities and prices need more general notation, purchases are not limited to steak and chicken. This is accomplished by letting subscripts denote specific goods and services. The ordering of the goods and services is not important, so the first good (i = 1) could be determined by alphabetical order, the amount purchased, or any other scheme. If there are n goods in the model, then the quantity demand of each can be shown as:

$$X_1 = f_1(P_1, P_2, ..., P_n, M)$$

(8-2)

$$X_n = f_n(P_1, P_2, ..., P_n, M)$$

A set of demand equations, or functions, which represents a generalization of the two-goods model and equations 8-1, is called a **demand system**. Variables on the right-hand side of equations 8-2 have effects on the X_i in a manner analogous to that of the two-goods model. Recall that a change is P_s alone alters the slope of the budget constraint and, thereby, the point of tangency and the quantities demanded. This is why P_s and P_c appear in both equations 8-1 and why P_i appears in each of the equations 8-2. The situation is similar for income and preferences.

Whether a two-goods or an n-goods model is used, the consumer is envisioned as maximizing utility subject to a budget constraint. Equations 7-3 and 7-4 are the decision-making rules for the more general model. The decision-making rule involves evaluating the value of the last dollar spent. Its diagrammatic counterpart is reaching the point of tangency. A fixed economic environment means the consumer has enough time to alter purchases until the values of the last dollar spent are equated. Any change in these determinants must lead to a change in the value of the last dollar spent for at least one good. When this occurs, the equality among them no longer holds, so the quantities purchased must change. The marginal utilities change as the quantities consumed change, until the values of the last dollar spent are equated again.

STUDY QUESTIONS

From Consumer Choice to Consumer Demand

1. Explain why the point of tangency determines the quantities of the two goods a consumer buys.
2. How do a budget constraint and a set of indifference curves portray a given economic situation for a consumer?
3. Why is a consumer's demand for a good determined by all prices, not just the own-price?
4. Distinguish between a functional and an explicit relationship. What are the advantages and disadvantages of each?
5. Why is consumer demand a flow per time period?
6. Explain how prices, income, and preferences determine the quantity demanded.

● Consumer Demand and Market Demand ●

Each separate equation in system 8-2 is called a **demand function**. The quantity demanded of a good or service per time period is determined by prices $(P_1,...,P_n)$, income (M), and preferences. While all of these have been shown to be important determinants of the quantity demanded, it is particularly interesting to study the relationship between demand and the market price of the respective good or service. A study of this relationship reveals how markets work.

A **demand curve** is defined as the quantity a consumer is able and willing to purchase at various market prices. The distinction between a demand function and a demand curve is found in the last phrase of the preceding sentence: at various market prices. In a demand curve, only the market price of the good or service being studied is allowed to change. All of the other determinants of the quantity demanded are considered fixed. Inspection of Figure 8-1 reveals this distinction. Each panel portrays, for the two-goods model, how a determinant of the demand function affects the quantity demanded. Specifically, Figure 8-1b shows the effect of a change in P_i on X_i and X_j, but because of the way a demand curve is defined, interest centers on the quantities of X_i alone.[1]

Only two variables are associated with a given demand curve: the price and the quantity demand of the good or service per time period. Each variable comprises an axis in a demand curve diagram. The vertical scale measures alternative prices, and the horizontal scale measures quantity per time period. Most demand curves are drawn as negatively sloped lines. There are two fundamental reasons for this, based on the traditional model of consumer choice. One is that as the price falls a good becomes relatively cheaper, so a consumer tends to substitute more of this cheaper good. This is called the **substitution effect**. The second is that as the price falls a consumer is able to buy more, because real income has risen. It is referred to as the **income effect**. Together, these reasons cause price and quantity demanded to change in opposite directions.

The rationale for a negatively sloped demand curve can be explained more clearly by focusing on the illustration contained in Figure 8-2. Panel (a) is the same as Panel (b) in Figure 8-1, with steak and chicken as the goods. Two budget constraints, drawn as b_1 and b_2, reflect a change in the price of steak. If the consumer has $50 to spend on X_C and X_S and the respective prices are $1.25 and $2.00, b_1 is the constraint and 11.25 pounds of steak are purchased. Should P_s become $1.25, then the diagram indicates that 14 pounds would be bought. This means that as the price of steak falls, the consumer unit's demand for steak increases.

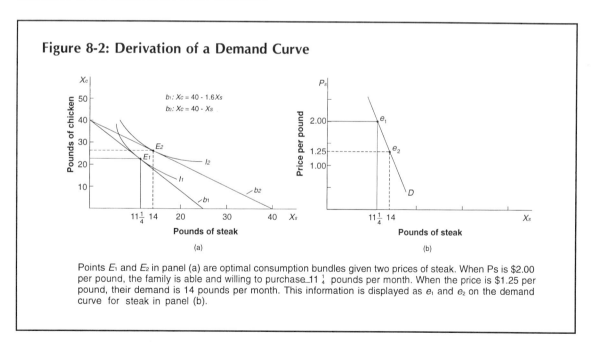

Figure 8-2: Derivation of a Demand Curve

Points E_1 and E_2 in panel (a) are optimal consumption bundles given two prices of steak. When Ps is $2.00 per pound, the family is able and willing to purchase 11 ¼ pounds per month. When the price is $1.25 per pound, their demand is 14 pounds per month. This information is displayed as e_1 and e_2 on the demand curve for steak in panel (b).

---

[1]   Figure 8-2 shows how a demand curve can be derived from a diagram like Figure 8-1b.

A more careful examination of panel (a) provides a basis for a better understanding of the substitution and income effects due to a change in price. The substitution effect induces the consumer to purchase more of the relatively less expensive item. When P_s is $1.25, steak has a lower relative price, and this is reflected in the fact that b_2 is flatter than b_1. The lower relative price alone induces a consumer to purchase more of the cheaper good (in this case X_s). This is consistent with the convexity of the indifference curves. Because as a budget constraint becomes flatter, it can only touch a given indifference curve farther to the right. The income effect arises from the change in real income associated with a price change. A decline in price enables a consumer to purchase more, and this is reflected in the fact that b_2 is farther away from the origin than b_1.

The information in panel (a) is summarized in panel (b). There are only two variables of interest: the market price, which has changed, and the quantity demanded, which has changed accordingly. This information on quantity and price is also presented in a demand schedule, shown as Table 8-1. Various market prices are displayed in column (1); the corresponding demand quantities are shown in column (2). Two of the combinations are the same as points e_1 and e_2 in Figure 8-2b. The other price-quantity pairs in the table are from other points of tangency like E_1 and E_2 that are not shown. This means that the demand curve indicates what the quantity demanded would be for many changes in the price of steak alone. Although the demand curve in Figure 8-2b is drawn as a straight line for the sake of convenience, a demand curve need not be a straight line.

Table 8-1: A Consumer's Demand.

(1) Market Price (in dollars)		(2) Quantity Demanded (in pounds)
2.50		9.50
2.25		10.30
2.00	e_1	11.25
1.75		12.16
1.50	e_2	13.08
1.25		14.00

Demand curves can be extremely useful for analyzing consumer behavior. The relationship between various market prices of a good and the quantities demanded by a consumer comprises a major component of the market system. Movement along a demand curve shows how a change in the price of a good brings about a change in the quantity demanded.

Consumer sensitivity to price change is reflected in the slope of the demand curve. The steeper the curve, the smaller a consumer's response (change in the quantity demanded) to a change in price. This is reflected in Figure 8-3, in which two alternative demand curves are drawn.[2] Both curves are

---

[2]   Since there is only one good being considered, there is no need for as an i subscript for price or quantity.

negatively sloped, but the flatter curve, D*, indicates much more sensitivity of the quantity demanded to changes in price. The price increase from P_1 to P_2 has a much more pronounced effect on the quantity demanded along D* than along D. Thus $(X_2^*-X_1)$ is larger than (X_2-X_1).

Figure 8-3: Slopes and Demand Curves

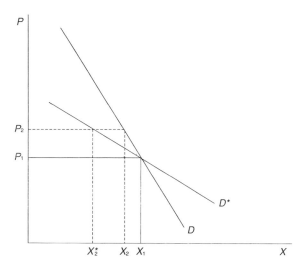

Slopes of demand curves show how sensitive consumer demand is to changes in price. The flatter the demand curve, the more responsive the quantity demanded is to changes in price. Curve D* indicates a much larger change in the quantity demanded because of the increase in price from P_1 to P_2.

Movement along a given demand curve is referred to as a **change in the quantity demanded**. This occurs whenever the only variable that changes in the consumer's economic setting is the price of the good. But the traditional model of consumer choice also identifies other determinants of the quantity demanded, summarized in equations 8-1 or 8-2.

What happens to a demand curve if one of these other determinants changes? The answer is that a new curve must be drawn. Because of the manner in which a demand curve is derived, any change in the point of tangency between a budget constraint and the indifference curves necessitates construction of a new demand curve. This is illustrated in Figure 8-4. Suppose the consumer unit's budget for chicken and steak increases to $80. The solid lines in panels (a) and (b) show the original information from Figure 8-2. The change in the budget creates a new budget constraint for each of the market prices of steak. Notice that because b_1 and b_1^* are parallel, they reflect the same relative price, but b_1^* is associated with a higher budget. Similar remarks hold for b_2 and b_2^*. Utility maximizing purchases occur at E_1^* and E_2^*, or 20 pounds and 30 pounds of steak, at the market prices $2.00 and $1.25 per pound. These are shown as points on a new demand curve, D*. A **change**

in demand occurs whenever any determinant of demand other than the good's own-price changes, because a new relationship arises between price and quantity.

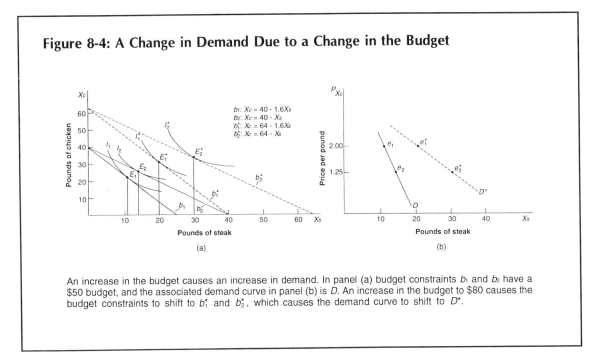

Figure 8-4: A Change in Demand Due to a Change in the Budget

b_1: $X_c = 40 - 1.6X_s$
b_2: $X_c = 40 - X_s$
b_1^*: $X_c = 64 - 1.6X_s$
b_2^*: $X_c = 64 - X_s$

(a)

(b)

An increase in the budget causes an increase in demand. In panel (a) budget constraints b_1 and b_2 have a $50 budget, and the associated demand curve in panel (b) is D. An increase in the budget to $80 causes the budget constraints to shift to b_1^* and b_2^*, which causes the demand curve to shift to D^*.

Distinguishing between movement along a given demand curve and a shift in a demand curve is very easy, given the traditional model of consumer choice as a reference. A change in the price alone simply involves movement along one demand curve and is referred to as a change in the quantity demanded. An increase in the quantity demanded is a movement down and to the right along a given demand curve, and a decrease in the quantity demanded is a movement up and to the left.

Any change other than a change in the good's own-price results in a new demand curve, or a new relationship between price and quantity. An increase in demand is represented by a shift to the right in the demand curve. Figure 8-5 illustrates. For any price, such as P_1, demand curve D_2 represents an increase in demand over D_1. Equations 8-1 and 8-2 identified the various changes in the economic environment that can cause an increase or a decrease in demand. For example, an increase in income makes the consumer able and willing to purchase more at each of the prices measured on the vertical scale. Hence, there is as an increase in demand.[3]

How these other determinants generate changes in demand depends on the good or service being studied. If a consumer decides that a good is not as desirable, then preferences have shifted away. At any market price the good is less desirable, so there is a decrease in demand.

---

[3]   In the absence of as an explicit mathematical formulation, all that can be argued is that a shift occurs. The amount of the shift and whether it is a parallel shift depend on the explicit form of the demand equation. The same is true of the other determinants.

Consider the demand for portable kerosene heaters. If the price of kerosene increased, how might this affect demand? This rise in operating cost is likely to produce a decrease in the demand for kerosene heaters. Later sections of this chapter and subsequent chapters indicate how the concepts of change in the quantity demanded and change in demand can be used to analyze many relevant consumer issues. Exercises provide the opportunity for you to apply the methodology.

The demand relationships presented so far pertain to an individual consumer unit. Individual demand is different from market demand for a consumer good or service. The **market demand** is the aggregate demand of the individual consumer units. Market demand refers to the quantities that all consumers are able and willing to purchase at various market prices per time period. Figure 8-6 and Table 8-2 illustrate. One family's demand for steak, taken from Figure 8-2, is reproduced as D_H in the figure and column (3) in the table. Aggregate demand for the two families is the sum of the quantities demanded by each family at the various prices. This is D_M in the figure and column (4) in the table.

Figure 8-5: A Change in Demand

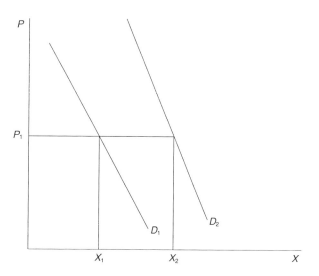

Moving along a given demand curve, such as D1 or D2, indicates how the quantity demanded changes as only the price of that good changes. All other determinants are assumed to be fixed. A change in one of the other determinants causes the demand curve to shift, or a different relationship between the market price and quantity arises. Shifts in the demand curve (from D1 to D2 or vice versa) are referred to as changes in demand.

Market demand curves also have negative slopes. D_M is falling to the right—columns (1) and (4) are changing in opposite directions. This is due to the combination of the income and substitution effects across consumers. Whatever causes a change in demand for an individual consumer also causes a change in the market demand. For example, if the first family's budget increases to $80, then the quantity demanded at every price increases for the first family, so the values in column (2) must

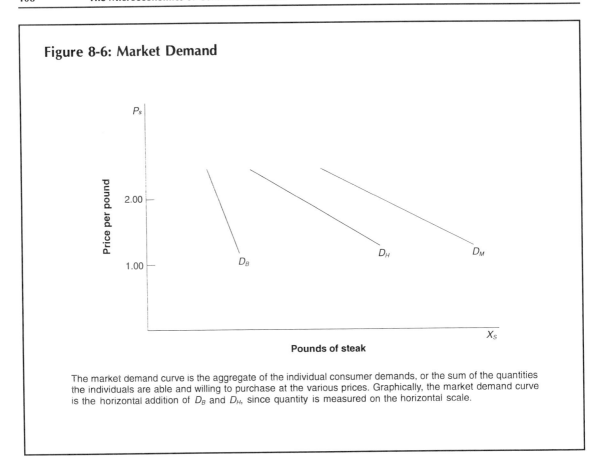

Figure 8-6: Market Demand

The market demand curve is the aggregate of the individual consumer demands, or the sum of the quantities the individuals are able and willing to purchase at the various prices. Graphically, the market demand curve is the horizontal addition of D_B and D_H, since quantity is measured on the horizontal scale.

be replaced with larger ones. This leads to an increase in column (4) quantities, or the increase in market demand in the figure. Determinants of market demand, then, are the same as those of an individual consumer unit's demand (i.e., own- and cross-prices, income, and preferences). However, one other factor can cause the market demand curve to shift—a change in the number of consumers. As the number of consumers increases (decreases), the demand in the market increases (decreases), causing D_M to shift to the right (left).

● **Supply** ●

A market exists whenever a buyer and a seller interact to have an exchange. Consumers are the buyers in the final goods markets. The preceding section identified the major economic determinants of consumer demand. In order to understand how final goods markets operate, one must also consider the seller's behavior. **Supply** is the quantity of a good or service, per time period, that a producer is able and willing to offer for sale at various market prices. Willingness and ability are just as important for the supplier as for the buyer when voluntary exchange occurs.

Key determinants of supply are the level of technology and the prices of the various factors used to produce the final goods and services. As noted previously, a technology is a way of combining

STUDY QUESTIONS

Consumer Demand and Market Demand

7. Distinguish between a demand relationship and a demand curve.
8. Why is it that changes in the own-price of a good do not cause a demand curve to shift but changes in the other determinants do?
9. Success in advertising is usually taken to mean that a consumer's preferences are change favorably toward the good being advertised. How does this lead to as an increase in demand?
10. Harvey Leibenstein, in his classic article "Bandwagon, Snob, and Veblen Effects in the Theory of Consumer Demand" (*Quarterly Journal of Economics,* 65 (May, 1950):183-207) deals with the following three effects: snob effect—as a good rises in popularity its utility to the consumer declines because the consumer values exclusiveness; bandwagon effect—a consumer derives utility from following the behavior of others; and Veblen effect—utility is derived from the status of the good. How could these effects be incorporated into functional demand relationships? How do they affect an individual consumer's demand curve?
11. What is the difference between the substitution effect and the income effect? How are they used to explain the negative relationship between price and quantity?
12. Distinguish between (1) a change in the quantity demanded and (2) a change in demand. Which phrase would you use to describe moving down a demand curve? Which would you use to describe a demand curve's shifting away from the origin?
13. Suppose the price of residential electricity rises. What happens to the demand for electricity and the demand for natural-gas home furnaces?

Table 8-2: Individual and Market Demand.

(1) Market Price	(2) Quantity Demanded by the First Family	(3) Quantity Demanded by the Second Family	(4) Market Quantity
2.50	9.50	16	25.50
2.25	10.30	20	30.30
2.00	11.25	24	35.25
1.75	12.16	28	40.16
1.50	13.08	32	45.08
1.25	14.00	36	50.00

resources to produce an output. Depending on the specific technology chosen, the amounts of the required inputs vary. Consequently, the costs of the inputs in conjunction with the way they are combined will determine the quantity supplied of a good.

Supply curves, which show the quantity supplied at various market prices, typically are drawn as positively sloped lines (see Figure 8-7). This implies that the seller is able and willing to sell more only at a higher price per unit. Assuming a producer is efficient, the only way supply can increase is if more resources are used. Thus, the individual producer must acquire needed inputs, which may be difficult to accomplish. A concave production possibility frontier reflects the difficulty in shifting resources from one sector to another. The alternative uses of scarce resources create the opportunity costs. The increased opportunity costs of shifting more resources into the production of a specific good or service is reflected in the positively sloped supply curve.

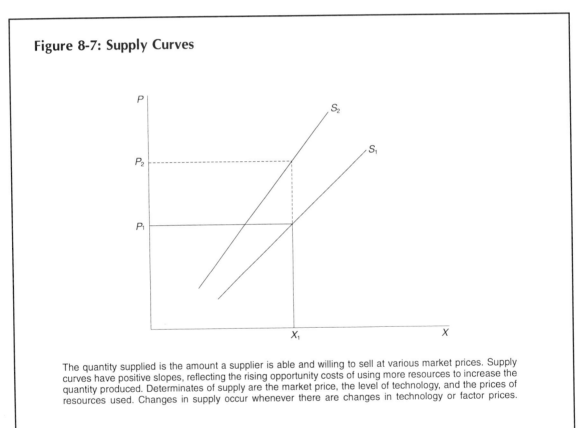

Figure 8-7: Supply Curves

The quantity supplied is the amount a supplier is able and willing to sell at various market prices. Supply curves have positive slopes, reflecting the rising opportunity costs of using more resources to increase the quantity produced. Determinates of supply are the market price, the level of technology, and the prices of resources used. Changes in supply occur whenever there are changes in technology or factor prices.

Movement along a given supply curve indicates how the quantity supplied varies as only the market price of the item changes. It is referred to as a **change in the quantity supplied**. An increase in the quantity supplied is reflected in a movement up and to the right along a given supply curve, and a decrease in the quantity supplied is shown as a movement down and to the left. Whenever there is a change in the quantity supplied, the implicit assumption is that the other determinants of supply remain unchanged.

These other determinants include the level of technology and the prices of the factors of production. Should any of these factors change, the willingness and ability of the producer to supply a given quantity at a given market price changes. Such a shift in the supply curve is referred to as a **change in supply**.[4] For example, if the wage rate increases, the production costs increase, so the same amount, such X_1, can be supplied only at a higher price, shown as P_2 in Figure 8-7. An upward shift in the supply curve would apply to any quantity and is called a decrease in supply. For any market price, the quantity supplied is smaller for S_2 than for S_1. As an increase in supply has occurred when the supply curve shifts to the right.

Derivation of a **market supply** curve follows the same process outlined for a market demand curve. Whenever there is more than one supplier, the market supply is the sum of the quantities the individual suppliers are able and willing to offer for sale at the various market prices. Market supply curves are positively sloped, and they shift whenever there are changes in technology or factor prices. Changes in the number of producers also can cause the market supply curve to shift.

STUDY QUESTIONS

Supply

14. How are a concave production possibility frontier, increasing opportunity cost, and positively sloped supply curves related?
15. Why are the level of technology and the prices of inputs determinants of the quantity supplied?
16. Technological change has decreased the cost of chips used to make computers. How has this affected the supply curve for computers of a specific quality (processor, speed, storage, etc.) over time?
17. Draw a diagram in which two supply curves cross. Which curve indicates a greater sensitivity to own-price changes?

● Market Adjustment ●

A single diagram can be used to portray demand and supply curves for a specific product, because the horizontal and vertical scales of the separate diagrams are the same. Conceptually, the use of one diagram permits an examination of how the two sides of the exchange process interact. The adjustment process is based on consumers and sellers reacting in a predictable way to prices. It is often called the **price-adjustment mechanism** or the **market mechanism**.

In order to appreciate how free markets operate, one needs to understand the meaning of "free". A **free market** is one in which there is no governmental intervention. Buyers and sellers interact on a voluntary basis. There is no central control, no overall coordination, and no central plan. However, one of the very interesting aspects of free markets is that they operate as though there were organized cooperation. For example, consider the market for lettuce in a urban area. Neither consumers nor sellers know how much lettuce is exchanged during a time period, such as a week. Consumers do

---

[4]   The amount of the shift and whether it is a parallel shift depend on the explicit form the supply equation.

not report their purchases to a central authority. Retailers may know how much they sell, but the do not have information on their competitors. However, the exchange process operates as though this information was known, because there does not appear to be any shortage or surplus of lettuce. Free markets work because buyers and sellers react in a stabilizing way to prices through the process outlined below.[5]

It is important to stress that buyers and sellers react independently to market prices. Their behaviors are dictated by different motives. This should be apparent from the way in which the demand and supply relationships have been developed. The determinants of demand are distinct from those of supply. Differences in the motivations generate the reactions to prices that bring the two groups together.

Figure 8-8 displays typical demand and supply curves that illustrate the adjustment process. Suppose the market price is P_1 in Figure 8-8. Given this price, the figure indicates that X_D is the corresponding quantity demanded by consumers, and X_{S1} is the market supply. There is as an excess supply, because $X_{D1} < X_{S1}$. Without any change in the marketplace, this situation would cause inventories to build up, because sellers are supplying more per period than consumers are able and willing to buy. Suppliers react to this situation by decreasing production, which leads to a decrease in the quantity supplied to the marketplace. The decrease in the quantity produced enables sellers to charge a lower price. As the market price falls, consumers respond with an increase in the quantity demanded, or they move down the demand curve. This adjustment process of decreasing the quantity supplied and increasing the quantity demanded persists as long as there is excess supply. Consumers and suppliers act independently in the sense that each group moves along its respective market curve. But their combined actions have the effect of eliminating excess supply.

Any situation in which the market price is below the one at which demand and supply curves cross is characterized by excess demand. Suppose the market price is P_2. Inspection of Figure 8-8 indicates that the quantity demanded, X_{D2}, is greater than the quantity supplied, X_{S2}. The shortage permits suppliers, or sellers, to increase the quantity supplied and charge more, which they do. Consumers react to the price increase by decreasing the quantity demanded. Such adjustments on the part of each group lead to the elimination of the shortage.

What happens when the market price is P_3? Demand equals supply. The voluntary actions of consumers lead to the same quantity as the voluntary actions of producers. No market adjustment occurs, because there is no surplus or shortage. P_3, X_3 reflects a balance between the two groups and is termed the **market equilibrium**. Unless something in the economic environment changes, this price will remain.[6] Notice that the market mechanism generates an equilibrium without any governmental intervention. Surpluses and shortages are eliminated through market adjustments of the price toward P_3 and quantity toward X_3.

Now that the price-adjustment mechanism has been outlined, it can be used to analyze the market behavior when other elements of the economic environment change. The adjustment process so far has focused on just the effects of a change in the own-price of an item, but it can be extended easily to the effects of changes in the other determinants of demand and supply. For example, suppose consumer income rises. In a free market there is no message sent to suppliers informing them that consumer income has risen, so how do suppliers become aware of the new situation?

---

[5]   The nature of some markets does not always foster stable exchange. Some agricultural markets and the stock market (see Chapter 17) are examples.

[6]   Another equilibrium, examined previously, is the point of tangency between the budget constraint and the set of indifference curves. Equating the values of the last dollar spent is the adjust mechanism.

Figure 8-8: Supply and Demand Curves

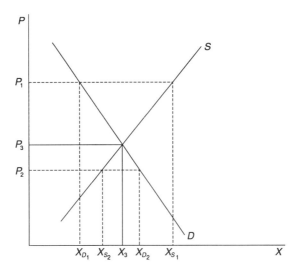

Demand and supply diagrams indicate how the two sides of an exchange interact. Whenever the price is above where D and S cross, there is an excess supply, as shown by P_1 and X_{S_1} - X_{D_1}. This means that inventories build up, and the suppliers' response is to decrease production. As the quantity supplied decreases, suppliers lower the price. Consumers react to lower prices by increasing the quantity demanded. Each group moves along its curve toward P_3. Whenever the price is lower than P_3, there is a shortage, as shown by P_2 and X_{D_2} - X_{S_2}. The adjustment process now works in reverse.

The market sends an indirect message, which produces the desired effect. Figure 8-9 shows how this occurs. An increase in income causes an increase in demand from D_1 to D_2. In other words, the relevant demand curve for the market becomes D_2 instead of D_1. Although there has been as an increase in demand, there is no immediate change in the market price. Rather, at P_1 there is a shortage equal to X_{D2}-X_1. The market then adjusts to the shortage in the manner outlined above. Sellers increase the price and the quantity supplied from X_1 to X_2. The new equilibrium price is P_2.

● Demand and Supply Applications ●

Application of demand and supply curves to market situations can provide many insights into the economic analysis of consumer markets. Three applications are outlined in this section, and others are identified in exercises and subsequent chapters. Each example generates a clear evaluation of the market situation. Applications presented here are rent control, seasonal gasoline prices, and food safety.

Figure 8-9: Market Adjustment to a Change in Demand

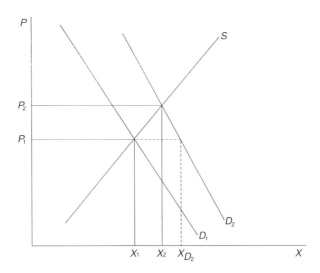

Shifts in either demand (D) or supply (S) create shortages or surpluses which cause the price adjustment. An increase in demand to D_2 cause a shortage at P_1 equal to X_{D_2} - X_1. The market mechanism leads to the new equalibrium P_2, X_2.

STUDY QUESTIONS

Market Adjustment

18. Explain why shortages (surpluses) are always characterized by a price below (above) the one at which demand and supply intersect.
19. Explain how free markets rely on the price-adjustment, or market, mechanism.
20. Why is an equilibrium price one at which demand and supply intersect?
21. Suppose there is a decrease in supply given an initial equilibrium. How does the market adjust?
22. Suppose it becomes very fashionable (bandwagon effect) to wear designer jeans. How does the market react?

● Rent Control

Rent control is the public regulation of rental housing costs within a local government's jurisdiction. The usual justification for the public intervention is that free-market-determined rents are so high that many consumers cannot afford to pay them. Demand and supply curves can be used to describe the situation. The horizontal scale in Figure 8-10 represents the quantity of standardized apartments over a period of time, such as six months, and the price axis measures the monthly rent.[7] Consumer market demand for apartments in an urban area is shown as D. The initial supply curve is shown as S_1. The equilibrium rent is R_1.

Figure 8-10: Rent Control

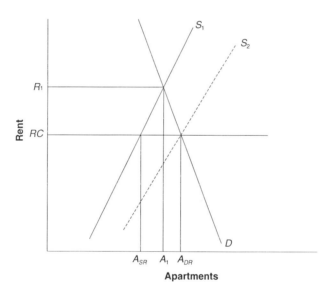

Rent control is a ceiling rent below the equilibrium level, causing a shortage of apartments equaling $A_{DR} - A_{SR}$. Fewer apartments are available with rent control than in the absence of rent control, as shown by the fact that A_{SR} is less than A_1. The real solution to the problem of high rents is to have an increase in supply such as S_2, but this is unlikely to happen as long as rents are beyond the landlords' control.

---

[7]   A standardized apartment is one possessing a fixed set of characteristics such as size, appliances, and plumbing.

Rent control establishes a ceiling , or the maximum rent that can be charged. In its simplest form, rent control requires landlords to roll back rents to what they were during as an earlier period, such a year ago. Line RC portrays the control. It indicates that regardless of demand or supply, rents are fixed at a ceiling.

The price adjustment mechanism is not allowed to work. Even though there is a shortage, it cannot be eliminated through rent increases. The excess demand for rental housing remains. Clearly, landlords have not benefited from rent control, but what about the tenants? Notice that the quantity of apartments supplied has decreased from A_1 to A_{SR}, some landlords decided to remove units available for rent. This means that some tenants have lost their housing. Furthermore, those who have managed to secure housing are confronted by a landlord who does not have to worry about finding a tenant, because of the excess demand. Such a situation could encourage the landlord to forgo repairs.[8]

No one has gained. The real solution to the problem is to have an increase in supply. If supply could increase to S_2, then the same rent as under rent control would occur without any excess demand. But what is the likelihood that the private sector will increase the supply of rental housing if investors are not allowed to determine rents in a free market? In the long run, the presence of rent control tends to perpetuate the consumer's problem. The real solution is to develop programs that encourage increases in the supply of rental housing. If there are some groups of consumers, especially low-income consumers, who cannot afford the short-term high rents, providing them with financial help through housing assistance programs would have more desirable long-run consequences.

● Gas Prices

Automobile gasoline prices typically follow a cyclical pattern. Winter months are characterized by a lower price per gallon than are the summer months. This is due to more vacation-oriented consumer travel (demand) in the summer. The situation is described in Figure 8-11. The price per gallon of regular unleaded gas is measured on the vertical scale, and the number of gallons supplied per month by refiners is measured on the quantity axis. D_W is winter demand for gasoline per month, and D_{SU} is the summer demand. D_{SU} tends to be more price sensitive than D_W as vacation plans can change with the price of gasoline.

Inspection of Figure 8-11 reveals that it is the change in demand that produces the change in the quantity supplied and the higher summer price. When the demand for gasoline shifts from D_W toward D_{SU} in the early summer months, shortages occur at the current market price. These shortages are accommodated through a depletion of the amount of refined gasoline held in storage. Refiners respond by increasing the production of gasoline and decreasing that for other refined fuels. Refiners receive an increase in price in order to increase unleaded gasoline production.

[8]   Unless rent control allows for as an increase in rents when repairs and improvements are made, landlords have no incentive to maintain property.

Figure 8-11: Gasoline Demand—Summer vs. Winter

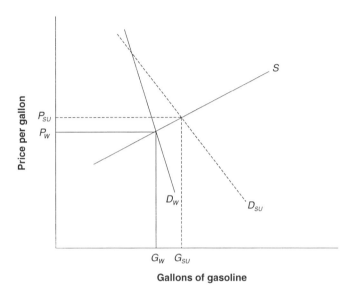

Summer demand for automobile gasoline, D_{SU}, tends to be greater than winter demand, D_W. D_{SU} tends to be more price sensitive, as consumers can decrease demand by postponing vacations or decreasing the distance traveled through a change in plans. The price rises from P_W toward P_{SU} as demand shifts from D_W to D_{SU}, causing supply to increase.

● Food Safety

In the spring of 1994, General Mills discovered that one of its suppliers of oats had used a pesticide which left a residue on the grain. The residue was present in Cheerios in very small amounts. How did this affect the market for Cheerios?

Assume the demand for a particular brand of cereal is very responsive to price changes, or the demand curve for Cheerios is fairly flat. Production and distribution technologies result in production costs that do not increase very much over a wide range of production, or the supply curve for Cheerios also tends to be fairly flat. The situation is reflected in Figure 8-12.

Market demand was not eliminated completely. Some consumers either were unaware of the situation or felt there was no real risk. However, there was a decrease in demand, reflected in D_2 versus D_1. General Mills removed boxes of contaminated product and also introduced new testing and production procedures to minimize the possibility of similar events occurring in the future. The increased production costs led to a decrease in supply, shown as the shift from S_1 to S_2. The market

Figure 8-12: A Food Safety Scare

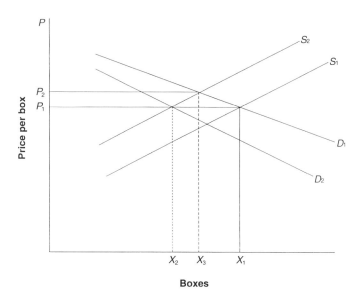

Accidental pesticide residues changed consumer preferences away from Cheerios, leading to a decrease in demand from D_1 to D_2. New production safeguards raised production costs, shown as the decrease in supply from S_1 to S_S. As consumer confidence returned, demand increased leading to a higher equilibrium price and a loss of market share that may be regained over time.

price returned to its previous level, but the quantity sold decreased considerably from X_1 to X_2, or there was as an erosion of Cheerios' market share. To the extent that General Mills is able to convince consumers of the renewed safety of Cheerios, then demand will increase toward D_1, causing a slightly higher equilibrium market price and an equilibrium quantity between X_2 and X_3.

● Summary ●

This chapter used the traditional model of consumer choice to identify the determinants of consumer demand. Demand is a function of prices, income, and preferences. A demand curve focuses on the relationship between the market price and the quantity demanded of an item. Substitution and income effects cause demand curves to have negative slopes. Market demand curves are the sums of the individual consumers' demand curves. Supply curves are positively sloped, reflecting the increased cost per unit associated with using more resources to increase production. The market mechanism outlines how buyers and sellers interact to bring about a market price where demand equals supply. The applications are rent control, seasonal gasoline prices, and food safety.

STUDY QUESTIONS

Demand and Supply Applications

23. What is the effect of setting a rent control ceiling that is higher than the equilibrium rent?
24. Suppose the demand and supply curves for computer repair technicians are drawn as typical demand and supply curves. If new certification standards involving more course work and practical experience are introduced in order for someone to be certified, what is likely to happen in this market? Who benefits and loses from the introduction?
25. If the bombing of the federal building in Oklahoma City in April, 1995 results in the government requiring manufacturers of nitrogen based fertilizers to include "identifiers" and retailers to keep sales records, how is this market likely to be affected?
26. Use demand and supply curves to show the effects of banning television advertising of children's cereals on the market for this good.

● Appendix: Linear Demand Equations ●

Given the two-goods model, suppose that the functional equations 8-2 could be expressed as explicit linear relationships. Equation 8A-1 below depicts this situation for a good X_i. Lower case letters represent the constant coefficients (parameters) of the independent variables. The intercept is a, and it is the quantity demanded if all the independent variables have values of zero. The coefficients of each independent variable show how values of the respective explanatory variables affect the quantity demanded. A positive coefficient indicates that the independent variable and the quantity demanded change in the same direction. A negative coefficient indicates that they change in the opposite direction.

(8A-1) $X_i = a + bP_i + cP_j + dM$

The theory of consumer choice hypothesizes the following signs for the coefficients. If a is positive, consumers demand the amount a when $P_i = P_j = M = 0$. If a is negative, consumers stop purchasing this good or service before all independent variables equal zero. The value of b is negative. Depending on considerations that will be explored in Chapter 9, c and d could be positive or negative.

Henry Schultz's classic study of demand in the United States provides a real-world illustration.[9] One part of his analysis pertained to the demands for beef and pork during the period 1922-1933. Estimated demand relationships for these two goods are presented below.

---

[9]   Henry Schultz, *The Theory and Measurement of Demand*. (Chicago: University of Chicago Press, 1938), p. 639.

$$X_{beef} = 66.40 - 1.90P_{beef} + 0.20P_{pork} + 0.07M$$
$$X_{pork} = 70.20 + 0.45P_{beef} - 1.18P_{pork} + 0.06M$$

X = annual per capita consumption (in pounds).

P = relative price, or P_{beef} and P_{pork} divided by a cost of living index.

M = annual per capita real income (income per person in dollars, divided by a cost of living index).

The intercept values are somewhat awkward to interpret without resorting to more advanced economics.[10] For present purposes, these values are considered to be the number of pounds the average person would consume at that time if the consumer had no current income and the prices were almost zero. Notice that the higher the prices of beef or pork are, the lower the demands are for the respective goods. As the price of either beef or pork increases by itself, consumers increase purchases of the other good. The implication is that as the relative price increases, consumers substitute more of the relatively cheaper meat. Higher real incomes lead to more consumption of both meats.

● Key Terms ●

Change in demand: a shift in the demand curve, caused by determinants other than the own-price of a good.

Change in the quantity demanded: movement along a demand curve, caused by a change in the price of that good.

Change in quantity supplied: movement along a supply curve, caused by a change in the market price of that good.

Change in supply: a shift in the supply curve, caused by a change in determinants other than the market price of a good.

Demand: the quantity of good or service a consumer is able and willing to buy.

Demand curve: a relationship between the quantity demanded of a good and its price.

Demand equations: equations that express the quantities demanded in terms of independent variables.

Demand function: the quantity demanded expressed as a functional equation.

Demand schedule: a table that shows quantity demanded and price.

Demand system: a set of demand equations or functions.

Dependent variable: a variable whose value is determined by values of the independent variable(s).

Explicit relationship: an equation that indicates exactly how independent variables determine values of the dependent variable.

Free market: buyers and sellers exchanging in the absence of governmental controls.

Functional notation: notation that indicates causality without stating the exact manner in which the variables are related.

Income effect: the effect of a price change on the purchasing power of a fixed amount of money.

Independent variable: a variable whose value determines the value of the dependent variable.

Market demand: the aggregate of individual consumer units' demand for a good or service.

Market equilibrium: when the quantity demanded equals the quantity supplied.

Market supply: the aggregate of individual producers' supply.

---

[10]   The elementary model does not accommodate the use of savings or borrowing to acquire goods.

Price-adjustment mechanism or market mechanism: the way in which buyers and sellers react to prices.

Substitution effect: as the price of a good or service falls, the consumer tends to substitute more of the relatively cheaper good.

Supply: the quantity of a good or service a producer is able and willing to sell.

Supply curve: the quantity supplied at various market prices.

Chapter 9

Applied Consumer Demand Analysis

Demand theory provides the structure for evaluating consumer behavior. This chapter extends the theory so it can be put to practical use. Three additional sets of factors affecting consumer demand are introduced: the effects of sociodemographic variables on consumer preferences, adjustments for trends and seasonality, and the effects of past behavior on current decision making. Real-world applications of demand theory provide estimates of the responsiveness of demand to changes in the various independent variables. For example, the theory presented in Chapter 8 indicated that an increase in the own-price of a good leads to a decrease in the quantity demanded. The responsiveness measure which is developed provides a standard way of interpreting the effect of a change in an independent variable on demand.

● Sociodemographic Variables ●

Is there any reason to expect that two consumer units would purchase the same bundle of goods and services? The answer, of course, is no, and there are many explanations. First, incomes are likely to be different. Even if earned incomes were the same for the two consumer units, unearned incomes (such as interest and dividends) might differ, causing differences in demand. Another source of variation is the amount of home production that occurs. If one consumer unit grows part of its vegetables, then it does not need to buy as much in the final goods market for food; therefore, purchases of other goods and services can be increased. Variations in marketplace demand can also be the result of differences in relative prices. Regional variations in energy prices, for instance, can cause differences in demand.

Consider two consumer units having the same total income as well as components, and reacting to the same market prices. Should one expect that the two units would have the same demand for final goods? The answer still is no. Even though the budget constraints are identical, there is no basis for assuming the preferences are the same. Differences in family size, age composition, and personal tastes affect the shape of indifference curves in a two-goods world and preferences in general.

Figure 9-1 illustrates the situation for the two-goods case. Let the goods be food, F, and all other goods, A. Imagine one unit's preferences are represented by the solid indifference curves, while those of another unit are dashed. Assume b is the budget constraint of either family. Optimal consumption differs because of differences in preferences.

The more general case can be discussed in relation to equations 7-3 and 7-4. They comprise the basic decision making rule, marginal utility divided by the unit price. We learned that economists refer to the ratio as the value of the last dollar spent, which is the equivalent of asking: is it worth the price? Differences in preferences are associated with differences in marginal utilities. Even though prices are the same, the marginal utilities differ among consumer units. These differences cause the differences in the values of the last dollar spent, so purchases differ. To put it another way, the differences in preferences cause the functional relationships of the demand equations 8-2 to vary, so that quantities purchased differ even though prices and income are the same.

Figure 9-1: The Optimal Purchase and Differences in Preferences

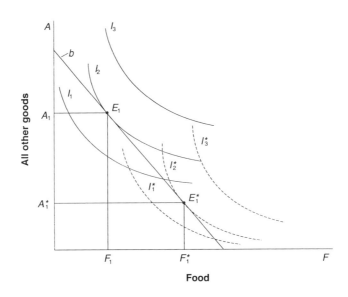

Even though two families may be identical in terms of their incomes, their consumption bundles may differ. The common budget constraint for the two families is denoted by b. However, the sets of indifference curves are different, leading to different optimal consumption bundles, E_1 and E_1^*.

Where does this leave the application of the model of consumer behavior? In the applied approach taken in the preceding chapter, the demand equations 8-2 were assumed to hold for the representative consumer unit, as well as in the aggregate. However, the individual characteristics of a consumer unit must now be incorporated into the model. The point is that the demand model must include personal preferences to the extent that they are determined by variables other than price or income, called **sociodemographic variables**.[1]

We are at the point where the demand equations have to be modified. There are three possibilities: adjust the dependent variable, incorporate additional independent variables, or allow the functional form to change. They can be shown as modifications of the representative consumer unit demand equations 8-2. Equations 9-1 through 9-3 provide a reference for the discussion of the rest of the chapter.

---

[1]   Sociodemographic variables do not include income and prices. Socio-economic variables include sociodemographic, income, and price measures.

The first entails defining a standard consumer and then expressing actual demand in terms of standardized units, X_i'. Or:

$$X_1' = f_1(P_1,...,P_n,M)$$

(9-1)

$$X_n' = f_n(P_1,...,P_n,M)$$

The second possibility is to include the sociodemographic variables as independent variables in the demand equations. Then variations in these variables automatically generate variations in the quantity demanded. To see how this approach is employed, let C demote a set of consumer characteristics such as the number of members, age distribution, and location. The same functional relationship for the quantity demanded of a particular good is assumed to hold as variations in characteristics are included as explanatory variables. The demand for a good or service by a consumer unit with sociodemographics B becomes:

$$X_{1,B} = f_1(P_1,...,P_n,M,C_B)$$

(9-2)

$$X_{n,B} = f_n(P_1,...,P_n,M,C_B)$$

The third possibility is to allow for differences in the explicit form of equations. Consumers can be grouped into cells on the basis of characteristics. Each cell is assumed to be represented by a specific relationship, although the relationship across cells may not be constant. Conceptually, this approach assumes that the f_i change as the characteristics of the cells change. Let B denote a specific cell for all consumer units having sociodemographic characteristics similar to those of the first family. The functional form of the demand equation now depends not only on the good but also on the cell, so a double subscript for the functional notation is required, or:

$$X_{1,B} = f_{1,B}(P_1,...,P_n,M,C_B)$$

(9-3)

$$X_{n,B} = f_{n,B}(P_1,...,P_n,M,C_B)$$

Equations 9-1,2 and 3 do not necessarily introduce sociodemographic variables in ways that preserve theoretical properties of demand relationships.[2] While an examination of these conditions is beyond the introductory scope of this text, the implications for empirical demand equations have straightforward empirical representations.[3] They correspond to parallel shifts in demand relationships, called translating, or to changes in the slopes called scaling.

An additional point must be made. In many applied settings, data limitations may not permit the identification of consumer unit characteristics, or interest may focus only on the behavior of the "average" consumer. In these cases, the quantity demanded and income data should be adjusted for size if at all possible. When aggregate consumption data are used, per capita figures are derived

---

[2]   One of the conditions is that the consumer be on the budget constraint, or all the money allocated to the expenditure for the goods is spent.

[3]   R. Pollak and T. Wales, "Demographic Variables in Demand Analysis," *Econometrica*, 49(1981):1533-51 is the seminal paper on these adjustments.

through dividing by the population. If consumer unit survey data are used, per person data are derived by dividing by the number of members in the consumer unit. These are only crude adjustments, because they do not take into account the effects on demand of age and sex. We return to this point in the Adult Equivalence Scales section.

STUDY QUESTIONS

Sociodemographic Variables

1. Why are sociodemographic variables included in demand relationships?
2. Identify the three conceptual approaches for the inclusion of sociodemographic variables in a demand equation.
3. Use the traditional model of consumer choice to explain how changes in prices, income, and sociodemographic variables affect the quantity demanded of a good or service.
4. Within the traditional model of consumer choice, how can the role of advertising be examined?
5. Consider food versus all other goods. Imagine the evolution of needs as a couple marries, children are born, and then the family grows older. What is the likely effect of these changes on preferences?
6. The post-World War II baby boom has pronounced effects on consumer demand. Explain why this sociodemographic variable needs to be included in forecasts of sales of consumer goods such as clothing, beverages, and furniture. How is health care likely to be affected?

● Trends, Seasonality, and Habit Persistence ●

Empirical demand analysis has to incorporate three other types of considerations. Two are time-related. The demands for some products increase or decrease over extended periods of time. Declining per capita red meat consumption and increasing per capita chicken consumption are two examples of such trends. Seasonality refers to regular periods of peaks and troughs in demand over time, as noted in the gasoline demand application in Chapter 8. Both of these time factors cause changes in demand and, therefore, should be included as independent variables in time-series studies of consumer demand.

Another component of consumer behavior is usually termed **habit persistence**, although the phrase is somewhat misleading. The basic idea is that a consumer tries to at least maintain the current level of utility. A consumer readily adapts to increases in utility but resists decreases. One reason for this is that many goods, such a housing, are purchased on a contractual basis. Another is that preferences may be determined partly by experience. One more factor is the cost to a consumer of changing purchases. In an imperfect world, risks and information costs confront a consumer who is altering consumption. These factors lead to some inertia on the part of a consumer making a purchase decision.

Habit persistence enters into the demand model because a consumer's past behavior is an excellent guide to what may occur in the current period. Thus, an additional explanatory variable needs to be introduced into the consumer decision-making model. Its inclusion requires a subscript to denote time. Let t represent the current period (today). Then t-1 refers to one period before today. If quarterly data are used, t denotes the current quarter and t-1 the preceding quarter. Equation 9-4 is a typical equation in a demand system, in which habit persistence is incorporated (excluding sociodemographics, trends, and seasonality).

(9-4) $\quad X_{i,t} = f_i(P_{1,t},\ldots,P_{n,t},M_t,X_{i,t-1})$

The relationship between $X_{i,t}$ and $X_{i,t-1}$ depends on the nature of the good being examined. Past purchases of nondurables and services are positively related to current demand. Consumers attempting to maintain the current level of utility must repeatedly purchase these items. The higher the demand for such quantities was in the previous period, the higher it is likely to be today. For example a consumer who enjoyed food away from home last period must purchase food away from home this period to help maintain utility.

Durable goods have a negative habit persistence relationship, because these goods are purchased not for their own value but for their service flows. A car is purchased not because it is a nice metal/plastic sculpture, but because of the transportation service flow it provides. Since durables by definition provide service flows over extended periods of time, they do not need to be repeatedly purchased. This leads to a negative relationship between current period purchases and those of the preceding period.

STUDY QUESTIONS

Trends, Seasonality, and Habit Persistence

7. Identify some consumer goods and services for which you feel there are positive and negative trends.
8. What type of seasonal pattern exists for residential electricity over a year?
9. What is habit persistence?
10. What is the basis for assuming that habit persistence is an important factor in studying consumer demand?
11. Distinguish between the effects on current consumption of past consumption of durables and of nondurables and services.

● Engel Functions ●

Most data sources that contain information about sociodemographic variables are cross-sectional. That is survey data are gathered on consumer units during a specific period to obtain information on the quantity purchased, income, and other characteristics. Because of the fixed time period, market prices are constant, so variations in the quantities purchased are assumed to be due to income and sociodemographic differences across consumer units. Under these conditions, empirical estimates of demand are constant price demand functions called **Engel functions**. This eliminates prices as independent variables in equations 9-1 through 9-4.

Figure 9-2 clarifies the distinction among the three possible ways of proceeding. First, the dependent variable, shown on the vertical scale, can be either in terms of quantities, X_i, or standardized quantities, X_i'. (How to generate X_i' values is outlined below.) Panel a reflects the changing functional form approach of equations 9-2 (scaling). Consumer units are grouped into cells on the basis of characteristics. The relationship between the quantity purchases of a particular good or service and income depends, in part, on the various cells. As cell characteristics change, the form of the relationship changes. Each cell has a different relationship between the quantity purchased and M.

Figure 9-2: Engel Curves and Family Characteristics

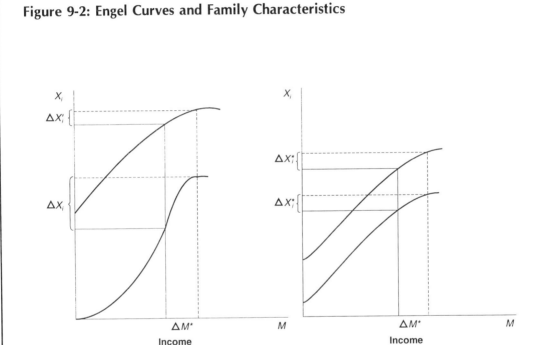

Family characteristics can affect the shape of Engel functions. In panel (a), family characteristics are assumed to affect the explicit form of the relationship between quantity (or expenditure) and income. Panel (b) shows parallel shifts in the Engel function due to family characteristics, so the effect of a change in income is the same change in quantity (or expenditure), ΔX_i^*.

The inclusion of characteristics as explanatory variables is shown in panel b (translating). Inspection of the two curves reveals they depict the same change in X_i due to a common change in M. That is, the slopes are identical. This means that income has the same incremental effect on X_i with or without adjustment for family characteristics. For example, the change in income ΔM^* produces the sane change in X_i, ΔX_i^* in both curves.

An alternative to measuring the quantity purchased is to multiply the quantity by price. This changes the dependent variable, or the vertical scale, to expenditure for the good or service. Because the price of the good is assumed to be fixed, the multiplication does not change the interpretation or shape of an Engel curve.

Prais and Houthakker conducted a seminal study of Engel relationships using British data for the period 1937-1939.[4] Among the estimated relationships was the simple linear form. In order to adjust for variations in household size, expenditure and income for each household were divided by the number of members, n. This produced a standardized quantity measure as well as income per person. The estimated linear Engel function for vegetables is shown below. This equation suggests that if a representative household had virtually no income for the time period, it would purchase Ł4.23 of vegetables.[5] Such purchases could be financed in the short run by savings or the sale of some assets. Each Ł1 increase in per capita household income would lead to a Ł.062 increase in vegetable expenditure.

$$P(X_{veg})/n = 4.23 + .062(M/n)$$

A more recent analysis of Engel functions was conducted on U. S. Households by Salathe.[6] The 1972-73 Consumer Expenditure Diary Survey was the data source. Household purchases were assumed to be functions of income and household size. Income squared and household size squared were included as explanatory variables to account for the differential impacts of high incomes and large households. The other independent variable included was a multiplicative interaction term of income and family size. The estimated Engel function for total food expenditure is shown below. The intercept can be interpreted as the limiting value of food expenditure when income and household size approached zero. Notice that income has a positive effect on food expenditure, but higher incomes have a slightly negative impact as reflected in the coefficient of M^2. Similar observations hold for household size. The combination of income and household size has a small positive effect on food expenditure.

$$P(X_{food}) = 4.256 + .965M - .00003M^2 + 6.314N - .293N^2 + .002M(n)$$

This Engel function is an example of the changing functional form approach. Household size appears as an explanatory variable, and M and n are together in the last expression. If this expression has been omitted from the equation, then M and n would have had separate influences. But because they were combined in the last term, each M(n) combination has a unique impact on per capita food expenditure.

4   S. J. Prais and H. S. Houthakker, *The Analysis of Family Budgets* (Cambridge University Press, 1955):108.
5   Ł denotes the British pound.
6   L. E. Salathe, *Household Expenditure Patterns in the United States*, National Economic Analysis Division; Economics, Statistics, and Cooperatives Service; U. S. Department of Agriculture Bulletin 1603.

STUDY QUESTIONS

Engel Functions

12. Distinguish between a demand function and an Engel function.
13. Explain why the dependent variable in an Engel function can be either a quantity or dollar value.
14. Suppose a consumer unit has a $30,000 income and two people. Another unit has three members. What are the predicted food expenditures based on the Salathe equation?

● Adult Equivalence Scales ●

The composition of consumer units affects purchases in the final goods market, or demand, in addition to prices and income, which prompted the introduction of sociodemographic variables. This section focuses on the first possible adjustment noted above, leading to equations of the form 9-1. One X', presented in the previous section, is to analyze demand per household member. A limitation is that all consumer unit members are treated the same way. For example, a one-year-old infant is counted the same as an 18-year-old, even though it is known that nutritional requirements vary with age. In fact, examination of budget data indicates that expenditures for various types of goods change according to the age-sex distribution of consumer units.

Adult equivalence scales are intended to relate each member of a consumer unit to a standard consumer. Then, demand (or expenditure) can be expressed in terms of the number of standard consumers within the unit. This standard traditionally has been an adult male. Because demographic data for households are required, most empirical work has used cross-sectional data. Much of the analysis has focused on the Engel function, modified so that it is expressed per adult equivalent. Equation 9-5 is the functional form of the Engel relationship using adult equivalence scales. Demand for X_i is adjusted by the number of household adult equivalents associated with that commodity, a_i. Income of the household is adjusted by an overall adult equivalence scale, a_0. Notice that under the condition that all members be treated the same way, equation 9-5 is the functional form of the Prais and Houthakker Engel function reported in the previous section.

(9-5) $X_i/a_i = f(M/a_0)$

One application of the approach is that of Salathe and Buse.[7] The U. S. Department of Agriculture's 1965 Household Food Consumption Survey provided data on types of foods consumed and costs during a seven-day period. Demographic data on respondents' households were recorded as well. The standard consumer was defined as an adult male between 20 and 55 years of age. Figure 9-3 reproduces the estimated scales for various food categories. They provide a mechanism for transforming household demands for foods into household demands for foods per adult equivalent.

---

[7]   L. Salathe and R. Buse, "The Relationships Between Household Food Expenditures and Household Size and Composition," *National Food Review*, (January, 1978):25-28.

Figure 9-3: Estimated Adult Equivalence Scales

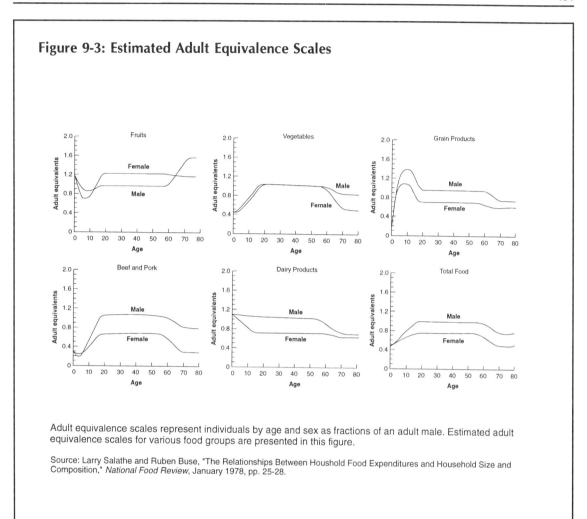

Adult equivalence scales represent individuals by age and sex as fractions of an adult male. Estimated adult equivalence scales for various food groups are presented in this figure.

Source: Larry Salathe and Ruben Buse, "The Relationships Between Houshold Food Expenditures and Household Size and Composition," *National Food Review*, January 1978, pp. 25-28.

The vertical axis in each panel is the adult equivalent scale. It represents a specific age-sex combination as a percent of the adult male. Notice that young children and females typically cost less to feed. Older adult males and females experience declines in food consumption. Grain products reach a maximum for both sexes around age 10. Dairy products show very little change for males, except after age 55. With respect to dairy products, females have a steady decline in adult equivalence to age 20, and thereafter there is little change. Fruits are a food category in which women have a consistently higher adult equivalence than males, except in the early and older age groups.

Adult equivalence scales can be used in many different ways. One application is the estimation of the effects of demographic change on consumer demand. Referring to Figure 9-3, it is clear that the quantity demanded of food items depends on the age-sex composition of the population. As this composition changes, the pattern of consumer demand changes. Another application is in the area of welfare programs. Income redistribution and transfer programs need to account for the age-sex composition of the recipient household. This is taken into account in programs such as Aid to Families with Dependent Children; Food Stamps; and Women, Infants, and Children. Recipients are supported according to the number of children. The basis for the amount of support is the food requirements of children by age.

These scales can be used to adjust for the composition of the consumer unit. They provide a methodology for comparing levels of utility, based on marketplace goods purchased. If the household is the consumer unit being studied, then **household equivalence scales** are a way of aggregating members adjusted for their sociodemographic categories. That is, household equivalence scales standardize the economic size of households. The approach involves defining standard adult consumption. Consumption for other members is estimated as the difference between actual expenditures and expenditures of the standard adult. Children's expenditures, then, are the difference between actual expenditures for various sociodemographic groups and the expenditures of the standardized adult members. Cross-section data sets, such as the Consumer Expenditure Surveys, are used to estimate typical expenditures. Results are then used to estimate the effects of selected individuals.

Table 9-1 presents estimated average expenditures for selected goods derived from the 1972-73 Consumer Expenditure Survey generated by Nelson.[8] The estimates are average consumption levels for a childless couple and a comparable couple with children. Goods for which the childless couple spends more are personal care, health insurance, dry cleaning, and public education. Alcohol and tobacco expenditures are higher for the childless couple.

Table 9-1: Estimated Average Consumption of Standardized Households for Selected Goods, Based on 1972-73 Consumer Expenditure Survey.

Category	Childless Couple	Two-Child Couple
Personal Care	$112	$101
Health Insurance	232	207
Dry Cleaning	78	72
Public Education	22	16
Alcohol	77	86
Tobacco	140	153

Source: J. Nelson, "Methods of Estimating Household Equivalence Scales: An Empirical Investigation," *Review of Income and Wealth.* 38,3(September, 1992): 295-310.

---

[8]   J. Nelson, "Methods of Estimating Household Equivalence Scales: An Empirical Investigation," *Review of Income and Wealth,* 38,3(1992):295-310.

STUDY QUESTIONS

Adult Equivalence Scales

15. Based on the discussion of this section, distinguish between an adult and an adult equivalence scale.
16. In an analysis of family expenditure for a market good such as food, why is per capita expenditure for the market good a better measure than total expenditure? Why is expenditure per adult equivalent a better measure, at least in theory, than per capita expenditure?
17. Distinguish between an adult equivalence scale and a household equivalence scale.

● Elasticity ●

The theory of consumer demand provides a very useful framework for analyzing consumer behavior. Each of the major determinants of the quantity demanded has been identified: prices, income, sociodemographics, trends, seasonality, and habit persistence. Equations 9-1 through 9-5 summarize the causal relationships. Variables on the right-hand side of each equation determine the dependent variable.

Causal relationships are used extensively in economic analysis, and economists have developed a very straightforward tool for measuring the degree of association between a dependent variable and each of the independent variables. This section first defines the tool and then discusses its usefulness with respect to the theory of consumer behavior.

Elasticity is defined as the percentage change in a dependent variable due to a percentage change in an independent variable. The general definition of elasticity is shown in equation 9-6, with DEP denoting the dependent variable and IND and independent variable. A very important feature of elasticity is the implied direction of causality. Percentage changes in the variable represented in the numerator are assumed to be caused by percentage changes in the variable represented in the denominator. Since two variables are involved, the elasticity measure, E, usually has two subscripts. The first subscript refers to the variable in the numerator, and the second subscript refers to the variable in the denominator.

(9-6) $E_{DEP,IND} = \%\Delta DEP / \%\Delta IND$

There are three reasons why elasticity is a useful tool. First, the elasticity measure can be used for any demand category. Given a demand system, the variable that appears in the numerator is the percentage change in the quantity demanded, which is one of the variables on the left-hand side of equations 9-1 through 9-5. Thus, the elasticity measure can be applied to such varied quantities as kilowatt hours of electricity, pounds of meat, or gallons of gasoline. Second, the elasticity measure can be used for any IND. Thus, the denominator of 9-6 represents the percentage change in any of the determinants of the quantity demanded included in the relationship. Third, elasticities can be interpreted easily as measures of responsiveness. This will become apparent as the discussion proceeds.

The usefulness of elasticity stems primarily from the fact that it is derived from percentage changes. Any percentage change is computed as the amount of change that has occurred divided by the level. For example, if a family's demand for steak decreases from 10.3 pounds to 9.5 pounds (see Table 8-1), the percentage change can be calculated as (9.5 - 10.3) pounds/10.3 pounds = -.092. Since pounds appear as the unit of quantity in the numerator and the denominator, they cancel, leaving a percent which is independent of the units. Because this occurs whenever percentage changes are derived, elasticity is always a ratio of two percentage changes, which is a pure number. This is why elasticity can be used so widely and interpreted so easily.

Several computational formulas exist for the calculation of percentage changes. Which formula to use depends on the availability of data and on whether explicit demand equations can be used. No matter how the values are computed, the interpretation is the same. Once an elasticity has been calculated, this number can be used as an important tool in the analysis of business generated or government generated consumer policies.

One point needs to be emphasized concerning demand elasticities. Each of the several independent variables could appear in the denominator of equation 9-6. Elasticity measures their effects on the quantity demanded one at a time. Since one independent variable is in the denominator, it is assumed that no change in any other independent variable occurs. This is implicit in the calculation, interpretation, and policy evaluation of any elasticity.

STUDY QUESTIONS

Elasticity

18. An elasticity is a measure of the causal relationship between two variables. What is the assumed direction of causality?
19. With demand elasticities, what always appears in the numerator?
20. Why is it necessary to assume that only one independent variable changes when using demand elasticities?

● Income Elasticity ●

Economic theory provides the framework for the causal relationship between income and the quantity demanded of a good or service. The **income elasticity** of demand is a numerical measure of the degree of responsiveness of consumer demand to income changes. Equation 9-7 is the expression for this elasticity. With respect to equation 9-6, notice that DEP has been replaced by the X_i, and IND is income, M.

(9-7) $E_{i,M} = \%\Delta X_i / \%\Delta M$

What values can this elasticity assume? Certainly, the closer $E_{i,M}$ is to zero, the smaller the effect of a percentage change in income is on the percentage change in the quantity demanded. In fact, $E_{i,M}$ is zero only when the numerator is zero, which implies that a percentage change in income has no effect on the quantity demanded when this happens. $E_{i,M}$ could be either negative or positive. A negative elasticity means that income and the quantity demanded change in opposite directions. For example, an increase in income could result in a decrease in the quantity demanded. Whenever the demand for a good declines as income rises, the good is called an **inferior good**.

A positive income elasticity means that income and quantity demanded change in the same direction. Whenever $E_{i,M}$ is greater than one, the percentage change in the quantity demanded is greater than the percentage change in income. Thus, as income rises, a consumer would spend proportionately more on this good. A good whose income elasticity of demand is greater than one is defined as a **luxury good**.

A **normal good** has a computed income elasticity of demand between zero and one. As income rises, consumers buy more of a normal good or service, although the percentage increase in quantity is less than the percentage increase in income.

Suppose a family's budget changes from $50 to $60, and the quantity demanded of steak (S) changes from 11.25 to 15 pounds. This information can be used to calculate the corresponding income elasticity of demand for steak, as shown below. $E_{S,M}$ = 1.67, which indicates that a 1 percent change in income induces the family to purchase 1.67 percent more steak. Thus, steak is a luxury good for this family.

$$E_{S,M} = [(15-11.25)/11.25]/[(60-50)/50]$$
$$= (1/3)/(1/5)$$
$$= 5/3$$
$$= 1.67$$

There are many ways to use a computed value for an income elasticity. For example, suppose you are in the marketing office of Electronic Games, Inc. Part of your responsibility is to forecast consumer demand for its games. Assume that the income elasticity of demand for them has been estimated to be 2.50. A recent business journal forecast that consumer income would fall .5 percent during the next six months. Based on this information and assuming there are no other changes, you forecast a decline of (2.5)(.5) = 1.25 percent in the quantity demanded of games.

STUDY QUESTIONS

Income Elasticity

21. Calculate the income elasticity of demand for a family if its income increases from $64 to $80 and its purchase of steak rises from 15 to 22.5 pounds.
22. Why could the income elasticity of demand be used to compare consumer demand for electricity, gasoline, fuel, and natural gas?
23. Suppose the income elasticity of demand for electricity is .9 and income is expected to rise by 7 percent during the next year. What would be the anticipated effect on electricity demand? Why is the "nothing else changes" condition critical?
24. How can luxury, normal, and inferior goods be identified via the income elasticity of demand?

● Price Elasticity of Demand ●

Consumer sensitivity to price change is measured by the price elasticity of demand. This elasticity's denominator measures the percentage change in price which, by itself, causes the quantity demanded to change. Equations 8-2 point out that the quantity demanded of any good is a function of all prices, so it is necessary to have a two-part classification. If the price change is for the good represented in the numerator, then its corresponding elasticity is called an **own-price elasticity**. If the price change is for another good, then its corresponding elasticity is called a cross-price elasticity. Each type of price elasticity is discussed below.

Figure 8-3 illustrated how the slope of a demand curve reflects the responsiveness of the quantity demanded to the own-price of a good. Own-price elasticity also distinguishes among demand curves, just as the slope does. However, as the following discussion reveals, the elasticity measure is a more powerful analytical tool because of the three advantages of elasticity: it can be interpreted easily, it is interpreted in the same manner regardless of the demand category, and it is consistent with other elasticity measures associated with consumer demand.

Equation 9-8 depicts own-price elasticity. The numerator, as for all demand elasticities, is the percentage change in the quantity demanded of good i, but the denominator is now the percentage change in price of that same good, i. This is why the same subscript is used in the numerator and the denominator. An own-price elasticity of demand, $E_{i,i}$, is usually negative, because the theory of consumer demand has led to the conclusion that own-price and quantity demanded change in opposite directions. The income and substitution effects that cause demand curves to have negative slopes also cause own-price elasticity to be negative.

(9-8) $E_{i,i} = \%\Delta X_i / \%\Delta P_i$

Interpretation of own-price elasticity begins with the recognition that -1 has a pivotal role to play. Whenever the absolute value of the percentage change in quantity is less than the absolute value of the percentage change in price, $E_{i,i}$ is between 0 and -1.[9] Demand associated with such an elasticity is termed **inelastic demand**. The closer $E_{i,i}$ is to 0, the smaller the absolute value of the percentage change in quantity demanded is relative to the percentage change in price. This indicates that consumer demand is becoming less responsive to price changes. When $E_{i,i} = 0$, an own-price change has no effect on the quantity demanded. This limiting case is termed perfectly inelastic. The closer $E_{i,i}$ is to 0, the more inelastic the demand. An own-price elasticity of less than -1 indicates that the absolute value of the percentage change in the quantity demanded is greater than the absolute value of the percentage change in price. Demand associated with such an elasticity is termed **elastic demand**. $E_{i,i}$ gets farther away from -1 as the quantity demanded becomes more sensitive to price change. In the limiting case $E_{i,i}$ is infinitely small, and demand is termed perfectly elastic. If the percentage changes in the numerator and denominator have the same absolute value, then $E_{i,i} = -1$; this case is called **unitary elasticity**.

Figure 9-4 provides additional insight into the interpretation of the own-price elasticity of demand. A demand curve is represented as a negatively sloped line; its exact position depends on the good being studied and the data being used to estimate the demand relation. The limiting cases for a demand curve are horizontal and vertical lines. Demand curve D_1 implies that regardless of the price, the quantity X_i^0 is demanded. Such a demand curve has an own-price elasticity of 0. D_2 implies that consumers are completely responsive to price changes. The associated elasticity approaches minus infinity, because with an infinitely small price increase consumers would switch completely to another good.[10] The steeper a demand curve is, the closer to 0 the elasticity and the more inelastic the demand. Thus, comparing own-price elasticities for various demand relationships allows one to compare immediately own-price sensitivities.

---

9   Reference is made to absolute values because one percentage change is positive and the other is negative.
10   There is no incentive for a seller to lower the price, because any quantity is demanded at the price $P_{i,2}$.

Figure 9-4: Elasticities and Demand Curves

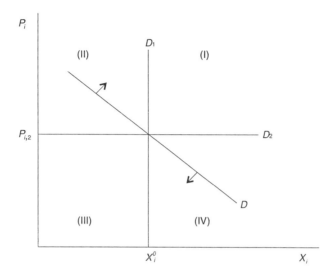

A perfectly inelastic demand is a vertical line. The own-price elasticity associated with this curve has the value of zero. Curve D_1 implies that X_i^0 is demanded regardless of price, or the quantity demanded by the consumer is not responsive to price. Just the opposite is implied by curve D_2, which is a perfectly elastic demand curve. Its own-price elasticity is minus infinity. The steeper a demand curve is, the smaller the consumer's sensitivity to price changes and the closer $E_{i,i}$ is to zero.

The own-price elasticity of demand is an extremely useful tool for assessing the effects of price changes on demand. The sales revenue of a firm is price times quantity sold. Notice that the two variables comprising revenue are the two variables included in the computation of $E_{i,i}$. This means that there is a direct relationship between own-price elasticity and revenue. Inelastic demand occurs when the absolute value of the percentage change in quantity is less than that for price. In this situation, raising the price, although lowering the quantity demanded, leads to increased revenue, because the positive percentage change in price more than offsets the negative percentage change in the quantity demanded. Just the opposite occurs with elastic demand. Lowering the price increases revenue.

An illustration of the computation and interpretation of the own-price elasticity is provided by the data on demand for steak in Table 8-1. Similar computations could be used for market demand. The own-price elasticity of demand associated with the decline in the price of steak from $2.25 to $2.00 per pound is shown below. Demand is inelastic. A 1 percent decrease in price, by itself, brings about a .83 percent increase in the quantity demanded.

$$E_{S,S} = (.95/10.3)/(-.25/2.25)$$
$$= (.092)/(-.111)$$
$$= -.83$$

The application of $E_{i,i}$ to consumer policy issues can be illustrated by returning to the Electronic Games, Inc., situation. Suppose the estimated own-price elasticity of demand for the games is -1.40. A new labor contract is being negotiated, and Electronic Games anticipates that the union demands will force the company to raise prices by 3 percent. Combining these two figures yields an estimate of the effect on quantity demanded: (-1.40)(3) = -4.2. Thus the expected effect of the price increase is a 4.2 percent decline in the quantity demanded.

A price change in a specific good j affects not only the quantity demanded of good j, but also the quantity demanded of each of the other goods. For example, a change in the price of electricity affects not only consumer demand for electricity, but also the quantity demanded of other goods, such as food and clothing.

The cross-price elasticity of demand measures the effect of a price change in one good on the quantity demanded of another. This elasticity is represented as equation 9-9. $E_{i,j}$ is the percentage change in the quantity demanded of good i (the first subscript) due to a percentage change in the price of good j (the second subscript). The closer $E_{i,j}$ is to zero, the smaller the causal effect. A cross-price elasticity can be either positive or negative. Negative cross-price elasticities occur when the price of good j and the quantity demanded of good i change in opposite directions. Whenever this occurs, the goods are **complements**. An increase in P_j causes less of good i to be purchased, because both goods (i and j) are consumed together. **Substitutes** are characterized as having positive cross-price elasticities. Two goods are substitutes to the extent that they satisfy the same need. If consumers substitute a competing good i when the price of good j increases, the corresponding elasticity is positive.

(9-9) $E_{i,j} = \%\Delta X_i / \%\Delta P_j$

We can calculate $E_{i,j}$ with the data provided in Figure 8-2. A rise in the price of steak from $1.25 to $2.00 per pound increases the family's purchase of chicken from 22 to 26 pounds. These data generate a positive cross-price elasticity, so chicken and steak are considered to be substitutes for this family. Based on this result, each 1 percent increase in the price of steak leads to a .15 percent increase in the purchase of chicken.

$$E_{C,S} = [(22-26)/22]/[(1.25-2.00)/1.25]$$
$$= .18/.6$$
$$= .30$$

Cross-price elasticities have many useful applications, as estimates of the effects of price changes in substitutes and complements can be crucial for any business. For example, suppose that Electronic Games has determined that the cross-price elasticity of demand for their games with respect to the price of electricity is -.8. The company anticipates that the price of electricity will rise 1.9 percent over the next year. These numbers suggest that the demand for Electronic Games will decline (-.8)(1.9) = -1.52 percent.

The most commonly used demand elasticities have now been presented. Table 9-2 summarizes the information. Elasticity refers to a causal relationship between two variables. With respect to demand elasticities, the numerator is the percentage change in the quantity demanded of a particular good. Variables that appear in the denominator dictate the specific demand elasticity.

Many variables besides income and prices have causal effects on the quantity demand. The calculation and interpretation of these elasticities follows the same general outline identified above. Zero is an important reference point, as this value denotes the absence of a causal relationship. The farther away an elasticity is from zero, the greater is the sensitivity of the quantity demanded to changes in the respective variable. A positive value indicates that the change in the quantity demanded is in the same direction as the change in the independent variable. A negative value indicates that the changes are in opposite directions. Family size, for example, has an impact on a

Table 9-2: Elasticity Summary

Type	Formula	Value	Interpretation
All	$\dfrac{\% \Delta\, DEP}{\% \Delta\, IND}$	$= 0$ < 0 > 0	No responsiveness DEP and IND change in opposite directions DEP and IND change in the same direction
Income	$E_{i,M} = \dfrac{\% \Delta\, X_i}{\% \Delta\, M}$	< 0 $0 < E_{i,M} < 1$ > 1	Inferior good Normal good Luxury good
Own-price	$E_{i,i} = \dfrac{\% \Delta\, X_i}{\% \Delta\, P_i}$	Always < 0 $= 0$ $0 > E_{i,i} > -1$ $= -1$ $-1 > E_{i,i} > -\infty$ $= -\infty$	Negative relationship Perfectly inelastic Inelastic Unitary Elastic Perfectly elastic
Cross-price	$E_{i,j} = \dfrac{\% \Delta\, X_i}{\% \Delta\, P_j}$	> 0 < 0	Substitutes Complements

family's demand for food, so an elasticity can be computed for these two variables. While it may not make sense to consider a percentage change in family size on an individual family basis, the approach does have validity within the context of market demand generated by many families.

● Summary ●

Sociodemographic, trend, seasonal, and habit persistence variables affect consumer demand. Elasticity measures the causal relationship between a dependent and an independent variable. Demand elasticities have the percentage change in the quantity demanded as the numerator and a percentage change in an independent variable identified by economic theory as the denominator. The farther away from zero an elasticity is, the more sensitive the quantity demanded is to changes in the independent variable. Income elasticity focuses on the effect of an income change by itself on the quantity demanded. Own-price elasticity measures sensitivity of the quantity demanded to a change in the price of the good. Cross-price elasticity refers to the effect of a change in the price of one good on the quantity demanded of another.

STUDY QUESTIONS

Price Elasticity

25. Use the data in Table 8-2 to calculate the various own-price elasticities for the market demand for steak.
26. Use the data provided below to show how the visual slope of a demand curve can be altered by changing the horizontal or vertical scale.
    P: 15 13 11 9 7 5
    Q: 0   4   8 12 16 20
27. With the use of algebra, rearrange equation 9-8 to show the relationship between the slope of a demand curve and own-price elasticity.
28. Distinguish among elastic, inelastic, and unitary demand.
29. The own-price elasticity of demand for food at home has been estimated to be -.05, and that of the demand for food away from home has been estimated to be 0.09. Evaluate these elasticities.
30. Explain the difference between cross-price elasticity of demand and own-price elasticity of demand.
31. How can the cross-price elasticity of demand be used to identify substitutes and complements?
32. Suppose the cross-price elasticity of demand for food at home with respect to the price of food away from home is -.06, whereas that of the demand for food away from home with respect to the price of food at home is -.75. Evaluate these elasticities.

● Appendix: Examples of Estimated Demand Elasticities ●

A study by Beierlein et al. of energy demand is an example of estimated elasticities.[11] Their particular study used an explicit relationship that is logarithmic. It can be shown that whenever this relationship is used, the estimated coefficients of the equation are elasticities. No further manipulation is required. Beierlein et al. used data for the northeastern United States for the period 1967-1977. Their estimated equations are presented below.

$$q_{G,t} = .462 - .232P_{G,t} + .318P_{E,t} - .187P_{O,t} + .010M_t + .917q_{G,t-1}$$
$$q_{G,t} = -.219 + .030P_{G,t} - .107P_{E,t} - .077P_{O,t} + .015M_t + .943q_{G,t-1}$$

Each coefficient can be interpreted as an elasticity. The own-price elasticities are between 0 and -1 (inelastic), with that of electricity being approximately one-half that of natural gas. Consumers appear to be about twice as sensitive to a percentage change in price of natural gas as they are to the same percentage change in the price of electricity. Cross-price elasticities indicate that natural gas and electricity are substitutes, while other fuels are complements. Natural gas demand seems to be much more sensitive to the price of other fuels. Both natural gas and electricity appear to be normal goods, although the income elasticities are close to zero. Habit persistence is included, and the elasticities

---

[11]   J. G. Beierlein, J. W. Dunn, and J. C. McCornon, Jr. "The Demand for Electricity in the Northeastern United States," *Review of Economics and Statistics*, LXIII, 3 (August, 1981):403-8.

indicate the very pronounced positive effect past demand has on current demand for the two types of energy.

The effect of children on spending patterns was studied by Douthitt and Fedyk using Canadian data for the Saskatchewan province from the 1982 *Survey of Family Expenditures*.[12] The analysis focused on nonfarm, dual headed families with all members present for the year. Adult equivalence scales were estimated and used to predict expenditures for various categories of goods. Table 9A-1 presents some of their estimated elasticities. They are for incremental effects for a "typical" family having expenditures of $31,200 (Canadian), the father was 39 and mother 36, and children were 11 and 9.

Table 9A-1: Estimated Expenditure (Income) and Household Size Elasticities for Selected Budget Categories.

	FOOD					CLOTHING		
Elasticity	Home	Away	Shelter	Transportation	Durables	Adult	Child	Other
Expenditure (Income)	.29	1.18	.81	.78	1.69	1.10	.45	1.23
Size	.54	-.42	-.29	.33	.19	.58	1.48	-.23

Source: R. Douthitt and J. Fedyk, "The Influence of Children on Family Life Cycle Spending Behavior: Theory and Applications," *Journal of Consumer Affairs*, 22,2(Winter, 1988):220-48.

Estimated income elasticities suggest that food at home expenditures were very inelastic and food away was a luxury, as were durables, adult clothing, and other expenditures. Increasing the typical family's size was estimated to lead to increased food at home, transportation, durables, and clothing expenditures and decreased food away, shelter, and other expenditures.

A complete demand system is a system of demand equations for which the sum of consumer expenditures across the included categories equals income. The desirable feature of these systems is they attempt to account for the simultaneous nature of consumer decision making. A complete demand system allows one to examine how any change in price, income, or other independent variables affects consumer demand for every good. Theoretically, as reflected in equations 9-1 through 9-4, every good and service purchased in the final goods market should be included. However, there are too many to work with empirically. The solution is to aggregate prices and quantities (or expenditures) into categories and to assume that the goods and services included in a study are separable from all other goods and services consumed.

---

[12]   R. Douthitt and J. Fedyk, "The Influence of Children on Family Life Cycle Spending Behavior: Theory and Applications," *Journal of Consumer Affairs*, 22,2(Winter, 1988):220-48.

A study by Huang and Haidacher provides an illustration of a complete system of demand elasticities.[13] Annual data for the United States for the 1953-1983 time period were used to estimate the model and derive the elasticities. Table 9A-2 presents the elasticities. It is called an elasticity matrix. While this table may appear imposing, there is nothing complicated about it. Each row refers to the quantity demanded of a specific category. A column represents an explanatory variable, of which the first five are prices. The rows and first five columns form a matrix of own- and cross-price elasticities. Own-price elasticities are on the diagonal, starting in the upper left-hand corner and falling to the right. Off-diagonal elements are the cross-price elasticities, with the column heading referring to the percentage change in a specific price and the row heading referring to the percentage change in quantity. The last column has the income elasticities for the five categories, where income is defined as the sum of the expenditures.

Table 9A-2: Estimated Price and Expenditure Elasticities for Meats.

Quantity	Beef	Pork	PRICE Other Meat	Chicken	Turkey	Expenditures
Beef	-.62	.11	.07	.06	.01	.45
Pork	.19	-.73	.05	.09	.02	.44
Other Meat	.54	.21	-1.37	-.16	.03	.06
Chicken	.29	.26	-.11	-.53	-.05	.36
Turkey	.21	.18	.06	-.17	-.68	.32

Source: K. Huang and R. Haidacher, "An Assessment of Price and Income Effects on Changes in Meat Consumption," *The Economics of Meat Demand.* R. Buse, ed., University of Wisconsin, Department of Agricultural Economics(1989):139-156.

Comparisons of the rows enable one to examine the sensitivity of the quantity demanded of a good to the various prices and income. With respect to own-prices (diagonal elements), other meat is the most elastic. Aside from the own-price (diagonal elements), the cross-price elasticities in the pork row are closer to zero than the other rows. This suggests that pork is the least sensitive to price changes in the other meats. Other meat is the least responsive to expenditure changes. Each column indicates how a percentage change in price or expenditure affects the quantity demanded of the meats. Notice the off-diagonal elements of the beef column are farther away from zero than are those of in the other price columns. This suggests that the price of beef has the largest impact on the percentage change in the quantity demanded of the other categories. Each of the categories is a normal good and other meat is the least responsive to percentage changes in income.

---

[13]   K. S. Huang and R. C. Haidacher. "An Assessment of Price and Income Effects on Changes in Meat Consumption." *The Economics of Mead Demand.* R. Buse, ed, University of Wisconsin, Department of Agricultural Economics, 1989.

One can also develop a demand system that is consistent with the human capital perspective. An interesting application is a study by Joerling.[14] His approach was to assume a family maximizes utility over its life cycle. Utility was a function of lifetime consumption, child services, the quality of children and leisure time. Constraints were income and the production of child services. Data for the empirical analysis were from a 1967-1970 survey of families.

The categories in Joerling's model were a composite of market goods (X), husband's leisure time (H), wife's leisure time (W), and the number of children (N). Determinants were the prices of each of the items and income. They were the price of the market good (P), husband's wage (HW), wife's wage (WW), the price of child services (PC), and income (M). The wage rates measured the opportunity costs of each spouse's time, and the cost of child services.

Table 9A-3 presents the estimated elasticity matrix for this demand system. Diagonal elements associated with the first four columns are estimated own-price elasticities. The demand for market goods is inelastic. The demands for leisure time are also inelastic. The husband's leisure time is estimated to be much more responsive to changes in HW than is the wife's leisure time to changes in WW. The number of children is estimated to be highly elastic, as its value is -2.44. Examination of the income elasticities indicates that market goods and spouses' leisure time are normal goods, while the number of children is a luxury. These estimates support the human capital approach to the analysis of family size. The rising price of quality children tends to decrease family size. The decline in the profitability of children has resulted in their being considered primarily a luxury good.

Table 9A-3: Some Estimated Socio-Demographic Elasticities

	P	*HW*	*WW*	*PC*	*M*
X	-.59	.09	.03	*	.58
H	.03	-.56	-.06	-.04	.59
W	.03	-.32	-.01	.01	.01
N	-.05	.01	.08	-2.44	2.52

*The estimated value is .0004.

Source: Wayne Joerling, "Lifetime Consumption, Labor Supply, and Fertility: A Complete Demand System," *Economic Inquiry* 20 (April, 1982): 255-76.

While a complete demand system approach possesses the desirable feature of accounting for the simultaneity of decision making, it does have disadvantages. Each system requires many theoretical assumptions, which can be quite restrictive. Data requirements are much more stringent than those for the estimation of one or two equations by themselves. Finally, the statistical procedures are more complicated and expensive to implement.

---

[14]   W. Joerling, "Lifetime Consumption, Labor Supply, and Fertility: A Complete Demand System," *Economic Inquiry* 20(1982):255-76.

● Key Terms ●

Adult equivalence scale: the representation of individuals, on the basis of sociodemographics, in terms of a standard consumer.

Complements: goods having a relationship such that the quantity demanded of good i and the price of good j have a negative cross-price elasticity.

Cross-price elasticity: the percentage change in the quantity demanded of one good due to a percentage change in the price of another good.

Elastic demand: demand for which the own-price elasticity is less than -1.

Elasticity: the percentage change in a dependent variable caused by a percentage change in an independent variable.

Habit persistence: tendency of consumers to resist decreases in utility.

Household equivalence scale: the sum of adult equivalence across household members.

Income elasticity: the percentage change in the quantity demanded due to a percentage change in income.

Inelastic demand: demand for which the own-price elasticity is between 0 and -1.

Inferior good: a good having a negative income elasticity of demand.

Luxury good: a good having an income elasticity greater than 1.

Normal good: a good having an income elasticity between 0 and 1.

Own-price elasticity: the percentage change in the quantity demanded due to a percentage change in the price of that good.

Sociodemographic variable: a variable other than price or income that affects consumer decisions.

Substitutes: goods having a relationship such that the quantity demanded of good i and the price of good j have a positive cross-price elasticity.

Unitary elasticity: the case in which the own price elasticity equals -1.

Chapter 10

Derived Demand Models

Chapter 7 outlined an economic model of consumer decision making which involved maximizing utility subject to a budget constraint within a single time period. Due to its long standing use in economics, it is referred to as the traditional, or classical, model of consumer choice. A critical feature of this model is the way the utility function (indifference curves) are developed. The willingness to trade (see Figure 7-2) is in terms of market goods (the axes), or utility (U) is derived from market goods (X), which can be expressed in functional notation for n goods as:

(10-1) $U = f(X_1,...,X_n)$.

The corresponding budget constraint is shown below for a given expenditure (M) and prices (P).

(10-2) $M = P_1X_1 + ... + P_nX_n$.

Maximizing equation 10-1 subject to equation 10-2 yields the demand equations, such as equations 8-2, which are given below.

(10-3) $X_i = f(P_1,...,P_n,M)$.

Two fundamental changes in the economic model are made in this chapter. First, a distinction is drawn between the generation of utility and the purchase of goods in the marketplace. Second, the amount of time available in the budget period is introduced as a constraint. These modifications create different perspectives on consumer behavior, but it is important to bear in mind that the underlying economic logic remains intact.

Figure 10-1 is a schematic presentation of the alternative models. Traditional demand models have marketplace goods as the independent variables in the utility function. The other models are called **derived demand** models because the consumer's demands for marketplace goods are derived indirectly from the demands for the independent variables that appear in the utility function. There are two basic types of derived demand models, and each is outlined in this chapter. Characteristics models are based on the idea that the properties of goods generate utility. Household production models assume the consumer transforms marketplace goods into commodities that the consumer uses to generate utility.

● Characteristics Models ●

Characteristics models assume the properties of goods generate utility, as opposed to the goods themselves. A **characteristic** is a property of a market good that a consumer values. For example, the traditional model would have a television as a market good in equation 10-1, whereas the characteristics model would have the properties of the television (size of screen, type of screen, remote control, etc.).[1] Market goods generate characteristics through a consumption technology.

---

[1]   There are two types of characteristics models: Houthakker-Theil and Lancaster. The distinctions between them are beyond the introductory scope of this book. See W. M. Hanemann "Quality and Demand Analysis," *New Directions in Econometric Modeling and Forecasting in U. S. Agriculture*. G. Rausser, ed., New York: Elsevier-North Holland, 1981 for a discussion. The Lancaster model is developed here.

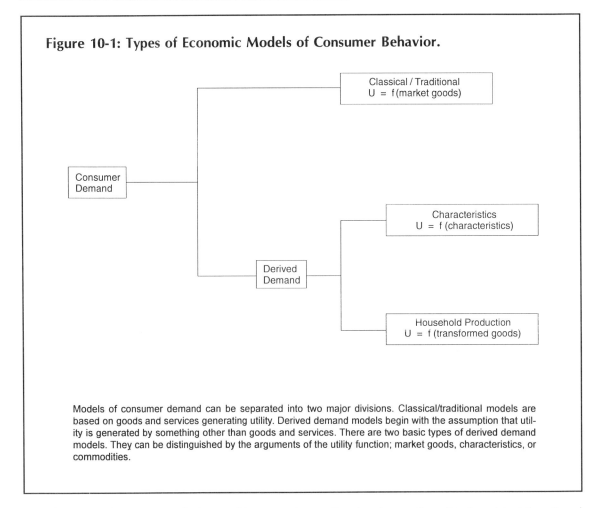

Figure 10-1: Types of Economic Models of Consumer Behavior.

Models of consumer demand can be separated into two major divisions. Classical/traditional models are based on goods and services generating utility. Derived demand models begin with the assumption that utility is generated by something other than goods and services. There are two basic types of derived demand models. They can be distinguished by the arguments of the utility function; market goods, characteristics, or commodities.

The revised consumer choice problem can be outlined quite easily with the aid of functional notation. Let C_i denote the ith characteristic, of which there are N. These characteristics generate utility, as represented below.

(10-4) $U = u(C_1,...,C_N)$

The **consumption technology** represents the transformation of market goods, X_i, into the desired characteristics. These transformations are shown as equations 10-5.

$$C_1 = c_1(X_1,...,X_n)$$

(10-5)

$$C_N = c_N(X_1,...,X_n)$$

Equations 10-5 are general representations of the manipulation of market goods into characteristics. Some of the X_i in a specific characteristic equation could have a value of zero. For example, if C_1 is shirt style and X_{12} is lawn fertilizer, the value of X_{12} in the C_1 equation is zero.

A consumer's ability to buy is represented as a budget constraint. It is the same as the traditional model's, or equation 10-2.

The economic problem of the consumer remains unchanged, which is to maximize utility, but now, in addition to the budget constraint, there is the consumption technology. Mathematical procedures for solving the problem are beyond the scope of the present introduction. However, it is possible, with the help of some simplifying assumptions, to identify the optimal choice.[2] Assume there are only two characteristics that generate utility, and there are five brands of market goods that can be transformed into these characteristics. Each brand is assumed to be transformed into the characteristics in fixed proportions. This last assumption means that no matter what quantities of the brands are purchased, the characteristics are always produced in the same ratio.

Suppose shirts produce the desirable characteristics of style (S) and comfort (Cm). There are five brands of shirts. Each brand can be changed into the characteristics in the amounts per shirt indicated in Table 10-1, Columns 2 and 3. Column 4 shows the proportions of S versus Cm for each brand. The notion of fixed proportions now can be explained. Regardless of how many shirts are purchased, a given brand is assumed to produce the indicated amounts of S and Cm per shirt, so the ratio remains unchanged. Columns 2-4 represent the consumption technology, or the way the market goods (brands of shirts) are changed into the characteristics S and Cm.

Figure 10-2 displays the same information. Units of S and Cm are measured on the noted axes. A ray from the origin represents a constant proportion of S versus Cm. Each of the five brands has an associated ray. Any point on ray E, for example, shows a combination of S and Cm in the ratio of 4S to 1 Cm. The rays depict the consumption technology. They represent the set of equations 10-5 for this illustration.

The budget constraint, equation 10-2, also needs to be incorporated into problem. It is expressed in terms of market goods, but the consumption technology and utility function are defined in terms of characteristics. This means that it is necessary to restructure the budget constraint so that it can be represented in terms of characteristics. Since the consumption technology does not depend on the quantities of characteristics used, an easy procedure is to determine how much of each characteristic can be purchased per dollar for each brand. Total expenditure can be generated through multiplication by the number of dollars budgeted. Columns 5-7 of Table 10-1 provide the requisite information. Dividing the market price of each brand (column 5) into the amount of each respective characteristic associated with a unit of the brand yields the characteristics per dollar. Lower-case letters are used to identify the points in Figure 10-2 that correspond to the results of columns 6 and 7. Characteristics S and Cm are desirable. The consumer wants to have as much of them as possible per dollar. Inspection of Figure 10-2 reveals that brands B and D are not good buys. Brand B is clearly a poor buy, because brands A and C provide more of both characteristics per dollar. The same is true for brand D.

A consumer has the option of buying more than one brand of shirt. Using two brands allows the consumer to create any combination of S and Cm between rays A and E. Conceptually, if the budget constraint represents a shirt budget for six months, the consumer can wear more than one brand of shirt during this period. Connecting all of the best buys per dollar generates the **efficiency frontier**. It is the counterpart of the budget constraint in the classical model. Points on the efficiency frontier between the rays represent combinations of brands. For example, point f is a combination of brands

---

[2]   A more advanced analysis can be found in H. A. J. Green, *Consumer Theory*, second edition (New York: Macmillan, 1976).

Table 10-1: Illustrations of the Characteristics Model

(1) Brand	(2) S	(3) Cm	(4) S:Cm	(5) P	(6) S/P	(7) Cm/P	(8) Point
A	9	36	1:4	9	1	4	a
B	24	48	1:2	24	1	2	b
C	45	45	1:1	15	3	3	c
D	30	15	2:1	10	3	1.5	d
E	40	10	4:1	10	4	1	e

S = style; Cm = comfort; P = price.

C and E such that their sum equals one dollar. Point f shows the amounts of S and Cm associated with spending $.50 on each of the two brands. Taking the results for columns 6 and 7 for brands C and E, one gets the following equations.

Point f:

$.5(3) + .5(4) = 3.5$ units of S per dollar.

$.5(3) + .5(1) = 2.0$ units of Cm per dollar.

Brand D was observed to be an inefficient purchase. In fact, it can be shown that a combination of brands C and E (point g) provides the same proportions of S and Cm as brand D, but the quantity per dollar is larger. Point g corresponds to spending $.40 on C and $.60 on E. Notice that point g is farther away from the origin than point d, so g is a better buy.

Point g:

$.4(3) + .6(4) = 3.6$ units of S per dollar.

$.4(3) + .6(1) = 1.8$ units of Cm per dollar.

$3.6/1.8 = 2/1$, the proportion represented by ray D.

Consumer preferences for the characteristics are based on assumptions analogous to those outlined in Chapter 7. This means that a set of indifference curves has the same properties as before. If the shape of the indifference curves remains constant along any ray from the origin, the examination of the efficiency frontier per dollar and indifference curves identifies the optimal bundle. The optimal position occurs at a point of tangency between the efficiency frontier and the set of indifference curves. Interpretation of this point is the same as in the traditional model. The slope of the indifference curve can be shown to be equal to the ratio of the marginal utilities. However, in the characteristics model they are in terms of the properties of the goods. The slope of the efficiency frontier is determined by the amounts of the characteristics that can be purchased per dollar, or the ability to trade characteristics. Consumer decision making still boils down to comparisons of the values of the last dollar spent. The difference is that they are in terms of characteristics, as opposed to market goods.

Figure 10-3 illustrates some possibilities. A single brand is purchased whenever the point of tangency occurs at a corner of the efficiency frontier, as is illustrated by the hypothetical indifference curve I_1. More than one brand is bought if the tangency occurs along a line segment of the efficiency frontier, such as the illustration of preferences associated with indifference curve I_2.

Figure 10-2: The Consumption Technology and the Efficiency Frontier

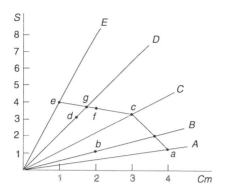

The efficiency frontier combines the consumption technology and the budget constraint. Five brands of shirts are associated with five separate combinations of the characteristics style (S) and comfort (Cm). Each brand is represented as a ray from the origin. No matter what quantity of a brand is bought, it is assumed to provide the same proportion of S and Cm. The quantity of the characteristics that can be bought per dollar is determined by dividing by the price given for each brand. These points, shown in Table 10-1, are labeled with lower-case letters. Connecting the outermost points generates the efficiency frontier. Brands B and D are observed to be inefficient. Combinations of brands produce points on the line segments of the efficiency frontier. Point f represents an expenditure of $0.50 for brands C and E.

Income changes cause the total expenditure frontier to change in a parallel fashion. Price changes affect the shape of the efficiency frontier, because they affect the amount of the characteristics that can be purchased. This is shown in Figure 10-4. Suppose the price of brand B falls to $12. The price change creates the new point b' on the B ray. Notice that this price change has caused brand A to become inefficient. Whether or not it affects consumption depends on the shape and location of the indifference curves. The characteristics approach to the analysis of consumer behavior leads to optimal consumption bundles in terms of characteristics.

The information associated with the points of tangency can be rearranged to express the market price of good as a function of the characteristics. This equation is called the **hedonic price equation**. It is one of the relationships that has been estimated in a wide variety of empirical studies.

An application of the characteristics approach to food demand is outlined below.[3] The starting point was the assumption that the nutritional composition of goods generated utility, as opposed to foods themselves. Data for the study were drawn from the 1977-78 Nationwide Food Consumption Survey, which was a representative sample of U. S. households. The survey collected information on foods consumed and the nutritional composition of foods. Nutrients were grouped into food energy (F), minerals (M), B vitamins (B), vitamin C (C), and vitamin A (A). Households which purchased at least 20 food items during a seven day period were grouped according to whether they met dietary

---

[3]   C. Cook and D. Eastwood, "Incorporating Subsistence into Hedonic Price and Nutrient Demand Equations," *Journal of Consumer Affairs*, 26,2(1992):288-304.

Figure 10-3: The Efficiency Frontier and the Optimal Purchase

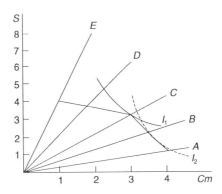

Optimal consumption is determined by a point of tangency between the efficiency frontier and the set of preferences represented by a set of indifference curves. Should a consumer's preferences be associated with a set of indifference curves of which I_1 is a member, then brand C is purchased. If I_2 is a member of the set of indifference curves, then a combination of brands A and C is purchased.

guidelines set by the USDA's Thrifty Food Plan. For households that exceeded the guidelines, the following hedonic price equation was estimated, where P is the unit price of a food. (The functional form excluded an intercept).

$$P = .0001(F) + .0002(M) + .0232(B) + .0011(c) - .0001(A)$$
$$[.33] \qquad [.11] \qquad [.35] \qquad [.05] \qquad [-.03]$$

Conceptually, the hedonic price equation relates the market price of a good to consumers' valuations of the characteristics it possesses. The coefficients are called marginal implicit prices because they are estimates of effects of the properties on the market price the buyer has to pay. Positive coefficients indicate positive valuations of the respective nutrients and suggest that consumers were willing to pay more in 1977-78 for foods containing more F, M, B, and C. The negative coefficient for A was considered to be the result of this vitamin adding a bitter taste to the foods that contained the nutrient.

Elasticities associated with the estimated coefficients are in brackets.[4] They are estimates of the percentage change in the market price associated with a percentage change in each of the nutrients. B, followed closely by F, have the largest impacts. M's elasticity is less than half those of F and B, and C's is about one-sixth. This low C elasticity was felt to reflect the consumer's perception that it is

---

[4]   More precisely, they are called flexibilities in demand analysis because price is the dependent variable. The logic behind the interpretation remains invariant, however.

Figure 10-4: The Efficiency Frontier and the Price Changes

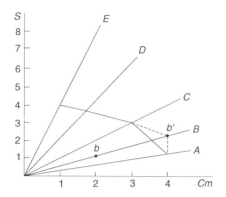

Price changes affect the shape of the efficiency frontier. Point b' represents a decline in P_B from $24 t0 $12. The price reduction allows more of S and Cm to be purchased per dollar. This causes the efficiency frontier to change, and brand A becomes inefficient.

found in so many foods, or easily supplemented, that less valuation was given to this nutrient before osteoporosis was publicized.

The characteristics approach offers some additional insights into the theory of consumer behavior. It provides an explanation as to why some goods can be grouped together by a consumer and also explains why some brands are not purchased. The model also introduces a different set of variables into consumer decision making. To the extent properties of market goods affect choices, this framework provides a more realistic way of analyzing consumer choice. This is particularly important in the next chapter where situations are identified for public intervention on behalf of consumer interests.

Finally, the introduction of new goods into the model can be accommodated easily in a diagram via a new characteristics ray. The traditional model requires a three-dimensional diagram for a third good, and it is not possible to have a diagrammatic presentation when there are more than three goods—mathematical techniques beyond the scope an introductory text are required. However, with the characteristics model there are the difficult problems of defining and measuring characteristics and dealing with a consumption technology.

STUDY QUESTIONS

Characteristics Models

1. Distinguish between a characteristic and a market good.
2. What are the similarities and differences between the traditional and characteristics models in the optimal position of a consumer?
3. Suppose a consumer has budgeted $100 for clothing. What does the total expenditure efficiency frontier look like for the data in Table 10-1?
4. A new brand of shirt (F) has just been introduced. If the new shirt possesses 40 units of S and 30 units of Cm and costs $10, what happens to the efficiency frontier?
5. Given the data provided in Table 10-1, suppose P_A rises to $12. What happens to the efficiency frontier? Referring to Figure 10-3, what happens to the optimal position if preferences are represented by I_1 instead of I_2?
6. Except in some unusual situations, the traditional model always has the consumer buying some of every good. That is, the point of tangency does not occur along any goods axis. How does the characteristics approach allow for zero purchases?
7. What advantages do the characteristics model have over the traditional model for someone writing advertisements?

● Household Production Models ●

● The Opportunity Cost of Time

Ever run out of time to get something done? Just about any production or consumption activity requires time as part of the process. Not only is time limited in supply, but it has alternative uses. The discussion of total utility in Chapter 4 identified the various ways in which a consumer unit must allocate the time of its members. Generally, the five types of utility are mutually exclusive with respect to use of time. Time spent generating market utility cannot be spent generating home-produced utility. Because of these competing alternative uses, the opportunity cost of time becomes a crucial part of decision making.

Therefore, time should be included as a constraint in the model of consumer choice. Whatever the budget period happens to be, there is a corresponding maximum amount of time available to generate the various types of utility. The sum of the time spent in these activities must equal the total time available. With T denoting total time and t_i $(i = 1,...,5)$ representing the five types of utility, the time constraint can be shown as

(10-6) $T = t_1 + ... + t_5$

Incorporating time into the model of consumer choice is more involved than just creating the time constraint in equation 10-6.[5] Time devoted to the marketplace determines the earned income, given

---

[5]   Notice that the discussion is within a one-period context. Time within a period must be allocated among competing uses. Decisions involving more than one period are the subject of Part V.

a wage rate. Time spent in home-production is a determinant of home-produced utility. The opportunity costs of the allocation decision also must be incorporated. For example, the decision to increase home production time can only occur through a reduction in time spent in other ways. Let us now look at these consequences.

● Household Production

Consumers have dual roles to play in our economic system. The consumer is both a buyer and a seller, as outlined in Chapter 2 and displayed in the circular flow diagram. Part II of this book has expanded on the dual functions. Through this book's development of the concept of total utility, it should be clear that a consumer unit must manage all of its resources as efficiently as possible in order to achieve the highest feasible well-being or utility. This section presents a more complete discussion of the dual economic roles.[6]

The household is assumed to obtain utility through the use of **commodities**, Z_i. These commodities are generated through **household production** processes in which market goods, X_i, and time, t_i, are combined. The Z_i are not the same as characteristics. For example, in the characteristics approach, the consumption technology transforms steak into characteristics such as taste and nutrition. In the household production approach, the household produces the commodity—a steak dinner—through combining steak purchased in a grocery store, other market goods, and the time of household members. Various production technologies are available to a household. For a steak dinner, options include oven broiling, charcoal broiling, or preparation by a restaurant. Each technology uses a different method of combining market goods and household time.

Household production imposes constraints on decision making. The market goods that are available to the household, along with the limited time of household members, determine how commodities are generated. A mowed lawn is an illustration. Given the size of the lawn (purchased as a real estate market good) and given the size and type of lawn mower, the time required for a person to mow the lawn can be determined. The size of the lawn also determines the quantity of hired lawn mower services the household would need to buy if someone else is to provide the commodity. These considerations indicate that the production of the commodity a mowed lawn is constrained by the acquisition of market goods, X_i, and the allocated time, t_i.

Such observations about household behavior can be summarized in a straightforward manner with the aid of functional relationships. Equation 10-7 is the utility function for a representative consumer unit. Utility, U, is derived from the use of the various commodities, of which there are N. Each of the commodities is produced by combining market goods and time.[7] These production functions are represented as equations 10-8. There is a total of n market goods that can be used in household production. Some of these may have a value of zero in the production of a particular commodity. This means the market good is not used in that particular commodity production process.

---

[6]   The seminal paper is G. Becker, "A Theory of the Allocation of Time," *Economic Journal* 75(1965):493-517. Subsequent development and extension is contained in G. Becker, *A Treatise on the Family*, (Cambridge: Harvard University Press, 1991).

[7]   Mathematical conditions are imposed on the production function in order to derive a solution to the model.

(10-7) $U = u(Z_1, Z_2, ..., Z_N)$
          $Z_1 = z_1(X_1, X_2, ..., X_n, t_1)$

(10-8)   .   .
          .   .
          .   .
          $Z_N = z_N(X_1, X_2, ..., X_n, t_N)$

Another constraint facing the household is the budget constraint. The purchase of market goods is limited by the available money, M. Two types of money income are identified. One is earned income, which is the equivalent of the wage rate, w, multiplied by the amount of time spent working, t_w. The second is the unearned income derived from savings and investments, V. Equation 10-9 is the budget constraint for a single person consumer unit.[8]

(10-9) $M = wt_w + V$

$$= \sum_{i=1}^{n} P_i X_i$$

The remaining constraint is the time constraint. There is a maximum amount of time per period that is available to the household. Time allocation is one of the key economic choice problems facing the household. Both household production and money income require time as a input. Opportunity cost is the key economic variable here. The opportunity cost of time spent in home production is the foregone income. Total time, T, must equal the sum of the production time plus time at work.

(10-10) $$T = \sum_{i=1}^{N} t_i + t_w$$

Households are assumed to maximize equation 10-7 subject to equations 10-8 through 10-10. Procedures for obtaining the solution are beyond the scope of this text. However, the solution has straightforward economic interpretations analogous to those of the traditional model. Utility is maximized when the household has allocated resources as efficiently as possible. The decision variables are how much of the X_i to purchase and how much time to spend producing each commodity and generating money income. Opportunity costs of the various courses of action determine what the household does. The value of the last dollar spent becomes the criterion used to attain the optimum. How much of the X_i to purchase is determined by relating the market prices, P_i, to the change in the production of a commodity and the consequent change in utility.

Let MU_{Zi} denote the marginal utility of Z_i. Let $MP_{Zi,Xj}$ represent how a small change in the market good X_j affects the production of Z_i. Then, $MU_{Zi} MP_{Zi,Xj}$ indicates how utility is altered by a change in X_j. The value of the last dollar spent is this product divided by the price per unit. For example, let h denote a commodity other than Z_i and let m be a market good input other than X_j. When the best purchases are made, the values of the last dollar spent are equated for both goods.

(10-11) $$\frac{MU_{Zi} MP_{Zi,Xj}}{P_j} = \frac{MU_{Zh} MP_{Zh,Xm}}{P_m}$$

---

[8]   Extension to multiple members requires wages rates and time variables for each person with appropriate summations.

Similar remarks apply to time allocation with respect to home production. The amount of time used as an input affects the production of commodities, and changes in the production of commodities affect utility. The opportunity cost of the time is the wage rate. Equation 10-12 depicts the optimal situation for commodity Z_i and time input t_i compared to another commodity Z_k and time input t_k.

$$(10\text{-}12) \quad \frac{MU_{Zi}MP_{Ziti}}{w} = \frac{MU_{Zk}MP_{Zktk}}{w}$$

Finally, the relationship between the time and market goods in production must be acknowledged. Reductions in home production time can increase income, which can allow more X_i to be purchased. This is reflected in equation 10-13 for commodities Z_i and Z_k, market good X_j, and time input t_k.

$$(10\text{-}13) \quad \frac{MU_{Zi}MP_{Zixj}}{P_j} = \frac{MU_{Zk}MP_{Zktk}}{w}$$

These equations may seem rather imposing, but they are not. Each relates the values of the last dollar spent. All that is being argued here is that a household must consider how productive the various inputs are in terms of their ultimate effects on utility. The effects must be weighed in terms of their respective opportunity costs. Replacing the equalities with inequalities indicates how the household can alter its production and resources to become better off. For example, if the $>$ holds then less time should be devoted to the production of Z_k and more X_j should be used to produce Z_i.

$$(10\text{-}14) \quad \frac{MU_{Zi}MP_{Zixj}}{P_j} \begin{array}{c} > \\ < \end{array} \frac{MU_{Zk}MP_{Zktk,}}{w}$$

A graphical illustration of the household production function approach can be created with the imposition of some additional conditions. Assume there are only two commodities and that a household has a fixed set of resources and abilities with which to produce Z_1 and Z_2. Assume further that there is a fixed technology for production. The household's production possibility frontier for Z_1 and Z_2 can now be developed, as shown in Figure 10-5. This production possibility frontier has properties identical to those discussed in Chapter 3. Movement along the frontier indicates how reallocating household resources changes the quantities produced of Z_1 and Z_2. This frontier represents the constraints facing a household.

Suppose for a moment that there is no market in which the Z_i can be purchased or an earned income can be generated. In this setting, the X_i represent some sort of endowment of goods (e.g., personal skills and training) which can be used to produce the commodities in the absence of any connection with a market. A set of indifference curves portrays the household's preferences for the commodities. Given one must remain on the production possibility frontier, the optimal position is achieved at a point of tangency, such as point E.

But it is not necessary for the family to be limited by this production possibility frontier when there are markets in which the X_i can be bought and sold. To see how the presence of markets enhances the household's well-being, assume the following. Given the presence of a market, the household could specialize in the production of a good or service, such as managerial talent. Through selling some of this business skill in the factor market, the household receives money, which could then be used to buy final goods to produce commodities.

Rather than producing and consuming at E, the household can move along the frontier to a point such as a in Figure 10-6, where $Z_{1,a}$ and $Z_{2,a}$ are produced by the consumer unit. The slope of the line b represents the market trade-offs between Z_2 and Z_1, given the prices of market goods and time. Trading in the market allows the family to move along b until the highest feasible indifference curve is attained at point e. This means that the family produces at a and consumes at e. Notice the presence of a market allows for specialization and enables the household to move beyond the limits of its production possibility frontier.

Figure 10-5: Household Production Possibility Frontier

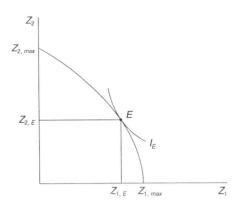

Assume that there are two commodities that generate utility. Given fixed household size, ability of members, and technology, $Z_{1, max}$ and $Z_{2, max}$ represent the most of either commodity alone that the household could produce if all resources were used exclusively for one or the other commodity. The slope of the frontier shows how Z_1 can be changed into Z_2. A set of indifference curves portrays preferences for Z_1 and Z_2. The utility maximizing position is at point E, where I_E is tangent to the frontier.

Line b just touches the production possibility frontier and I_e. This is the graphical counterpart of equations 10-10 through 10-13. The tangency at a reflects production trade-offs being equal to the commodity prices. The tangency at e reflects willingness to trade along I_e being equated to commodity prices. Since b is a straight line, the trade-offs at a and e must be the same. This is equivalent to equating the values of the last dollar spent for market goods and time. Exercises at the end of this section indicate the many ways in which this model can be applied.

● Household Production and the Recent History of U.S. Consumer Units Revisited ●

The household production model provides a very useful framework for a more complete analysis of the observed changes in resource allocation within consumer units than was described in Chapters 5 and 6. Key elements in decision making are represented as equations 10-11 through 10-14. They involve incremental valuations of utility generated by commodities (MU_{zi}), the marginal products of the market goods (MP_{xj}) and time (MP_{tk}), and the opportunity costs of market goods P_j and time, w. That is, both the numerators and denominators of the relationships have changed in recent decades.

Technological change affects the marginal products of goods and time. For example, new durables have emerged (such as microwaves and lawn trimmers), and others have new features (such as washing machines and driers). Often these changes have reduced the amount of time required, or

Figure 10-6: Household Production and Markets

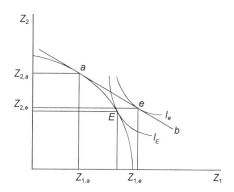

The ability to interact with markets enables a household to move away from its frontier. Rather than remaining at point E, the consumer can specialize in the production of Z_2. Line b depicts the cost of producing Z_2 and Z_1, with given market prices. Through reallocating resources, the household can change production to point a. By trading in the market, the household can exchange the amount $(Z_{2,a} - Z_{2,e})$ for the amount $(Z_{1,e} - Z_{1,a})$, making the family better off.

increased the marginal products of time spent in these home production activities.[9] These increases, by themselves, increased the respective numerators of the relationships, thereby helping to generate the observed changes in resource allocation.

Durables have tended to decline in price, following their introductions, especially when adjusted for quality. For example, televisions are now cable ready, come with remotes, and have circuits that require less repair. As some P_j's decline relative to other goods, consumers have an inducement to reallocate time and expenditures.

Time reallocation between home production and marketplace activities is also part of the decision making environment. The opportunity cost of not working has increased with rising educational attainment and the availability of part time employment. That is, w has tended to increase for the adult members of the typical consumer unit. Increases in w, assuming nothing else changes, cause the right-hand side of equation 10-13 to fall, or the $<$ inequality depicted in equation 10-14 prompts reallocation.

Altogether, the changes in the economic environment have led not only to changes in marginal utilities, marginal products, prices, and wages, but the real incomes of typical households have risen. Consumers have responded by changing the optimal mix of market goods and labor. A direct consequence of the reallocation is the increased time pressure on parents, especially mothers, to manage responsibilities in the home and at work.

Changing food consumption patterns support the household production framework. The rise in the dual career household has enabled many consumers to increase their earned incomes. A way of

[9]   Estimates of household production have been published in K. Bryant, C. Zick, and K. Hyoshin, *The Dollar Value of Household Work*, Ithaca: Cornell University, College of Human Ecology, 1992.

reallocating time is to purchase more expensive but use less time for food preparation. This is consistent with research of Smallwood et al. who found that annual per capita spending for food at home by urban households has increased 55 percent between 1980 and 1992 and that for food away from home increased nearly 69 percent.[10] Other studies show that the share of the food dollar going to food away from home increased with income.[11] Supermarkets have also expanded their offerings of highly processed foods such as precut fresh produce and prepared meals. In fact, the supermarket industry is competing directly with fast food retailers because working women are estimated to spend on average approximately 15 minutes preparing a meal.[12] Consequently, a growth area for the supermarket industry is the provision of high quality meals.

STUDY QUESTIONS

Household Production Models

8.   Distinguish among utility functions 10-1, 10-4, and 10-7.
9.   Distinguish between equations 10-5 and 10-8.
10.   What is the difference between marginal utility and marginal product?
11.   How is the household production approach consistent with the concept of total utility?
12.   How can the purchase of a microwave oven, a market good, affect the home production model of consumer behavior?
13.   A homemaker is considering going back to school to earn an MBA in accounting. Assuming she graduates, how will her new degree affect household decision making?
14.   A family wants to add a porch to its home. How can the production function approach be used to explain the factors involved in doing it yourself versus contracting for the work?
15.   Use the home production function framework to explain why a family would purchase a lawn mower. Then explain why the family might prefer to spend more for a riding lawn mower.

● Summary ●

The characteristics model of consumer behavior assumes people derive utility from the properties that goods possess. The consumption technology represents the way in which market goods are transformed into characteristics. A budget constraint limits the purchase of market goods. The efficiency frontier depicts the combined budget constraint and consumption technology. It shows how

[10]   D. Smallwood, N. Blissard, J. Blaylock, and S. Lutz, *Food Spending in American Households: 1980-92*, USDA/ERS Statistical Bulletin 888 (October, 1994).
[11]   The Food Institute. *Food Retailing Review 1994 Edition*, Fair Lawn, NJ: The Food Institute, 1994.
[12]   R. DeSanta, "Supermarket Food Service—Its About Meals, Not Deals," *Supermarket Business*, (June, 1995).

much of the characteristics can be bought per dollar. Utility maximization occurs at a point of tangency between the indifference curves and the efficiency frontier.

The household production function approach assumes households produce desired commodities through production processes which combine market goods and time. Efficient decision making entails comparing the marginal products of the inputs in terms of their ultimate effects on utility relative to their opportunity costs. The presence of markets enables households to consume beyond their production possibility frontiers.

● Key Terms ●

Characteristic: a property of a market good that is assumed to generate utility.

Commodity: a market good that has been transformed through home production into a utility-producing item.

Consumption technology: a process through which market goods are transformed into characteristics.

Efficiency frontier: locus of maximum combinations of characteristics per dollar.

Hedonic price equation: representation of the price paid for a product as a function of the good's characteristics.

Household production: process of combining market goods and household time to generate commodities.

Chapter 11

The Economics of Information: A Basis for Public Intervention

Economic theories of consumer choice serve four very useful purposes, three of which have been covered in previous chapters. First, economic theory provides a structure for understanding and evaluating consumer behavior. Second, the theory establishes a basis for generating empirical estimates of consumer responsiveness to changes in the economic environment. Third, the models establish conditions under which the consumer is as well off as possible through maximizing utility subject to constraints. Fourth, the models can be used to determine when public intervention on behalf of consumers is justified.

The fourth purpose is discussed in this chapter. Utility maximization, regardless of which approach is used (traditional or derived demand), leads to a decision making rule that entails some form of the value of the last dollar spent. Graphically, this involves moving along the constraint(s) (i.e., to the ability to exchange determined by the budget and consumption or production technologies) to reach the highest level of satisfaction (i.e., willingness to trade). Mathematically, decisions hinge on incremental changes in utilities and corresponding opportunity costs.

Three assumptions are implicit in the analyses of the models outlined in the preceding chapters. One is the consumer is capable of determining the marginal utility associated with the arguments of the utility function. Another is the relevant opportunity costs are directly related to market prices. The third is that consumer sovereignty prevails. This chapter questions how appropriate these assumptions are in real-world buying situations. To the extent the assumptions do not hold, there are economic justifications for public intervention.

Clearly, less than optimal decisions are likely to occur whenever the consumer is making choices and the assumptions do not hold. If a consumer is unable to determine the relevant marginal utility or opportunity cost, incorrect resource allocation decisions may be made. Such decisions reduce total utility. One way of addressing the situation is to provide the missing information through advertising. However, the implicit assumption is that advertising provides accurate, useful information.

● The Consumer's Price ●

A consumer decides whether to allocate resources (e.g., buy a market good, acquire a characteristic, or produce a commodity) by comparing the change in utility in relation to the cost of the change. Market prices are at the center of the cost, as they appear in the budget constraints of the three types of models. Up to this point the assumption has been that for each food considered in the decision-making process, there is only one price, which is the unit price of the good in the marketplace. The usual justification is that consumers will pay only the lowest price, so higher priced sellers will not remain in the market for long.

But **price variation**, the charging of different prices per unit for a good of constant quality at a single point in time, is a characteristic of markets. Consequently, an adequate overview of how consumers function in a market system must include an examination of the causes of price variation.[1] Reasons for price variation can be separated into two categories: the economic considerations of the seller and the determination by the consumer of the appropriate price measure to be incorporated into the budget constraint. Economic considerations of the seller can be subdivided into differences in seller cost and market instability.

Differences in seller cost may occur if the unit cost is a decreasing function of the size of the retailer. In this situation, larger firms are able to sell each unit of the good at a lower price than a smaller firm. High-volume retailers often state in their advertising that they are able to "charge less" because they sell so much. Car dealers, tire stores, and discount stores frequently use this approach. Two caveats are noted. First, just because a seller advertises such pricing behavior, it does not mean that it actually occurs. Second, a business may have a very low price for one good, but other goods may have relatively high prices and/or related goods may be priced above competitors.

Unstable markets are characterized by variations in price. To the extent that supply and demand fluctuate, the price-adjustment mechanism is always causing the market to move toward a new equilibrium price. The entry of new sellers into the market contributes to the instability, as new entrants typically try to attract customers with lower prices. The exit of firms with going-out-of-business sales can be a cause of price instability. Unstable markets are also characterized by many competing brands trying to underprice one another. Finally, if the use of one good is tied closely to the use of another, then the market is likely to be unstable and price variation is more likely to occur. For example, if the price of electricity goes up, it may induce some retailers to lower the price of portable electric heaters.

The consumer has no control over these variables, but the price is used in the budget constraint and becomes part of the optimal decision making rule of the value of the last dollar spent. If the numerator reflects the incremental benefit then the denominator should reflect the entire opportunity cost to the consumer associated with the benefit. The **consumer's price** is defined as this entire opportunity cost. Since the consumer's costs include more than just the market price of a good that is to be acquired, the incorporation of opportunity costs into the analysis of consumer behavior provides a much clearer perspective on the cost considerations associated with the acquisition of goods.

Geographic separation among stores and consumers necessitates the inclusion of travel costs in the consumer's price. Such costs are determined by transportation mode and time. The former refers to the cost of using a particular transportation mode such as a bus or a car, and the latter reflects the opportunity cost of time spent shopping. Large shopping malls may not offer the lowest market prices, but they do provide proximity to residences as well as a variety of stores, which keeps transportation costs down. Convenience stores are able to charge slightly higher prices because the prices for the consumer are competitive by virtue of the lower travel cost.

How does a consumer know where the lowest price for a good can be found? Acquiring price information can be costly. Travel costs may be involved in gathering information, depending on how the various retailers in a market are geographically distributed. In addition, more time must be spent in stores. This time has an opportunity cost, since it could be used in other activities. The consumer must determine how much search should occur before a purchase is made.

---

[1]   The seminal work is that of G. Stigler, "The Economics of Information," *Journal of Political Economy* 69(1961):213-25.

The fundamental rule of search is that a consumer should continue this activity as long as the expected gains from the continued search are greater than the costs. This is applying the value of the last dollar spent rule to finding the lowest price. The gain is the marginal utility associated with locating a lower price so the same money can control more market goods. The consumer's price for additional search, the **search cost**, is the increased travel and time costs of the continued effort. Advertising plays a very beneficial role within this context. To the extent that advertising conveys accurate information, it greatly diminishes the cost of search to obtain the lowest price. For example, grocery store ads in newspapers provide information that enables a consumer to compare prices while at home.

Variations in search costs can compensate for variations in market prices. Higher priced stores typically provide more information about goods and more consumer assistance. The consumer spends less time finding someone to answer questions and paying for the good. Consumers who place high values on time may prefer this type of store because of the reduction in time required. Even though the market price is higher, the consumer's price may be lower than at a discount store. Notice that these considerations lead to the common situation in which a variety of stores offer basically the same good but specialize in other aspects of the consumer's price.

A recent study of price dispersion illustrates the extent of price variation.[2] The analysis was based on the annual price data gathered by *Consumer Reports* and covered the years 1987-91. Table 11-1 presents the dispersion data for the noted electronic products. Average price dispersion was calculated as the difference between the average price of all brands of comparable quality and the average price of the two lowest priced brands. Differences were divided by the average price of all brands to obtain relative measures. Each entry in the dispersion column represents the percentage lower price a consumer could have paid on average if one of the two lowest priced brands was bought. For example, consumers could have paid 16 percent less on average in 1987 for a camcorder by purchasing one of the two lowest priced comparable quality brands.

Inspection of the table reveals two important points. First, the percents are fairly large, suggesting that shopping around for these products can lead to significant savings. Second, the price dispersions within each category do not display consistent evidence of decreasing price variation over time.

So far, the assumption has been that if a consumer is willing to pay the travel and time costs, the lowest consumer's price can be found. This does not necessarily occur, however, because of some additional factors. One additional factor is that the market may not provide all of the needed price information. Durables are the prime category. Regardless of which model of behavior is used, deriving utility from a durable involves other market goods, depreciation, and maintenance. Without such information, one cannot determine all the relevant components of the consumer's price. This increases the likelihood that incorrect values of the last dollar spent are used in decision making. All purchases are affected, not just those for which actual consumers prices are unknown. The reason stems from recognizing that all values of the last dollar spent are equated, so if one is incorrect, the equating process affects all the choices. Therefore, the consumer could be made better off through the provision of relevant consumer's price information, assuming that the cost of the additional information is the less than the consumer's valuation. The next section identifies some features of information that are useful to consumers and comprise a framework for providing information through public policies.

---

[2]   A. Jannuzzi and R. Dardis, "Consumer Losses from Price Dispersion in the Consumer Electronics Market," *Consumer Interests Annual*, T. Mauldin, ed., Columbia, MO: American Council on Consumer Interests (1994):210-15.

Table 11-1: Estimates of Price Dispersion for Selected Consumer Electronics

Product	Year	Price Dispersion
Camcorder	1987	.16
	1990	.19
	1991	.21
CD Player	1987	.35
	1989	.17
	1990	.16
	1991	.29
Color TV	1987	.21
	1988	.15
	1989	.14
	1991	.27
Receiver	1988	.27
	1989	.29
	1990	.16
	1991	.14
TV/VCR	1990	.12
VCR	1989	.06
	1990	.12
	1991	.13

Source: A. Jannuzzi and R. Dardis, "Consumer Losses from Price Dispersion in the Consumer Electronic Electronics Market," *Consumer Interests Annual*, T. Mauldin, Editor, Columbia, MO: American Council on Consumer Interests (1994): 213.

The household production model provides two additional reasons for price variation for some goods. One is based on the opportunity cost of time. A consumer with a high opportunity cost (high wage) may find it desirable to purchase market goods that require smaller time inputs in order to obtain the same commodity. For example, supermarkets are finding consumers are willing to pay a premium for more highly processed foods such as precut produce and high quality meals prepared in the store.

STUDY QUESTIONS

The Consumer's Price

1. Distinguish between the consumer's price and the market price. Why is the consumer's price appropriate for consumer decision making?
2. What are the market factors causing market price variation?
3. Suppose you are going to buy a pair of shoes. What are the advantages of shopping in a large mall?
4. Why is it that higher income consumers tend to buy in higher priced stores?
5. How can advertising serve a useful role for consumers?
6. From a consumer perspective, what is the rationale for allowing the phone company to charge fees to businesses for publishing special listings in the yellow pages?
7. What are the key elements of the consumer's price when a car is purchased?
8. How are opportunity cost and the consumer's price related?

● Incremental Effects on Utility and Price Information ●

A consumer's ability to maximize utility subject to a budget constraint depends on the ability to assess properly the incremental effects of choice variables on utility as well as the consumer's prices of the choices.[3] Should the consumer be unable to do this, then the values of the last dollar spent will be incorrect, which leads to less than optimal purchases. Consequently, it is crucial the consumer be able to determine accurately the numerators as well as the denominators of the ratios. This section identifies instances in which the consumer may not be able to determine marginal utilities. The discussion also focuses on another key function of advertising—that of providing relevant information.

When decisions are made about what market goods to buy, all three models (traditional and two derived demand) of consumer behavior implicitly assume the consumer knows how the good will affect utility. That is, the person is able to relate a unit more or less of the good to a change in utility. Unfortunately, the amount of information that a consumer can acquire about a good varies considerably across the spectrum of items available for purchase. Consequently, it is very useful to categorize goods on the basis of their information content.[4] A **search good** is one whose qualities can be assessed prior to purchase. An example is a CD player. Style, size, features, and other attributes can be determined in a store. Since a consumer is able to evaluate these factors prior to purchase, the marginal utility can be determined fairly accurately before the good is bought. That is, the consumer can determine the marginal utility of the player directly in the classical model or marginal utility and the consumption or the production technologies in the derived demand models.

---

[3] Consistent with Chapter 7, it is not necessary that the consumer be able to associate precise numerical values for marginal utility. Rather, all that is necessary is that a consumer can arrive at an assessment of the effect of an incremental unit of the good, characteristic, or commodity.

[4] P. Nelson, "Information and Consumer Behavior," *Journal of Political Economy*, 78(1980):311-29.

An **experience good** is one whose properties the consumer is not able to assess until the good is used. Thus, the consumer must purchase the good and then determine whether the purchase was desirable. Because the good's characteristics cannot be determined prior to purchase, the consumer is unable to assess marginal utilities before money is spent. Less than optimal purchases arise as a result. Food items are examples. Suppose a new brand of beer is introduced. How do you know if you will like it? Because of their increased complexity, many new consumer durables have characteristics of experience goods. To the extent a consumer is unable to assess the characteristics of a good before purchase, the marginal utility can be over- or under-stated, leading to a less than optimal purchase.

A **credence good** is one whose qualities a consumer is unable to assess even after using it.[5] If a dentist informs you that a crown is needed rather than a filling, how do you know the dentist is right? Or, suppose your car is not running well, and you go to a garage for repairs. How can you tell if the all the repairs are needed? In both situations even after the work has been completed, it is difficult or impossible to determine if the amount of work was appropriate.

Information content is more complex in the derived demand frameworks. In these models the consumer must also be knowledgeable about the consumption or production technologies. Both have search, experience, and credence features that are extensions of the present discussion.

This classification scheme, based on the informational properties of goods, provides a convenient framework for a discussion of how much shopping around a consumer should do in order to determine properly the marginal utility associated with buying a good. Whenever a search good is involved, the consumer is in the best position, because comparisons of price and quality can be made. Information acquisition can continue with a search good as long as the person anticipates a net gain from continuing the search.

Since experience goods normally are purchased prior to determination of the marginal utility, the consumer must estimate the gains and losses of the purchase. Gains (losses) occur whenever the new good turns out to be better (worse) that the brand presently used. As long as the expected gains of trying a new product are greater than the consumer's price, the consumer should make the purchase.

Credence goods present the most uncertainty for the consumer, as the marginal utility of the purchase is extremely difficult to ascertain, even after the good has been purchased. A buying strategy in this situation is to obtain a second opinion if it is felt that the additional information is worth the cost of its acquisition.

Many marketplace goods are associated with more than one of the three categories. For example, canned coffee has search, experience, and credence aspects. The price per pound, type of bean, and processing can be determined prior to purchase. But each person must drink the coffee to determine quality. An assessment of the nutritional and medical effects of drinking coffee requires research by experts.

Advertising can have a very important and useful role to play on behalf of consumers in need of information. Search goods' advertisements should stress the price competitiveness and quality of a product. Advertising campaigns for experience goods should be directed toward inducing the consumer to try the product via low prices or free samples. The quality of credence goods generally is more difficult to advertise. Instead, product standards and licensing have been used to ensure quality. These policy tools are discussed in the next section, but it can be noted here that some

---

5   M. R. Darby and E. Karni, "Free Competition and the Optimal Amount of Fraud," *Journal of Law and Economics* 16(1973):67-87.

suppliers of credence goods try to convey quality by advertising how long they have been in business, licenses earned, or standards attained. Examples can be found in building trade ads. It is important for the consumer to recognize that, to the extent that ads transmit needed information, they provide the valuable service of enabling consumers to assess incremental effects on utility more accurately and to reduce search costs.

Notice that this discussion of the economics of information does not conclude that a consumer should become completely informed about every item purchased. It is unrealistic to expect a consumer to become knowledgeable about each item purchased. Goods are too numerous and diverse. Furthermore, it can be in the consumer's self-interest to terminate the information-gathering process short of acquiring all available information. Information should be acquired as long as the consumer feels that the gains are at least equal to the associated costs. Since each consumer has a different preference structure as well as a different opportunity cost of search, the amount of information acquired before purchase will vary across consumers.

Being informed is a crucial aspect of making optimal purchases. It is necessary to acquire information about both price and quality in order to determine the appropriate value of the last dollar spent. Consumers are in a position to do this with items that are purchased regularly. But infrequently purchased goods pose more of a problem. It is unrealistic to expect consumers to be knowledgeable about all of the very wide variety of goods purchased. It is difficult to know what information is relevant, where to get it, and how to interpret it. On the other hand, sellers are knowledgeable and can control the information they present, especially in retail stores, in order to portray their products in the most favorable light. Thus, it is necessary that consumers not be intimidated by sales personnel, try to get as much information as possible prior to going into a store, and feel free to ask many questions.

A buying strategy for purchasing durables might be as follows. Prior to visiting showrooms, try to get as much information as possible. Determine how much can be spent. Identify the product features that are most important. Read publications, such as *Consumer Reports*, that periodically evaluate durables. Have a list of questions ready to ask the salesperson.

The impact of information on consumer markets was shown in a study by Archibald, Haulman, and Moody.[6] They examined the effect of quality ratings for jogging shoes on advertising and price. Jogging shoes are experience goods, because the only way a jogger can determine how a pair feels is to run in them. The study included 34 makers of 178 models, and these data show how complex the information problem can be for this market. Quality ratings for the shoes were provided by *Runner's World*, advertising expenditures were obtained from manufacturers, and price data were collected from retailers and *Runner's World*. A conclusion of their research was that the publication of the ratings affected advertising behavior. After the ratings were published, ads became less misleading, they were good indicators of quality shoes, and they identified good buys.

● Product Standards and Disclosure Information ●

The value of the last dollar spent is the consumer's guiding principle for spending a limited income as wisely as possible. The preceding two sections have discussed instances in which the normal functioning of private markets does not enable consumers to use this principle properly.

---

[6]   R. B. Archibald, C. A. Haulman, and C. E. Moody, Jr., "Quality, Price, Advertising, and Published Quality Ratings," *Journal of Consumer Research* 9 (1983):347-56.

STUDY QUESTIONS

Incremental Effects on Utility and Price Information

9. If you are going to purchase a notebook computer, how would you go about finding the best buy? Identify the search, experience, and credence features.
10. Explain why overstating incremental effects on utility are as detrimental as understating them.
11. Explain why miscalculations about incremental effects on utility are as detrimental as not being able to calculate consumer's prices.
12. The research department of E-Z Products, Inc. has just developed a new detergent for washing wrinkle-free cotton fabrics. Tests have indicated that this new product removes more stains than other detergents. As a member of E-Z's marketing department, what type of advertising campaign would you outline for the new product?
13. Identify the search experience, and credence aspects associated with the purchase of a CD player.
14. Identify the search experience, and credence aspects associated with the purchase of an automobile using a household production framework.

Product standards and disclosure information are the two basic avenues the public sector has for intervening on behalf of consumers. The legal system provides the mechanism for enforcing public intervention as well as the vehicle by which consumers can seek redress.

● Product Standards

Product standards establish minimum performance requirements. They affect both the numerator and the denominator of the value of the last dollar spent. The consumer's price is reduced in two ways—the risk of being adversely affected by a defective product is decreased, and search costs are reduced because certain product features are standardized. These effects serve to enhance well-being because a consumer can assess the marginal utility more accurately and the consumers price can be lowered.

Warranties are one vehicle for the implementation of product standards. A warranty protects consumers from defective products, usually durable goods. There are two basic types of warranties. An **express warranty** is a written statement attached to the good, containing specifics about the corrective procedures the manufacturer will follow in the event of product failure. Express warranties should be read very carefully, as there can be significant differences among warranties of different brands of the same product. An **implied warranty** refers to the presumption that any good placed for sale is reasonably well made for its intended use. Both types of warranties serve to reduce search costs and contribute to the likelihood that a purchased item is going to meet a consumer's need or be returned.

Many regulatory agencies established by the public sector have created specific product standards. The Food and Drug Administration was created in 1906 to prevent unsafe processed foods and drugs from being marketed. Meat inspection by the U. S. Department of Agriculture began at the same time. The Federal Trade Commission (FTC) was established in 1914 to deal with restraints of trade. Since then, the FTC has expanded its purview to include advertising.

Most regulation of advertising can be viewed as the setting of product standards. By outlawing false and/or deceptive ads, the FTC has created standards for the presentation of information. Bait-and-switch tactics have been declared illegal. Advertisements about sales must contain information about the number of units available. The FTC also requires advertisers to be able to document all claims in the event they are asked to do so by the FTC. Two other product standards that you may have encountered are building codes and automobile mileage requirements for the fleets of cars sold in the United States.

Another very important federal consumer agency is the Consumer Product Safety Commission (CPSC), created in 1972. This agency oversees the production and sale of consumer products that are potentially hazardous. Included in the agency's responsibilities are the protection of consumers from unreasonable risk, research into the cause and prevention of accidents, and the creation of safety standards. One of the ways in which the CPSC gathers information is from hospital emergency rooms and accident reports. Data are compiled, analyzed, and used to generate product warnings found in *Safety News.*

Licensure can be considered a form of product standards. It is used primarily with credence goods. When it is difficult or impossible to evaluate quality, **licensure** is used to certify the quality of the provider of the service. Many building and repair trades have licensed workers to try to convey to image that only quality work occurs. Other examples are medical professionals, lawyers, accountants, and financial planners.

A complete overview of product standards should encompass their detrimental features as well. Consumer choice is restricted by the setting of product standards. The range of goods available in the marketplace is curtailed if the standards ban some of the lower quality products. This can decrease utility for those consumers who preferred the lower quality. Furthermore, producers, in trying to manufacture products that comply with standards, may incur higher costs which they will attempt to pass on to consumers through higher market prices. Such price increases can more than offset the decline in search costs mentioned above, so the consumer's price may actually increase. Product standards can also increase the monopoly power of some producers. This occurs when the imposition of standards causes some manufacturers to drop out of the market, leaving fewer producers. Increased concentration may allow the remaining firms (in the limiting case there is only one) to charge a price in excess of the economic costs of production. This situation, as well as its implication for consumers, is discussed in Chapter 13. Finally, there is the potential for the standards to focus on criteria that are not valued as highly by consumers as by the agencies. A result is frustration with the agency as well as the potential problems just noted.

On the one hand, the credence properties of the goods and services provided by occupations such as the medical, legal, and accounting professions support the argument for regulatory boards. But on the other hand, regulatory boards can encourage monopolistic practices, as when regulatory constraints on professional advertising restrict the possibility of comparison shopping or pricing is controlled.

An illustration of the first problem is found in a study by Maurizi, Moore, and Shepard.[7] They examined the effect of the removal of a ban on advertising by eyewear providers in California. More specifically, they estimated the impact of the elimination of the advertising ban during the first year in which advertising was allowed. The ban was removed in July, 1976. The authors compared a survey of providers in the summer of 1977 to a survey conducted in 1975. Their conclusion was that the increased advertising led to lower market prices. Providers of eyewear who advertised charged, on average, 17 percent less than nonadvertisers for contact lenses. Such a result points to the significant adverse effect regulatory policies can have on consumer markets.

The second problem occurs with regulatory commissions set up to regulate public utilities. Initially, the organizations protect consumer interests, but often they end up protecting the interests of the utilities. This point has a long-standing history in the public finance literature.

● Disclosure Information

Since the market system failures presented in this chapter stem from information problems, a major public policy goal is to make information available to consumers prior to purchase. Some of this disclosure information can and has been provided by the private sector.[8] Independent, privately operated consumer product testing groups do supply a great deal of information on a wide variety of goods such as automobiles, personal computers and software, athletic equipment, etc. However, the sales of their publications generate most of the support for their work. Since consumers must pay for the information received, many consumers may not have access to it. Another problem is that sometimes the private sector does not have relevant information available.[9] These deficiencies have led to imposition by the public sector of disclosure information requirements.

Disclosure information requirements mandate specified information be prominently displayed or available to the buyer at the point of sale. Disclosure information can enhance either the numerator or the denominator of the value of the last dollar spent. There are two basic ways in which the consumer's price is affected in a positive manner. First, search costs are reduced. Public provision of information decreases the amount of search a consumer must do, saving time and travel costs. Unit pricing is an example; it allows consumers to compare brands and sizes more accurately in less time. Gasoline octane ratings on fuel pumps are another disclosure aid. Second, disclosure information may shed light on operating costs and thus allow consumers to factor them into their decision making. For instance, mileage ratings for automobiles allow consumers to assess the fuel costs of driving various cars. Some disclosure information affects both search and operating costs. "EnergyGuide" labels provide information on the energy costs associated with the normal operation of selected appliances.[10] This information was not available prior to the enactment of governmental regulations requiring labels. The consumer's search costs are decreased because the labels show the range of energy costs for the type of appliance, along with the place the specific brand falls in the range.

---

[7]   A. R. Maurizi, R. L. Moore, and L. Shepard, "The Impact of Price Advertising: The California Eyewear Market After One Year," *Journal of Consumer Affairs* 15,2(Winter, 1981):290-300.

[8]   An example is Consumer's Union, which publishes *Consumer Reports*.

[9]   Operating costs of durables are examples.

[10]   The appliances are refrigerators, water heaters, clothes washers, room air conditioners, dish washers, furnaces, and freezers.

The numerator of the value of the last dollar spent is affected in a positive manner, because consumers have better assessments of products and the ways they function. Knowing more about products enables consumers to make more accurate evaluations of the marginal utilities. Care labeling for clothing is an illustration of successful disclosure information. Warnings on cigarette packages and alcoholic beverages and labeling of the ingredients and nutritional contents of foods are two other examples.

There are drawbacks associated with the use of disclosure information. One is the generation of information can be expensive, although the cost is usually less than that associated with setting product standards. Price increases may result when manufacturers experience increases in production and marketing costs to comply with disclosure requirements. If the public sector bears the cost, then the ultimate impact is in the form of higher taxes.

Aside from the cost considerations, one must evaluate the actual information provided. Could the information hurt sales? For example, safety feature information could alert buyers to potential dangers of the product not associated with normal use. Is the information presented in an understandable manner? Is the information too technical to be of use to the ordinary user? Are consumers interested in the information provided? Answers to these questions are not always in the affirmative. Failure to use the information means the resources that were used to provide the information could have been allocated more efficiently to other activities.

Product standards and disclosure information can be combined to generate more comprehensive public intervention programs. Product standards can be used to eliminate those items that are unsafe and/or cannot meet minimal performance expectations. Disclosure information can be used to enable consumers to evaluate more accurately those brands that meet or exceed the minimum standards. Such a scheme allows for minimal constraints on consumer choice while at the same time providing consumers with the requisite input to make informed choices. One always needs to bear in mind, however, that any public policy has costs, and intervention should only occur when the benefits exceed the costs.

STUDY QUESTIONS

Product Standards and Disclosure Information

15. Distinguish between product standards and disclosure information.
16. Identify the advantages and disadvantages of product standards and disclosure information.
17. What criteria should be used in determining whether public regulation of a retail market should occur?
18. What economic arguments can you present on behalf of consumers regarding the need for setting product and disclosure standards for the funeral industry?

● Economic Models of Consumer Choice, Information, and Public Policies: Some Applications ●

The three basic models of consumer choice (traditional and two derived demand) provide different perspectives on key elements of decision making. They also comprise three ways of analyzing marketplace behavior. Viewed from a policy perspective, the selection of the appropriate framework depends on the problem under investigation. Should interest center on the demand for final goods, then the traditional model has the appropriate conceptual framework, and the corresponding demand relationships are outlined in Chapters 7-9. If the concern is with the properties of goods and their relationship to consumer behavior, then the characteristics model of Chapter 10 is the one to use. Interest in household resource allocation (in both factor and final goods markets) is most compatible with the household production model of Chapter 10. Regardless of the approach taken, sociodemographics can be introduced into the empirical research. Examples of studies using these models are outlined below.

A traditional demand equation framework was estimated by Eastwood to analyze consumer acceptance of a the type of fresh beef packaging.[11] Vacuum packing has several advantages over conventional shrink-wrapped plastic. These include less opportunity for spoilage and contamination, longer shelf life, both sides are visible, and freezing is not necessary. The major drawback is the color because the air-tight seal prevents the beef from turning bright red, the traditional signal for freshness and quality. Therefore, an information gap was present when the packaging was introduced. A supermarket started carrying four vacuum packed cuts of steak: filet mignon, round, chuck, and cubed, and at the same time, the cuts were available in conventional packaging at the same price per pound. Supermarket scan data were used to estimate the demand relationships for the quantity sold per week per customer, where the quantity sold was a function of selected steak prices, amount of newspaper advertising, lagged sales, and seasonality variables. Results suggested that consumers were reluctant to try vacuum packed fresh beef, which is consistent with the experience good nature of steak. That is, in the absence of any information, consumers were unwilling to buy the vacuum packed steak to see if they liked it. Newspaper advertising for each of the cuts was found to have a positive effect on sales. An interpretation is these ads conveyed price information that consumers found useful in their decision making.

Changes in food consumption over time have been related to diet and health concerns. Capps and Schmitz studied meat demand with information about cholesterol.[12] They used an index of cholesterol information, based on the number of articles about this nutrient which appeared from 1966 through 1988, as an independent variable in their model. A conclusion they reached was that cholesterol information was a determinant of meat consumption over this time period. The increased information was estimated to have had positive effects on poultry and fish consumption, but negative effects on pork consumption.

Food handling practices have received a great deal of attention recently, with concern about promoting safe handling practices. A way of providing information is to include a label on packages of fresh meat. In 1993 the U. S. Department of Agriculture announced a new labeling requirement

---

11   D. Eastwood, "Consumer Acceptance of a New Experience Good: A Case Study of Vacuum Packed Fresh Beef," *Journal of Consumer Affairs*, 28,2(1994):300-12.

12   O. Capps and J. Schmitz, "A Recognition of Health and Nutrition Factors in Food Demand Analysis," *Western Journal of Agricultural Economics* 16(1991):21-35.

for fresh meat and poultry with the objective of giving relevant information to food preparers in the home. Teague and Anderson describe a process of using focus groups to help design the label format.[13] Their work indicated that the message had to be brief, use some symbols, and should explain why the message is important.

Jensen and Kesavan examined the effects of calcium-related nutrition information provided by the National Dairy Board's commodity promotion program.[14] They used results of a 1985-86 national telephone survey that focused on dairy consumption. Respondents recalled television or other calcium advertising about dairy products, and information was also gathered on dairy consumption. Results indicated the promotions had positive impacts on consumer attitudes which led to increased dairy consumption.

With respect to nutrition labeling, research suggests this disclosure requirement has a positive influence on decision making, aside from the obvious benefits to consumers who have medical concerns associated with the contents of foods. Wang, Fletcher, and Carley, using data from the 1987-88 Household Food Consumption Survey, found that food labels were more likely to be used by households that consumed more food at home, higher income households, and larger households.[15] As educational attainment increased, so did the likelihood of using labels. Households headed by whites were more inclined to use them. They also concluded that food labeling is more effective in nonmetropolitan areas and in the midwest region.

Another application examined the mother's choice of whether and how soon after the birth of children she engaged in paid work.[16] Decision making was based on the opportunity cost of time framework. The opportunity cost of staying home was measured as the after-tax wage rate the mother would have earned if she was employed. The opportunity cost of time spent working was the value of the woman's time spent working at home, which was based on the marginal utilities of the commodities and the marginal products of the mother. Proxies for this opportunity cost were the level of education, household income, the federal marginal tax rate, home ownership, and the number and ages of children. Data were drawn from a longitudinal survey of a representative sample of U. S. households. Results were that by the start of the fifth month following birth, half the mothers had started paid work. Women who worked during pregnancy (i.e., had already allocated time to marketplace work) were 6.5 times more likely to work following delivery. The probability of employment declined by 36 percent for each $1,000 increase in unearned income. Home ownership was associated with a 25 percent greater likelihood of marketplace work following delivery. Increases in the marginal tax rate were estimated to increase the probability of marketplace work by 5 percent.

Not all advertising is necessarily in the consumer's interest. For example, an article by Bannor in the Wall Street Journal noted that the message in a promotion is important, although the content of the ad and the movie are secondary.[17] The strategy is one of stressing the shows as spectacular events, utilizing the bandwagon effect. Critics felt Congo was not a very good movie, but an advertising blitz

---

[13]   J. Teague and D. Anderson, "Consumer Preferences for Safe Handling Labels on Meat and Poultry," *Journal of Consumer Affairs*, 29,1(1995):108-127.

[14]   H. Jensen and T. Kesavan, "Sources of Information, Consumer Attitudes on Nutrition, and Consumption of Dairy Products," *Journal of Consumer Affairs*, 27,2(1993):357-76.

[15]   G. Wang, S. Fletcher, and D. Carley, "Consumer Utilization of Food Labeling as a Source of Nutrition Information," *Journal of Consumer Affairs*, 29,2(1995):368-80.

[16]   J. Joesch, "Children and the Timing of Women's Paid Work After Childbirth: A Further Specification of the Relationship," *Journal of Marriage and the Family*, 56(1994):429-40.

[17]   L. Bannon, "The Hyped and Hypeless: Fate of Two Films," *Wall Street Journal* (July 5, 1995):B1.

helped encourage many people to see it. On the other hand, some higher quality films (at least according to the critics) had very low advertising campaigns and low attendance.

STUDY QUESTIONS

Economic Models of Consumer Choice, Information, and Public Policies: Some Applications

19. The U. S. Department of Agriculture recently introduced the requirement that supermarkets provide nutrition information for fresh produce items. What are the arguments in favor and against this requirement?
20. Health insurance companies often require second opinions on nonemergency surgery. Is this an appropriate policy or is it an attempt to take away a person's decision making control?
21. What economic arguments can you present for automobile seat belt and air bag regulations?
22. Why are bank and real estate companies required to use standard forms for the recording of financial information when buying and selling homes?

● Summary ●

Consumers evaluate the value of the last dollar spent to achieve the highest level of utility given constraints. This chapter has focused on some instances where the normal operation of private markets does not enable consumers to evaluate the values of the last dollar spent precisely. The deficiencies stem from consumers' not being able to determine the consumer's price, properties or goods, production technologies, or marginal utilities. These situations increase the likelihood that consumers make less than optimal purchases. Product standards and disclosure information requirements are two main public policy vehicles for addressing the market system failures.

● Key Terms ●

Consumer's price: consumer's opportunity cost associated with the acquisition and use of a good.
Credence good: a good whose quality cannot be determined even after it is used.
Disclosure information requirements: requirements that specified information about products be prominently displayed or available to the buyer at the point of sale.
Experience good: a good whose quality can be determined only after it is used.
Express warranty: a manufacturer's written statement concerning the repair of a product.
Implied warranty: the presumption that any good offered for sale works satisfactorily in its intended use.
Licensure: a product standard for the provider of a good.
Price variation: charging different prices per unit for a good of constant quality.
Product standards: minimum performance requirements for goods.
Search cost: travel and time costs associated with acquiring information.
Search good: a good whose quality can be determined prior to purchase.

Chapter 12

Supplier's Cost, Profits, and Competition

A consumer's utility maximizing choice is based partly on the ability to trade, which is determined to a large extent by market structure. If there is only one seller, the consumer's position in the exchange process is much different than if there are many suppliers. Market structure affects trade-offs because of the separate motivations of buyers and sellers. A supplier's objective is to maximize profits, while a consumer's motivation is to maximize utility. The interaction of these two motivations dictates the outcome of an exchange.

This chapter examines market structure and its implications for consumers. Suppliers' costs, in conjunction with various market settings, determine the profit maximizing behavior of businesses. Consequently, businesses react to consumers in different ways, depending on the competitive environment. The chapter begins with an overview of the relevant cost considerations. Then the profit maximizing behavior of a business is outlined. Finally, different types of market structure are incorporated into the exchange process so the consumer implications of competitive situations can be discussed.

● Production Cost ●

In the consideration of production cost, time generally is divided into three periods. The **market period** is so brief that there is not enough time for new units to be made; hence any sale that occurs must deplete the inventory of finished goods. If it takes five months to build a house, the market period for housing is five months or less. The **short run** is a production period where there is at least one fixed factor. If a business has an existing plant, there is not enough time to construct a new facility, but the business can vary other inputs, such as employment. The **long run** is characterized by there being no fixed factor. A business can vary plant size as well as all other inputs into the production process. Most economic analyses center on the short run and the long run, because these periods are associated with decisions about resource allocation. Since market period exchange occurs as a result of past production, resources have already been allocated and used.

The profitability of a business depends on the cost of providing the good or service to consumers. The problem of production costs is associated with the basic economic problem of scarcity. Given unlimited consumer wants and limited resources with which to satisfy those wants, economics is concerned with efficient resource allocation. Opportunity cost is at the heart of production cost, because scarce resources have alternative uses. Viewed from this perspective, production cost should reflect the value of all the resources used to furnish the good or service to the consumer. This notion of cost is broader than the accounting concept, and the distinction between the two will become apparent shortly.

The **total cost**, TC, of producing a good equals the opportunity cost of all the resources used. As production increases, total cost increases. If a firm is efficient, the only way to produce more is to use more resources. Table 12-1 provides short-run cost information for a hypothetical firm. Imagine that this business has an existing plant and can vary production by varying employment. Let X denote the quantity of output produced. No subscript is needed, as only one consumer good is considered in this chapter. Column 2 of this table indicates how total cost increases as output increases.

Table 12-1: Short Run Production Costs

(1) X	(2) TC	(3) AC	(4) MC
0	30		
1	38	$38.00	$ 8
2	44	22.00	6
3	48	16.00	4
4	50	12.50	2
5	54	10.80	4
6	60	10.00	6
7	68	9.71	8
8	78	9.75	10
9	90	10.00	12
10	104	10.40	14
11	120	10.91	16
12	138	11.50	18
13	158	12.15	20
14	180	12.86	22
15	204	13.60	24

X = quantity produced; TC = total cost of production; AC = total cost divided by the quantity produced (average cost); MC = the change in cost associated with a change in production (marginal cost).

Average cost, AC, shown in column 3, is the total cost divided by the number of units produced. A glance down this column shows that the average cost falls at first, reaches a minimum, and then rises. The rationale for this pattern is based on the law of diminishing returns. Labor is the variable factor of production, and plant size is the fixed factor. As more labor is hired, the firm may approach the best combination between the fixed and variable factors. But above some employment level, continued increases in labor carry the firm away from the best combination.

How is this law reflected in the short-run cost? Marginal cost, MC, indicates how total cost changes as production changes. It is the change in total cost divided by the change in output. Column 4 displays the typical pattern for marginal cost. Marginal cost falls until it reaches a minimum, because as the firm hires more workers, it approaches the best input combination between the fixed and variable factors of production. But beyond the point where the law of diminishing returns takes effect, increasing employment begins to raise the marginal cost. The more employment rises beyond this point, the larger the marginal cost becomes. That is, a positive relationship between output and marginal cost exists beyond the point where the law sets in.

Compare the average cost and the marginal cost columns. Observe that as long as the marginal cost is less than the average cost, the average cost is falling. When marginal cost is greater than average cost, the average cost is rising. Whenever changes are less than the average, the average falls, and vice-versa.[1] The average cost depends on the marginal cost, and the marginal cost depends on the law of diminishing returns.

The information contained in Table 12-1 can be presented as a graph. Rather than just unit changes, it is possible to consider fractions of units produced, such a kilowatt-hours divided into minutes and seconds. Table 12-1 does not provide such a continuous breakdown. However, the marginal cost and average cost curves drawn in Figure 12-1 represent continuous measurements of output and cost. Notice that the average cost is somewhat U-shaped and that the marginal cost rises after the rate of production of four units, passing through the lowest point of the average cost curve.

Figure 12-1: Illustration of Average Cost and Marginal Cost

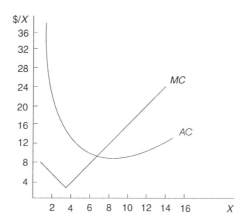

Average cost is the total cost of producing a level of output divided by the number of units produced. Marginal cost is the change in the total cost divided by the change in production. Because of the law of diminishing returns, the marginal cost curve has a positive slope. The marginal cost curve passes through the lowest point of the average cost curve.

Economic cost can now be distinguished from accounting cost. Economics is concerned with all resources associated with a production activity. Included in economic cost is the payment for services of the owner(s). The owner may be an individual who provides labor to the firm but is paid after other (contractual) production costs have been covered. Or the owners may be shareholders (see Chapter 17) who have placed money in the corporation and whose payment occurs after other (contractual) production costs have been paid.

---

[1]   Suppose a test is given to two students. The grades are 10 and 90, so the total is 100 and the average is 50. A third student takes the exam and receives a 20. What are total for the three students, the marginal score, and the new average score?

An accountant would term these monies profit. An economist considers them to be factor payments, just like expenses, for the use of other resources. The labor provided by an owner has alternative uses. Similarly, the shareholder's funds could be used by another business. This means that part of the *accounting profit* is a payment for the use of resources similar to other employee services or sources of money. Only when payment to the owner(s) exceeds the normal payment is an *economic profit* earned. This normal payment is considered to be an economic cost to the firm representing the opportunity cost of the resources of the owner(s). Frequently, it is referred to as a **normal profit**. Throughout the remainder of this chapter, cost is assumed to include the normal profit, and "profit" is used to refer to payment to the owner(s) exceeding a normal profit.

STUDY QUESTIONS

Production Cost

1. Identify the market period, short run, and long run for the following consumer goods: an automobile, a personal computer, a college education.
2. Why does the law of diminishing returns apply in the short run but not in the long run?
3. Why are opportunity cost and the economic concept of production cost related?
4. Why does the marginal cost curve have a positive slope, and why does the marginal cost equal the minimum average cost?
5. Consider the data provided below, where X = quantity and TC = total cost. Calculate AC and MC and compare them.

X	TC	X	TC
0	50	40	350
4	106	44	414
8	150	48	490
12	182	52	578
16	202	56	678
20	210	60	790
24	214	64	914
28	230	68	1050
32	258	72	1198
36	298	76	1358

● Principles of Profit Maximization ●

The **sales revenue** of a firm is the money received from the sale of its product in the marketplace during a period of time. It is the price per unit multiplied by the number of units sold, assuming there is only one product. The number of units sold is determined by market demand. If P denotes the market price and X denotes the units sold, then sales revenue, R, equals P·X.

No matter what the type of market structure, the profit of a business is the difference between sales revenue and cost. There are two conceptual ways of describing how a business reaches the profit maximizing level of production. One is to imagine that the firm calculates the costs and the revenue associated with each level of output. Profit maximization is the point where the largest difference is found. Another way of arriving at the profit maximizing output is to use incremental decision making. This approach assumes the business is in operation. The task is to determine what would happen to profits if production changes incrementally. Both revenue and cost are affected by the amount produced, so profit changes as revenue and cost change. Whether an additional unit should be produced depends on whether the incremental unit would add more to revenue than to cost.

The second approach focuses on the change in revenue per unit sold. **Average revenue**, AR, is the sales revenue divided by the number of units sold. Since AR = R/X, AR = P. This simply means that the market price is the same as the average revenue. If 25 units are sold at $2 each, R = $50, and AR = $2. Changes in production and the ensuing changes in the number of units sold cause changes in the sales revenue. **Marginal revenue** is defined as the change in sales revenue divided by the change in production.

Whenever marginal revenue is greater than the marginal cost, the firm should increase production. Increasing production increases both revenue and cost, but the increase in revenue is greater than the increase in cost, so profit rises. Whenever marginal revenue is less than the decline in cost, profit can be increased by decreasing production. Decreasing production decreases revenue and cost, but the decline in revenue is less than the decline in cost, so profit increases. Through this marginal analysis, then, the business arrives at the profit maximizing output.

Regardless of the market structure, marginal analysis can be used to locate the level of production that maximizes profit. But this is only part of the story. The price that the firm can charge has to be determined. This involves the interaction of buyers and sellers in a market, and the outcome can depend on the influence of each group. These influences are determined by market structure, the focus of the next section.

● Types of Competition ●

There are two extreme forms of competition. They comprise the bounds of actual market structure in which consumers and businesses operate. One extreme demonstrates the virtues of competition. The other permits identification of the problem a monopoly creates from the consumer perspective. The distinction is whether a single firm exerts a direct influence on the market. A firm, under any form of competition, is assumed to maximize profit.

This section shows the hypothetical firm, with the costs depicted in Table 12-1 and Figure 12-1, operating first at one extreme and then at the other. Since the only difference between the two situations is the market structure, this approach demonstrates the effects of different competitive environments. After the two extremes have been presented, an overview of the middle ground is given.

STUDY QUESTIONS

Principles of Profit Maximization

6. Distinguish among sales revenue, economic cost, normal profit, and economic profit.
7. Explain how a business could earn an accounting profit and at the same time earn an economic loss.
8. What is meant by the expression "profit maximizing output"?
9. Why is average revenue the same as the market price?
10. Identify the two conceptual ways a business could go about locating the profit maximizing output.

● Pure Competition

Pure competition is one extreme form of market structure. It arises whenever the following four conditions hold. First, there are many buyers and sellers of the good or service. Second, the good or service produced by the sellers is homogeneous. This simply means that there are no different brands of the item. Each producer creates a product that is indistinguishable from the outputs of other producers. Third, there is free entry and exit. Any firm that wants to enter the market can do so at existing prices, and any firm can leave whenever it wants without having to worry about long-term commitments and contracts. Finally, consumers and sellers are considered to have perfect information about the product and the market price.

These conditions dictate how the consumer and firm view their market positions. Neither has independent control of the market. Both must consider a market price as given. The consumer determines how much to buy based on the considerations outlined in previous chapters. The firm determines how much to produce based on an effort to maximize profit. Because there are many buyers and sellers, the quantities exchanged in the marketplace are very large relative to the output produced by an individual firm. For example, the market may exchange millions of pounds of fish fillets per week, while an individual firm may be able to process only a few thousand pounds per week. No matter how much a single firm produces, there is no effect on the prevailing market price and supply.

Given a market price, the firm identifies the **profit maximizing output**. Since profits are the difference between revenue and costs, one way of proceeding is to calculate this difference for every level of production to find the largest one. This is illustrated in Table 12-2, which reproduces the cost data of Table 12-1 along with some revenue data. Assume the market price for the product is $15 per unit. This information can be used to generate the firm's revenue for each level of production, as shown in column 3. Subtracting cost from revenue yields the economic profit (or loss), and the largest profit is associated with producing 10 units.

The other way of locating the profit maximizing output is to use marginal analysis. Marginal cost has already been explained, so all that remains to be done is to compute marginal revenue, and it is shown in column 6. Sales revenue increases $15 with each additional unit sold, because the firm is

Table 12-2: Revenue and Profit, Pure Competition

(1) P	(2) X	(3) R	(4) TC	(5) π	(6) MR	(7) MC
15	0	0	30	-30		
15	1	15	38	-23	15	8
15	2	30	44	-14	15	6
15	3	45	48	-3	15	4
15	4	60	50	10	15	2
15	5	75	54	21	15	4
15	6	90	60	30	15	6
15	7	105	68	37	15	8
15	8	120	78	42	15	10
15	9	135	90	45	15	12
15	10	150	104	46	15	14
15	11	165	120	45	15	16
15	12	180	138	42	15	18
15	13	195	158	37	15	20
15	14	210	180	30	15	22
15	15	225	204	21	15	24

P = price per unit; X = quantity; $R = P \cdot X$ = (revenue); TC = total cost; π = profits $(R - C)$; MR = marginal revenue; MC = marginal cost.

such a small part of the market that every unit it offers for sale has no perceptible impact on the market price. That is why column 6 displays a constant change in revenue for each additional unit of production.

Comparing columns 6 and 7 reveals how profit changes as production changes. As long as marginal revenue is greater than marginal cost, an increase in production leads to an increase in profit. For example, by increasing production from one to two units, a company increases revenue by $15 and costs by $8. The result is that profit rises by $7. Continued marginal revenue/marginal cost comparisons lead to further expansions of production up to 10 units. It is not profitable for the firm to produce 11 units, because marginal cost exceeds marginal revenue by a dollar, leading to a decline in profit.

Marginal analysis can be used in a diagram to locate the profit maximizing output. A graphical illustration can be an excellent tool for presenting a consumer's perspective on market structure. Figure 12-2 displays all the pertinent information regarding pure competition. Panel (a) is a conventional demand and supply diagram. The price-adjustment mechanism leads to the market equilibrium price-quantity combination of P_1 and X_1^*. Panel (b) has the same vertical scale as panel (a), the price per unit. However, the horizontal scale in the second panel represents the much smaller quantities associated with an individual firm's range of production, X.

The market price is determined by the price-adjustment mechanism. As in Table 12-2, the equilibrium price established in the market is assumed to be $15. Average cost and marginal cost for the hypothetical firm are displayed in panel (b). Since the cost and revenue are expressed in dollars per unit, there is no reason why average revenue and marginal revenue cannot be included in a

Figure 12-2: Pure Competition and Short-Run Profit

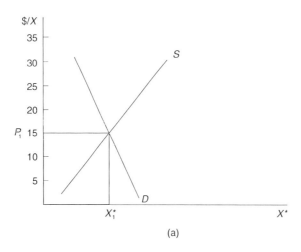

(a)

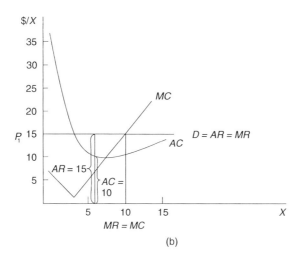

(b)

In a purely competitive market, the equilibrium price is achieved through the price adjustment mechanism, panel (a). The profit maximizing output is where $MR = MC$, or $X = 10$ in this illustration. If $MR > MC$, as at $X = 6$, the firm can increase profit by increasing production, because revenue increases faster than cost. Just the opposite applies to a level of production in excess of $X = 10$.

graph. No matter now much is produced, average revenue and marginal revenue remain fixed at $15, and this is reflected by the horizontal line. In effect, the purely competitive firm considers the market demand to be fixed at $15. Charging a higher price would result in consumers' buying the homogeneous product elsewhere. There is no reason to charge less than $15, as the firm's entire production can be sold at this price.

Comparison of average revenue to average cost at any level of production reveals the firm's profit. Whenever average revenue is above (greater than) average cost, the firm must be making more than a normal profit. For example, at a production level of 6 units, average revenue ($15) is greater than average cost ($10). That is, each of the 6 units brings in $5 more of revenue than of cost, leading to a total profit of $30.

Just as marginal revenue and marginal cost columns in a table can be compared to locate the profit maximizing output, marginal revenue and marginal cost curves can be compared. For example, at 6 units, the marginal revenue ($15) is above (greater than) the marginal cost ($6), so the firm could increase profit by expanding production. At 12 units, marginal revenue is below (less than) marginal cost, so the firm could increase profit by decreasing production. The firm is led to the profit maximizing output characterized by the interaction of marginal revenue and marginal cost.[2]

Short-run profit maximizing behavior leads the business to produce the output that equates marginal revenue and marginal cost. This is the diagrammatic equivalent of locating the output where the marginal revenue curve intersects the marginal cost curve. Should this intersection occur at a market price (average revenue) that exceeds average cost, then the firm earns an abnormal profit. If the intersection is associated with a market price below average cost, then the firm minimizes its loss by operating at the output where marginal revenue equals marginal cost.

What happens in the long run? With the assumption of free entry and exit and the economic definition of cost, this question can be answered easily. Whenever a firm earns a short-run abnormal profit, new firms are encouraged to enter the market. The entry of more firms into the market generates the familiar adjustment outlined in Figure 12-3. Starting in panel (a) with the market price P_1, the firm earns a short-run abnormal profit indicated in panel (b). But the entry of new firms causes an increase in supply, shown as S_2. The market adjusts with a lower price. At price P_2, the best the firm can do is minimize its loss, because average revenue is less than average cost. So some firms leave the market, causing a decrease in supply. Abnormal profits and losses, then, cause entry and exit, which generate changes in the market price and the firm's level of production.

When do entry and exit stop? They no longer occur when firms break even. That is, if the typical firm in the market earns a normal profit, it has no incentive to exit, and there is little incentive for others to enter. The long-run equilibrium occurs when average revenue equals average cost. This also is the profit maximizing output, because marginal revenue equals marginal cost. Figure 12-4 illustrates. The horizontal price line just touches the average cost curve. At this point average revenue equals average cost, so the firm earns a normal profit. Furthermore, marginal revenue equals marginal cost, so the profit maximizing firm voluntarily operates at this level of production.

Notice throughout the discussion of the adjustment process that both the producer and the consumer react passively to market prices. Whatever the market price is, the consumer makes a determination of how much to buy. At the same time, the producer takes the market price as given and determines how much to supply. The consumer is maximizing utility, and the producer is maximizing profit. Although their objectives are different, a market equilibrium is found. Neither the consumer nor the producer has any extra power or control in the marketplace.

---

[2]   Profit is not maximized at the lowest AC because MR > MC.

Figure 12-3: Entry and Exit in Pure Competition

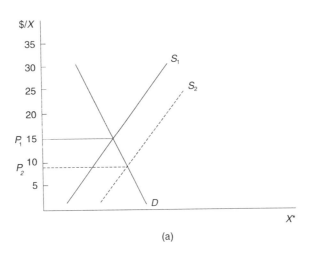

(a)

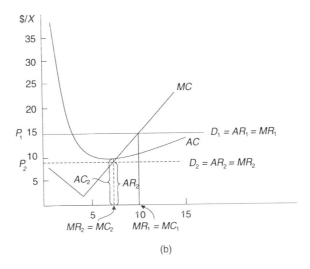

(b)

A purely competitive business can earn an abnormal profit in the short run. At the market price P_1, the firm maximizes profits at ten units and $AR > AC$. This encourages entry of other firms and results in an increase in market supply, shown as S_2. At the market price P_2, the profit maximizing output does not generate enough revenue to cover the entire production cost, $AC_2 > AR_2$. This encourages firms to exit and results in a decrease in supply.

Figure 12-4: Long Run Equilibrium, Pure Competition

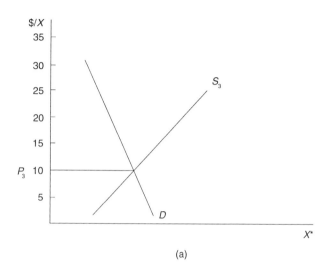

(a)

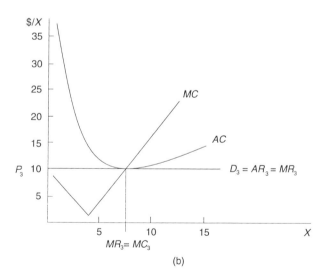

(b)

Entry and exit stop when the representative firm earns a normal profit. This occurs where $AR = AC$. At the market price P_3, the firm maximizes profits by producing $7\frac{1}{2}$ units per period. The corresponding AR and AC are just under $10.

● Monopoly

The other theoretical extreme is a monopoly. A **monopoly** is a single seller of a good or service for which there is no close substitute. One way to envision a monopoly is the consolidation of all the purely competitive firms into a single producer. This means that the monopolist's control is the equivalent of the collective power of all the purely competitive firms. Consequently, the monopolist reacts to the entire market demand. The relevant demand curve now is negatively sloped, whereas the demand curve for the purely competitive firm was horizontal.

Measures of sales revenue are calculated as before; but because of the negative slope, average revenue and marginal revenue are no longer constant. Table 12-3 illustrates. The first two columns of this table represent the market demand for the product. Each pair is a point on a demand curve. Notice that price and quantity change in opposite directions. Column 3 is the sales revenue.

Table 12-3: Monopoly Revenue

(1) X	(2) P	(3) R	(4) MR
0	$30	$ 0	
1	28	28	28
2	26	52	24
3	24	72	20
4	22	88	16
5	20	100	12
6	18	108	8
7	16	112	4
8	14	112	0
9	12	108	-4
10	10	100	-8
11	8	88	-12
12	6	72	-16
13	4	52	-20
14	2	28	-24
15	0	0	-28

X = quantity demanded (sold); P = price per unit; R = price times quantity sold (revenue); MR = the change in revenue associated with a change in quantity (marginal revenue).

An important fact becomes apparent in this example. A monopolist is not able to charge just any price. The price a monopolist can charge is limited by consumer demand. Any price of $30 or more results in there being no quantity sold. Thus, there is an upper limit to the price that can be charged.

The monopolist in this illustration must settle on a price between $0 and $30 per unit, and consumers decide how much to buy.

Average revenue is the same as the market price of the good. For example, when 6 units are sold at $18 each, the sales revenue is $108, and the average revenue is $108/6 = $18. The demand curve represented by columns 1 and 2 also is the average revenue curve.

Any negatively sloped demand (average revenue) curve indicates that in order to sell more goods, the seller must lower the price. But the price must be lowered on all the units sold, not just the last one. Marginal revenue measures the net effect of having to lower the price to sell more. For example, in order to sell 2 units instead of 1, the table indicates that the seller must lower the price from $28 to $26. This means that both units must be sold at $26. A $2 loss is associated with selling the first unit at $26 instead of $28. Selling the second unit at $26 generates a net change in revenue of $24.

Marginal revenue for the illustration is presented in column 4. It is the change in column 3 divided by the change in column 1. Each of the numerical values in column 4 can be interpreted in the above manner. Marginal revenue falls as sales increase, because as more units are sold, the loss in revenue due to the lower price acts as a larger and larger drag. In fact, when more than 8 units are sold, the effect of lowering the price more than offsets the gain of increased sales. This is why marginal revenue is negative and why total revenue falls beyond sales of 8 units.

Figure 12-5 indicates the relationships among demand, average revenue, and marginal revenue for the data associated with Table 12-3. The use of smooth curves implies continuous measurements of dollars and quantity. Demand and average revenue have been found to be identical, and they are labeled as such. Marginal revenue can be included, because it measures the change in dollars per unit as the number of units sold changes. For example, the marginal revenue of $20 in the table refers to changing sales from 2 to 3 units; for approximately 2 ½ units, the marginal revenue is $20. The marginal revenue curve must lie below any negatively sloped demand curve, because marginal revenue measures the net effect of lowering price to increase sales.

The profit maximizing monopolist locates the optimal output in the same way that the purely competitive firm does. Profit is equal to sales revenue minus cost, regardless of the type of market structure, so the firm attempts to locate at the level of production associated with the largest difference. Table 12-4 combines the cost data of the hypothetical firm, now considered to be a monopoly, with the associated demand and revenue data. Column 5 indicates that the profit maximizing output occurs at 6 units of production. This conclusion can also be drawn from a comparison of columns 6 and 7. Production expands as long as marginal revenue is greater than marginal cost. Starting with the short-run situation where the plant is available for use but is not producing, the monopoly would increase production until the level of 6 units is reached. Similarly, if the level of production is above 6 units, the monopoly would conclude that profits could be increased by decreasing production.

Figure 12-6 displays all the relevant information in graphical form. Marginal analysis can be used to locate the profit maximizing output quickly. It is the output at which marginal revenue equals marginal cost at 6 units. But what price is to be charged? The price is determined by consumer demand, which in the present example allows 6 units to be sold at $18 each. Whether the firm is losing money, breaking even, or earning an abnormal profit is determined by a comparison of the average cost to average revenue. An abnormal profit is received in the present situation, since the average cost is less than the average revenue at 6 units of production and sales.

The purely competitive firm can earn an abnormal profit in the short run, but this will end as new firms enter the market. Can a monopoly earn an abnormal profit in the long run as well as the short run? Yes, as long as there is no entry. If the monopoly can maintain its position as the single supplier

Figure 12-5: Illustration of Monopoly Demand and Marginal Revenue

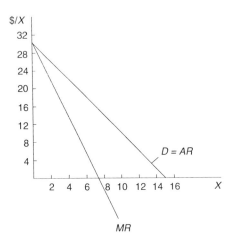

Data from Table 12-3 are used to draw the demand curve and the marginal revenue curve for a monopoly. Because marginal revenue measures the net effect of having to lower prices to sell more, *MR* lies below *D*.

of a product, it can earn an abnormal profit indefinitely. Barriers to entry include legal constraints, patents, and situations in which the lowest cost of production is attained by a single producer.

Pure competition and monopoly represent extreme forms of market structure. Indeed, it is hard to imagine situations in the real world where they apply. But they define the boundaries of the continuum of market structures. At the one extreme, consumers have power equal to firms; at the other, the monopoly has consolidation of producer power. The advantages and disadvantages of the different forms are discussed from a consumer perspective in the next chapter. The two extremes permit a clear statement about why competition is desirable and why monopolies may need to be regulated in order to serve consumer interests better.

● Imperfect Competition

Most consumer activity in final goods markets occurs in situations that are between pure competition and monopoly. This middle ground is called **imperfect competition**, and it is divided further into two areas. One is called monopolistic competition, and the other is referred to as oligopoly.

Monopolistic competition is one step removed from pure competition. In this type of competition, the assumption of a homogeneous product is dropped, but all of the other conditions remain. Monopolistic competition assumes there are many brands of virtually the same good or service. In this situation the demand curve for a brand is not a horizontal line, because some consumers may prefer

Table 12-4: The Profit Maximizing Output, Monopoly

(1) X	(2) P	(3) R	(4) TC	(5) π	(6) MR	(7) MC
0	$30	$ 0	30	$ -30		
1	28	28	38	-10	28	$ 8
2	26	52	44	8	24	6
3	24	72	48	24	20	4
4	22	88	50	38	16	2
5	20	100	54	46	12	4
6	18	108	60	48	8	6
7	16	112	68	44	4	8
8	14	112	78	34	0	10
9	12	108	90	18	-4	12
10	10	100	104	4	-8	14
11	8	88	120	-32	-12	16
12	6	72	138	-66	-16	18
13	4	52	158	-106	-20	20
14	2	28	180	-152	-24	22
15	0	0	204	-204	-28	24

X = quantity; P = price per unit sold; $R = P \cdot X$ = revenue; TC = total cost; π = profits = $(R - C)$; MR = marginal revenue; MC = marginal cost.

a specific brand for one reason or another. However, each demand curve is relatively flat (or fairly elastic), reflecting the availability of competing brands. The marginal revenue curve lies below the demand curve, because the latter has a negative slope.

The profit maximizing output occurs where marginal revenue equals marginal cost, and the corresponding price is determined by the demand curve. Figure 12-7 shows how a firm operates in this type of market. Starting with demand curve D_1 in panel (a), the firm maximizes profit by producing X_1, and the market price is P_1. Because average revenue is greater than average cost at this output, the firm earns an abnormal profit. Other firms enter the market, reducing the market share of each brand. Consequently, there is a decrease in demand for the representative firm's brand, D_2 in panel (b). The firm minimizes its loss by producing X_2, and the market price is P_2.

Long-run stability occurs when there is no entry or exit. This happens when the representative firm just breaks even. Panel (c) illustrates the situation. At the profit maximizing output, the firm is able to charge P_3. Since average revenue equals average cost, the firm earns a normal profit. It has no incentive to leave, and no new firm enters.

Figure 12-6: Monopoly Profit Maximization

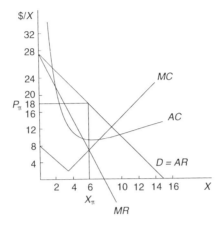

Just like a purely competitive firm, the monopoly arrives at the profit maximizing output through comparing marginal cost. MR = MC at six units. Each unit can be sold at $18. This average revenue ($18) is greater than average cost ($10), so the monopoly earns an abnormal profit.

In monopolistic competition, consumers as a group maintain much of their power, as in pure competition. The seller gains some control, the extent of which depends on brand loyalty. Should consumers view brands as very similar, the demand for a brand will be very close to the horizontal demand of pure competition. Increasing brand loyalty allows the firm to be more of a monopoly. Brand loyalty, then, becomes an important consideration for the firm, and this is reflected in its advertising. Additionally, firms engage in nonprice competition (such as service) in order to attract buyers.

Oligopoly is defined as a market in which there are few sellers of the same good or service. The key feature is the interdependence among sellers. This setting should be quite familiar to consumers, as many items are available in only a few stores within a shopping area. How does a firm operate in this environment, and what are the implications for the consumer? Any model of this market structure must account for the way one firm views the actions of its competitors. There are several ways in which such interdependence can be incorporated. One of the more interesting approaches, especially from a consumer perspective, considers the firm's expectation about consumer reactions to price changes.

Figure 12-7: Monopolistic Competition

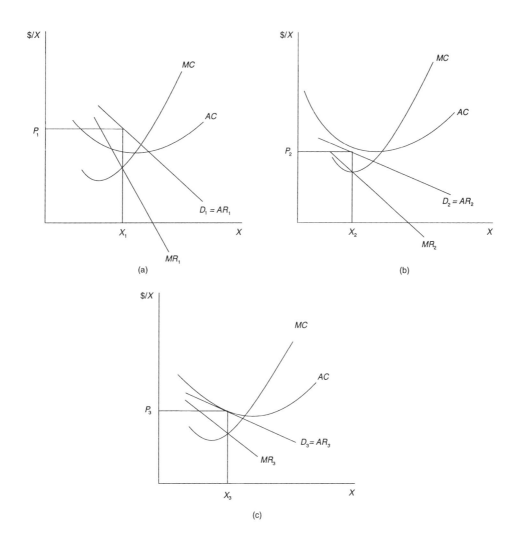

The demand curve for a brand in monopolistic competition represents that brand's share of the market. In panel (a), the profit maximizing output is X_1, and the corresponding price is P_1. The firm is able to earn an abnormal profit. This encourages entry and reduces the share for each brand. In panel (b), D_2 represents the decrease in demand. The profit maximizing output is X_2, and the price is P_2. The firm now operates at a loss, which causes exit. Panel (c) portrays the long-run equilibrium. The profit maximizing output is X_3, and the price is P_3. The firm breaks even because average revenue equals average cost.

How is one firm likely to view raising the price it charges for its good or service? A reasonable expectation is that the firm would feel that competitors would not raise their prices, and consumers could switch to other firms. Lowering the price is considered to be disadvantageous as well, because competitors would lower theirs, thereby counteracting any sales increase.

Figure 12-8 illustrates the demand curve for this situation. Above the current price P_1, the curve is very flat (elastic), reflecting consumer sensitivity to an increase in price by a single firm. Below P_1, the curve is fairly steep (inelastic) because the lowering of a price is likely to be replicated by competitors, the increase in sales is likely to be small.

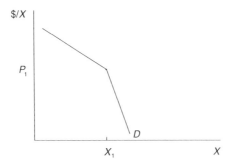

Figure 12-8: Oligopoly Demand Illustration

Oligopoly causes firms to recognize their interdependence. Demand curve D portrays one view of the interdependence. A firm may feel that raising the price above the current price P_1 would drive customers away to competitors. The demand curve above and to the left of D_1 implies that sales fall off rapidly as the price charged by a single firm rises. A lowering of the price by one firm would be followed by a similar action by competitors, so the quantity demanded would not increase very much with a price cut.

The consumer's position is difficult to evaluate in this model. On the one hand, consumers have some control. Price increases are likely to be infrequent, and the firm must be sensitive to consumers. Consumers also may benefit from nonprice competition. On the other hand, there is little incentive for a firm to lower price, even when permitted to do so by a reduction in cost. In addition, the limited number of competitors is an ever-present concern. Their interdependence could develop into a kind of monopoly called a **cartel**. Cartels are illegal in the United States, but it is difficult to prove in court that firms are acting in collusion. The formation of a cartel places the consumer in the position of having to buy from a monopoly.

STUDY QUESTIONS

Types of Competition

11. Under pure competition, why is average revenue equal to marginal revenue?
12. Why can a purely competitive firm earn an abnormal profit in the short run but not in the long run?
13. Assume that the market price for a good is $10. Use the cost data from problem 5 to approximate the profit maximizing output first as revenue less cost and then with marginal analysis.
14. Explain why the firm in problem 13 does not produce at the lowest unit cost.
15. If a demand curve has a negative slope, why does the marginal revenue curve lie below it?
16. Interpret the marginal revenue in Table 12-3 associated with increasing production from 8 to 9 units.
17. How can marginal revenue be less than zero?
18. Use the revenue data provided below, where X = quantity and P = price, to calculate revenue and marginal revenue.

X	P	X	P
0	20	40	10
4	19	44	9
8	18	48	8
12	17	52	7
16	16	56	6
20	15	60	5
24	14	64	4
28	13	68	3
32	12	72	2
36	11	76	1

19. Combine the data from problems 5 and 18 to locate the profit maximizing output first as revenue minus cost and then with marginal analysis.
20. Distinguish between monopoly and monopolistic competition.
21. Draw the long-run purely competitive equilibrium. Then show how the market would adjust if there was an increase in the price of a variable factor of production, resulting in an increase in average cost and marginal cost.
22. How do free entry and exit affect profit in the short run and long run?
23. In what respects does a consumer's leverage in the marketplace change with the type of market structure?

● Summary ●

A firm's motivation in the marketplace is directed toward maximizing profits. In economic analysis, production costs should reflect the opportunity costs of all the resources used. Thus, economic cost includes a normal profit for a business. Comparing average revenue to average cost allows one to determine whether the firm breaks even, has an abnormal profit, or incurs a loss. The profit maximizing output is always where marginal revenue equals marginal cost. Free entry and exit force the firm to break even in the long run. In pure competition consumers, as a group, have market power equal to that of sellers. A monopoly has consolidated power in the marketplace.

● Key Terms ●

Average cost: total cost divided by the number of units produced.

Average revenue: sales revenue divided by the number of units sold.

Cartel: a group of sellers agreeing to act as a monopoly.

Imperfect competition: forms of competition between pure competition and monopoly.

Long run: a period in which no factor of production is held constant.

Marginal cost: a change in total cost divided by the corresponding change in production.

Marginal revenue: a change in sales revenue divided by the corresponding change in units sold.

Market period: a period so short that there is not enough time to produce new units.

Monopolistic competition: the type of competition in which there are many brands of virtually the same product.

Monopoly: a single seller of a good or service for which there is no close substitute.

Normal profit: the opportunity cost to a business for the use of the owner's resources.

Oligopoly: a market in which there are few sellers of the same good.

Profit maximizing output: level of production at which the difference between sales revenue and cost is a large as possible.

Pure competition: a competitive situation in which buyers and sellers acting independently cannot affect the market.

Sales revenue: the price of a good multiplied by the number of units sold.

Short run: a period in which there is at least one fixed factor of production.

Total cost: the entire opportunity cost of producing a good or service.

Chapter 13

Consumers and Market Structure

Why is a monopoly generally considered to be bad? Or, for that matter, why is competition usually considered to be good? These questions are answered in this chapter. Market structure is examined to identify the implications of the various forms of competition for consumer well-being. Pure competition provides the most desirable environment; a monopoly is the least desirable situation.

Although many people think that consumers would be better off with the regulation of monopolies, the issue is not as clear-cut as it may seem. The problem with a monopoly does not stem directly from its profit maximization. Purely competitive firms also maximize profits, and the consumer is shown to be as well off as possible in a competitive market. The problem with a monopoly lies in the divergence between price and marginal cost, as this chapter explains.

Monopoly regulation usually is accomplished by price regulation. Two forms price regulation are outlined, and some caveats associated the regulations are noted. The problems of overregulation are identified, and the motivation behind deregulation is explained.

● Benefits of Competition ●

The virtues of competition stem from the equilibrium reached in the long run through pure competition. Properties of this equilibrium have very significant implications with regard to the price-adjustment mechanism's efficacy for consumers. Pure competition, then, serves as a standard for the evaluation of how the actual operation of markets can be improved to enhance the consumer's position in the exchange process.

Figure 13-1 displays the long-run pure competition equilibrium as point E. It is reached through a series of short-run adjustments to profits on the part of businesses. In the short run, a purely competitive firm can make an abnormal profit, or it can operate at a loss. An abnormal profit means that the firm is receiving a better than average rate of return on all of the resources it is using. A loss really refers to an economic loss, because the firm may be earning an accounting profit, but one that is less than what the owner's resources could have earned elsewhere.[1]

Free entry and exit eliminate abnormal profits and losses in the long run. Abnormal short-run profits encourage entry into the market by other firms until these profits erode away in the long run. Short-run losses foster exit until the remaining firms break even in the long run. This means that the purely competitive business must break even in the long run. Sales revenue must equal total cost; or average cost, AC, must equal average revenue, AR.

Because there are many buyers and sellers of a homogeneous good, the demand curve for an individual business is a horizontal line. The horizontal line indicates that it is not possible for a single firm to sell anything at a price above the prevailing market price. Consequently, the demand curve is perfectly elastic. In addition, marginal revenue equals average revenue, because each unit can be

---

[1] For example, if the average rate of return is 10 percent and the owner invests $50,000, the firm ought to earn a $5,000 return. Should the firm earn only $3,000, the business has an economic loss of $2,000.

Figure 13-1: Pure Competition, Long-Run Equilibrium

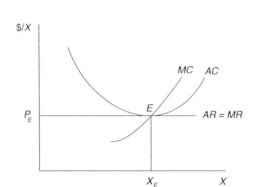

The long-run pure competition equilibrium is shown as point E. Free entry and exit force the firm to break even, so $AR = AC$. The business operates at the lowest point on AC, because the demand curve is a horizontal line. Consumers pay the lowest possible price per unit, P_E. Since $P_E = MC$, the value consumers place on an additional unit equals the cost of producing that incremental unit.

sold at the existing price. There is no need for a single firm to lower the price to sell more. The demand curve just touches the average cost curve, because the firm must break even. No portion of the demand curve can lie above the long-run average cost, or an abnormal profit would be earned. Similarly, the demand curve cannot lie entirely below the long-run average cost, or a loss would occur.

Profit is maximized at that output where marginal revenue equals marginal cost. This occurs at point E in Figure 13-1. Notice that at this point several key economic relationships are equated. Price, average revenue, marginal revenue, marginal cost, and average cost all have the same value for the level of production X_E.

Examination of point E reveals the virtues of the long-run pure competition equilibrium. The firm operates at the lowest possible cost per unit. Since marginal revenue, which equals average revenue, is a horizontal line, marginal revenue can equal marginal cost, and the firm can break even only at the lowest point on the average cost curve. Not only does the firm operate at the minimum average cost, but the consumer pays this minimum cost. That is, the long-run pure competition equilibrium is associated with the market price being equal to the minimum average cost.

Another very desirable feature of point E is that marginal cost equals price. While the profit maximizing output always occurs where marginal revenue equals marginal cost, the price that the business can charge equals marginal cost only when marginal revenue equals average revenue. This condition is restricted to cases of horizontal, perfectly elastic, demand. It should be apparent, based on the model of consumer choice, that the price a consumer is able and willing to pay depends on the consumer's valuation of the good. Marginal cost is the cost of producing an additional unit. Consequently, the value a consumer places on the good is the same the cost of producing an additional unit of that good.

These desirable features of the long-run pure competition equilibrium form the basis for the argument that the more competition there is, the better off consumers are. Neither consumers nor sellers exercise any individual control. Rather, the price-adjustment mechanism serves to accommodate the interests of individual buyers in maximizing utility and sellers in maximizing profit. A full appreciation of this rationale must await an examination of the implications for consumers of the other types of competition. However, even at this juncture, it should seem reasonable that the more competition there is, the closer a market should be to functioning on a purely competitive basis.

STUDY QUESTIONS

Benefits of Competition

1.   Explain how a purely competitive market would adjust if the typical firm earned a short-run abnormal profit.
2.   Why must a purely competitive firm operate at the minimum long-run average cost but not necessarily at the minimum short-run average cost?
3.   What is the significance of price being equal to marginal cost?
4.   Identify the desirable features of the long-run purely competitive equilibrium.

● Imperfect Competition ●

Monopolistic competition is one step removed from pure competition. The assumption of a homogeneous good is relaxed, but all the other assumptions are retained. Instead of a homogeneous good, there is a slightly differentiated product, so each producer offers a brand. The demand curve facing a representative firm represents a brand's share of the market for the good.

A slightly differentiated product changes the demand curve facing the representative firm. It is not a horizontal line, although it remains highly elastic. To the extent that consumers prefer a particular brand over available substitutes, there is a limited ability for a single seller to raise the price somewhat and still have customers. The crucial feature is that as long as the demand curve is not horizontal (perfectly elastic), marginal revenue must lie below average revenue.

As in the case of pure competition, free entry and exit cause the firm to break even in the long run. Consequently, the demand curve must touch the average cost curve, but not cross it. The firm breaks even at this point, because average revenue equals average cost. Figure 13-2 portrays this long-run monopolistic competition equilibrium. The firm produces output X_e, because marginal revenue equals marginal cost at this level.

The long-run monopolistic competition equilibrium differs in several important ways from the corresponding pure competition solution. These differences can be seen by comparing operations of the same hypothetical firm in a purely competitive market and in a monopolistically competitive market. Figure 13-1 can be compared to Figure 13-2.

Because the demand curve in monopolistic competition is negatively sloped, it can only touch the average cost curve somewhere to the left of the minimum average cost. The firm in the long run operates at a higher unit cost than under pure competition. In addition, consumers must pay a higher price per unit, even though the firm is only breaking even. Since the market price reflects consumers'

Figure 13-2: Monopolistic Competition, Long-Run Equilibrium

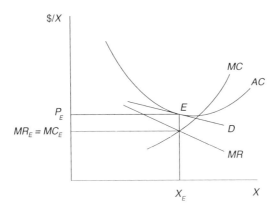

The long-run monopolistic competition equilibrium is shown as point E. Demand is highly elastic, but not perfectly elastic. Consequently, MR is below D. Free entry and exit cause the firm to break even. Profit is maximized at E because $MR = MC$. However, $P_E > MR = MC$.

valuations of the good, the fact that this price is greater than marginal cost suggests that there would be a net gain to society of more were produced. However, the monopolistically competitive business has no incentive to produce more, because the gain would not accrue to the business. Notice that these results are a consequence of the negatively sloped demand curve rather than profit maximization per se.

The extent to which the long-run monopolistic competition equilibrium differs from the pure competition solution depends on the slope of the demand curve. Figure 13-2 approaches Figure 13-1 as the demand curve approaches a horizontal line, becoming more and more elastic. Thus, introducing more competition into a market results in a closer approximation of the pure competition solution. Implicit in this view are the notions that competition will, in fact, occur and that the competition is directed toward serving consumers.

Oligopoly is much more difficult to analyze with respect to a long-run solution. The problem is to account for the interrelationships among the few sellers. Furthermore, barriers to entry and exit are often present, so it is not necessary for the firm to break even. The oligopoly solution lies somewhere between the monopolistic competition result and the monopoly result, which is presented in the next section. Certainly, the divergence of the oligopoly long-run equilibrium from the long-run pure competition solution is likely to be more pronounced than that of monopolistic competition, because the demand curve is likely to be steeper.

STUDY QUESTIONS

Imperfect Competition

5. How does the introduction of a slightly differentiated product affect the revenue of a firm?
6. Why is having price greater than marginal cost less desirable than having price equal marginal cost?
7. If both the purely competitive and the monopolistically competitive firms break even, why is the pure competition solution better for consumers?
8. As the number of competing sellers decreases, what is likely to be the effect on the demand curve facing the typical firm, and why is this detrimental for consumers?

● Why Regulate a Monopoly? ●

A monopoly, as the sole seller of a product for which there is no close substitute, reacts to the entire market demand curve. This by itself is not a reason for regulation. Even though there is only one seller, the price that a monopolist can charge is dictated by the position of the demand curve. Nor is the problem one of profit maximization alone, because purely competitive firms also maximize profit. In fact, profit maximization is an automatic incentive to be as efficient as possible. Remember, the basic economic concern is the efficient use of resources, and within this context an abnormal profit (either in the long run or the short run) could reflect the firm's efficiency.

The economic basis for regulating a monopoly lies in the divergence between price and marginal cost. Figure 13-3 illustrates the problem for the hypothetical firm, now considered to be a monopoly. As in all profit maximizing situations, the optimal output occurs where marginal revenue equals marginal cost. The market price is determined by the position of the demand curve. The average cost curve is used to determine if the monopoly is making an abnormal profit. Because the average cost curve is below the demand curve at the profit maximizing output, Figure 13-3 shows the monopoly making an abnormal profit.

The difference between this pricing problem and that of monopolistic competition is a matter of degree. The only seller of a product for which there is no close substitute is often associated with a demand curve that is considerably steeper (more inelastic) than the curve for a firm in monopolistic competition. Consequently, the divergence between price and marginal cost is apt to be much larger—and the social gain would be much larger if the monopoly were regulated. Administratively, regulating a single seller is much easier and less costly than regulating several sellers.

The effect on society of regulating a monopoly is not limited to the market for the monopoly's product. Optimal consumer choice occurs through equating the values of the last dollar spent on all goods. Any change in the profit maximizing price or quantity of a monopoly alters the numerator and denominator of the ratio. Marginal utility is affected by changes in the quantities consumed. Changes in the market price affect the consumer's price.

Whenever the value of the last dollar spent changes, the equalities among goods are disrupted. A consumer's purchases change until the equalities are restored. For example, if a local cable television company is forced to lower its price, a consumer unit could decide not to change its set of

Figure 13-3: Monopoly Profit Maximization

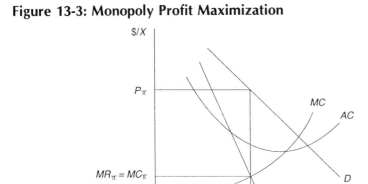

Profit is maximized by equating MR and MC. The monopolist can charge the price P_π, and X_π is sold. This monopolist earns an abnormal profit, since P_π is above the average cost (AC) of producing X_π. If barriers to entry are present, the abnormal profit can be earned in the long run. The profit maximizing position is characterized by $P_\pi > MR_\pi = MC_\pi$, and $P_\pi > AC$.

channels received but to use the savings to purchase other goods. Thus, the effects of the pricing problem are not limited to monopolies alone.

There are two ways to regulate the price a monopoly charges. These are illustrated in Figure 13-4, where representative revenue and cost curves are drawn. The profit maximizing output, X_π, occurs where marginal revenue equals marginal cost, and the corresponding price is P_π. An abnormal profit is obtained, because the average cost associated with X_π is less than the price.

One pricing scheme for regulating monopolies is to use **average cost pricing**. This is determined by the intersection of demand with average cost. Under such a policy, the monopolist is forced to break even, because a regulatory agency requires that P_{AC} be the price per unit. Given P_{AC}, the only level of production for which production equals demand is X_{AC}. However, one difficulty remains. The marginal cost associated with the average cost pricing situation in Figure 13-4 is greater than the price that consumers are able and willing to pay. There would be a net benefit if production were curtailed.

Marginal cost pricing, in which marginal cost is equated with demand, eliminates the imbalance between the consumer's valuation of a unit and the cost of producing that incremental unit. The regulated price is the one at which the marginal cost and demand curves cross. Notice that in Figure 13-4 the monopolist with this pricing scheme would receive an abnormal profit.

The most common justification for allowing monopolies is that certain production technologies favor large facilities. For example, mail, electricity, telephones, water, cable television, and natural gas services can operate most efficiently as single sellers in a market. This situation is depicted by a graph in which the lowest point on the average cost curve is associated with a large rate of production, and the market demand curve lies to the left of and below the minimum average cost.

Figure 13-4: Monopolies and Price Regulation

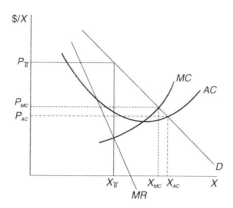

The economic basis for regulating a monopoly is because price exceeds the cost of producing an additional unit (i.e., $P_\pi > MC_\pi$). In average cost pricing, the price is set where average cost and demand intersect, shown as P_{AC}. X_{AC} is the corresponding production that would occur. But P_{AC} does not equate price with marginal cost. the only way to do this is to set the price where demand and marginal cost intersect. This price is denoted as P_{MC}, and X_{MC} is the production.

In the absence of regulation, the monopoly represented in Figure 13-5 obtains an abnormal profit. Average cost pricing causes the monopoly to break even (i.e., earn a normal profit), but the price still exceeds marginal cost. Marginal cost pricing eliminates the economic pricing problem, since price now equals marginal cost. However, marginal cost pricing has introduced another problem. The monopoly is losing money. Marginal cost pricing under the given conditions does not permit the monopoly to cover the economic cost.

A monopoly in this pricing situation receives a **subsidy**, consisting of public funds that supplement revenue or help the business cover costs. Before one can argue that marginal cost pricing is better than average cost pricing, it is necessary to evaluate the source of funding for the subsidy. This opens a Pandora's box with the question of whether the subsidy is generated in an equitable manner. It could be that the adverse effects of raising the subsidy more than offset the gains of the price regulation. For example, the cost of a property tax to pay for mass transit losses may exceed the savings from lower transit fares.

Most monopolies in the Unites States have agencies that control their pricing behavior. Examples are the Federal Communications Commission, the Postal Service, and utilities. A **regulatory agency** serves as a buffer between the monopoly and the public. These agencies control entry into a market and the extent of competition in it. They are also mandated to protect buyers from unfair practices and implement regulated prices. Every time a monopoly wants to change the existing market price, rate hearing are held. A crucial aspect of this process is the focus on the normal profit of the monopoly. The hearing provides the monopoly with the opportunity to demonstrate the price needs to be changed so a fair rate of return can be earned. Others attending the hearings can present opposing points of view. The regulatory agency then decides the appropriate price for the monopolist to charge.

Figure 13-5: Large-Scale Production and Price Regulation

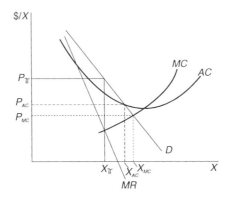

One reason monopolies exist is because of large scale production efficiency. This occurs when the market demand can be met at lowest cost with only one producer. Suppose D represents the market demand for X. In such a situation the demand curve lies below the average cost curve at a minimum level of production. Average cost pricing has the monopoly breaking even. Marginal cost pricing has the desirable feature of equating price and marginal cost, but necessitates subsidizing the monopoly, as P_{MC} is less than the average cost of production.

STUDY QUESTIONS

Why Regulate a Monopoly?

9. Distinguish between average cost and marginal cost pricing.
10. Why is a monopoly unwilling to lower prices in the absence of regulation?
11. Explain why profit maximization alone is not a reason for monopoly regulation.

● Identification of Monopoly Power ●

When does the divergence between price and marginal cost become large enough to justify public control? The crux of the issue is determining whether one firm or a small group of firms has the ability to exert undue influence in a market. Conceptually, the problem is to develop criteria that permit a market to be characterized as very near the theoretical extreme of monopoly. There are two crucial aspects to the criteria. First, the market share held by the largest firms must be measured. This can be done in several ways. Second, the market must be defined. Each aspect is outlined below. Unfortunately, some unresolved problems associated with each aspect make it very difficult to identify exactly when public intervention is warranted.

A commonly used measure of market control is the **concentration ratio**. It is defined as the proportion of market sales controlled by the largest producers of a good. Table 13-1 presents concentration ratios for some selected industries in the United States for 1967, 1977, and 1987. Sales are measured as the value of shipments, and the concentration ratio is the percentage of total shipments made by the four largest firms in each industry. The closer a percentage is to 100, the greater is the potential for monopoly power.

Table 13-1: Concentration Ratios for 1967, 1977, and 1987.

Industry	1967	1977	1987
Cookies and crackers	59	58	58
Bottled and canned soft drinks	13	15	30
Greeting card publishers	67	77	85
Laundry equipment	78	89	85
Household refrigerators and freezers	73	82	85
Envelopes	32	28	31
Tires and inner tubes	70	70	69
Meat packing plants	26	19	32
Motor vehicles and car bodies	92	93	90
Luggage	34	40	41

Note: Based on the value of shipments of the four largest firms.

Source: U. S. Bureau of the Census, *1987 Census of Manufacturers*. Subject Series. Concentration Ratios in Manufacturing, Table 4. (GPO, 1988).

No cut-off ratio exists at which public intervention should occur. Several factors cause the ambiguity. One has to do with the definition of a market, discussed below. Another is that concentration ratios omit the costs and profits of the businesses. A third is that the value of shipments is not the same as sales, because inventories of goods can change. Fourth, fluctuations in business activity can also affect the ratios. Thus, focusing on concentration ratios alone gives an incomplete picture of the control that a group of firms has in a market.

Even with these limitations, concentration ratios can provide some insight into the competitive situation. This is especially true of industry ratios over time. A rising concentration ratio suggests a decreasingly competitive environment. For example, in Table 13-1, cookies and crackers experienced virtually no change in its concentration ratio over the 20 year period, whereas the ratio for bottled and canned soft drinks was relatively low, but it increased somewhat over the first 10 years and doubled over the next decade.

Merger activity is another signal of increased concentration. Firms can gain monopoly power by purchasing competitors. Table 13-2 contains some recent merger data for food businesses. Notice that brewers have very few mergers, whereas food processing firms had many. Care must be used in interpreting these data because there is only a small number of national breweries, whereas there are many small food processors. Combining concentration ratio data with merger activity is one way of tracking changes in competitiveness. This information is used by regulatory agencies, such as the Federal Trade Commission, to monitor the level of competition.

Table 13-2: Food Business Mergers and Acquisitions, Selected Categories: 1990-1994.

Category	1994	1993	1992	1991	1990
Bakers	16	6	9	4	12
Brewers	1	3	1	1	1
Food Processing Firms	106	114	84	73	66
Packaging Suppliers	14	14	12	8	11
Supermarkets	42	19	15	16	15

Source: The Food Institute, *Food Institute Report*, April 10, 1995.

Abnormal profit is another measure of monopoly power. The idea behind this approach is that businesses with monopoly power are able to charge prices that exceed marginal cost. Consequently high rates of return can be used as a measure of monopoly control. This approach has several problems. One is the absence of a cut-off to indicate the rate of return at which significant monopoly power is present. Wide variations in acceptable accounting procedures cause rates of return to vary, making comparisons difficult. Differences in product mixes and in the sources of financing also cause variations in profits. Thus, profit rates as a measure of monopoly power require subjective evaluation.

Closely related to the problems of measuring control are the problems of defining a market. Part of the difficulty centers on identifying which goods are in direct competition. How are they to be grouped? For example, is hamburger in competition with fish or chicken? If there were one hamburger seller, whether it could operate as a monopoly would depend on whether fish and chicken were substitutes. Substitution among final goods rests with individual consumers through their purchases. Thus, cross-price elasticities of demand can serve as a guide to the availability of substitutes. The closer elasticities are to zero, the more likely it is that the product has no close substitutes. Subjective evaluation is needed again because no cut-off values for cross-elasticities exist to signal monopoly power.

Geographic distribution is a complicating factor in defining a market. As shown in Chapter 11, the consumer's price includes transportation costs. Sellers also must transport goods. The extent to which consumers are willing to travel, coupled with the extent to which sellers recognize their spatial boundaries, determines the geography of a market. Different products have different market sizes based on variations in the properties of the specific good. For example, high fashion clothing is relatively easy to transport; furniture is not. Consequently, the definition of a market also depends on the characteristics of the goods being studied.

The preceding observations indicate a few of the difficulties encountered in trying to measure monopoly power. The tools available are less than ideal. Furthermore, they are subject to interpretation. But all is not lost. The tools can serve as foundations for the dismantling monopoly practices.[2] Contrary to popular perception, monopoly practices are not restricted to large, national corporations. They also arise in small geographic markets for products manufactured and distributed on a regional basis. From a consumer perspective, both types of monopolies are detrimental because they allow price to exceed marginal cost. The appropriate consumer-oriented policy initiative is to use these tools, as precisely as possible, to document instances in which markets are moving away from competition toward monopoly. Price regulation can be considered when the divergence between price and marginal cost has become large enough to warrant action.

STUDY QUESTIONS

Identification of Monopoly Power

12. Concentration ratios for the four largest U. S. automobile manufacturers have been in excess of 90 percent (see Table 13-1). What arguments can you develop to support the position that the automobile industry does not need to be regulated?
13. Even though there are many dry cleaning services across the nation, why should the Federal Trade Commission be concerned with their competition in a metropolitan area?
14. How would you go about building a case to support the charge that a local cable company operates as a monopoly?

● Two Exchange Problems ●

Two other instances of market system failure are becoming increasingly important to consumers. One, called a **public good**, pertains to situations where the supply of a good or service cannot be restricted to individuals who purchased it. An example is a person who is concerned about safety and has a street light constructed. All the neighbors receive a benefit from the light. The other pertains to situations where all of the costs of production are not covered by the business or some benefits from consumption are received by others. An example of the former is pollution and of the latter is a well landscaped lawn. Both situations come under the heading of an **externality** because some of the benefits or costs are not reflected in the market price.

Figure 13-6 depicts the problem of a public good. We saw in Chapter 8 (Figure 8-6 and Table 8-2) that market demand is found by adding together all the quantities that individual consumers are able and willing to buy at various market prices. Since Q is on the horizontal scale, this amounts to a horizontal addition, as shown in panel (a) of the diagram. Taking the additional liberty of assuming that panel (a) of Figure 13-6 represents the market for a purely competitive good, then we have seen that P_E is the equilibrium price, and Q_E is the equilibrium quantity. Consumers individually decide how much to buy at P_E (q_1 and q_2), and the sum over consumers is Q_E.

Panel (b) pertains to a public good. Although D appears to be a typical demand curve, its interpretation is different because of the nature of the public good. If Q is a public good, the

---

2   For example, see M. C. Howard, *Antitrust and Trade Regulations: Selected Issues and Case Studies* (Englewood Cliffs, NJ: Prentice-Hall, 1983).

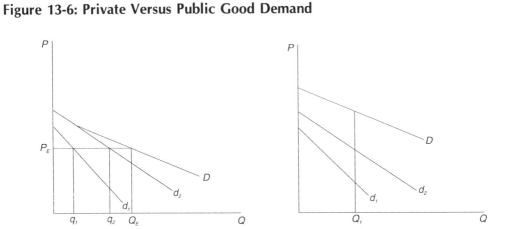

Figure 13-6: Private Versus Public Good Demand

(a)   (b)

Panel (a) shows exchange in a purely competitive market. Market demand, D, is the sum of the quantities demanded by individual consumers at the various market prices. The equilibrium price, P_E, is associated with the equilibrium quantity, Q_E. Given P_E, consumers determine how much to purchase. Panel (b) reflects a public good where consumption cannot be restricted. If Q_1 is produced, then the total value of it is the vertical sum.

horizontal addition makes no sense because everyone consumes the same amount. What is the total amount that consumers would be able and willing to pay? The total value would be the sum of all the individual valuations which is the vertical distance.

The problem is there is no way to charge individual buyers unless the individual demand curves are known, and it is in consumers' self interest to indicate they have very small valuations of the public good, let others pay, and consume the same level. If consumers have approximately equal valuations, then there could be fairly wide-spread agreement on the quantity supplied and an average assessment. If there is disagreement over valuations, then many people will be dissatisfied with the quantity supplied and with the price charged (or taxed).

The problem of externalities arises from the inability of the market system to capture all of the costs or benefits associated with production and the benefits or costs of consumption. (This is different from the public good situation where everyone consumes the same amount.) Misallocation of resources occur in either situation. To outline the problem, consider external costs.[3] Assume they rise with the level of production. It follows that the marginal cost curve of the firm is below the marginal cost to society. That is, the social cost includes the private cost plus the externality. This means that the supply curve associated with market exchange understates the cost, or the supply curve for society lies above the supply curve for the market. This is shown in Figure 13-7 where S_S lies above S. In the

---

[3]   Similar logic applies to other externalities in that resource misallocation occurs. The market supply or demand curves are not the same as the social curves, thereby causing the market equilibrium to be different from the social equilibrium.

case of pure competition, the market equilibrium price and quantity are shown as P_E and Q_E. However, if social costs were included, then P_S and Q_S are the equilibrium amounts. This means the market is over producing and charging too low a price, so there is a misallocation of resources. Two ways to achieve a better allocation are to impose a tax to raise the effective price to P_S and to impose product standards.

Automobile pollution standards are an example. Consumers have tended to ignore the external costs of driving (producing a transportation service). These have become so large that the public sector has intervened and mandated mileage and emission standards. Impacts include the increased purchase price of new automobiles and higher maintenance costs.

STUDY QUESTIONS

Two Exchange Problems

15. Identify some public goods that are provided by various levels of government.
16. Parking garages in metropolitan areas often charge lower rates for all day parking and for monthly parking. What is the economic reason for the private sector to work this way? How does this practice relate to an economic analysis of rush hour congestion?
17. Can you develop an economic argument for the creation of neighborhood beautification groups?

● Problems With Regulation ●

A complete overview of monopoly regulation requires consideration of opposing views. While there are sound economic principles in support of public control, there also are some important economic problems created by regulation. The problem of having to subsidize some monopolies has already been discussed. Other difficulties are identified below.

What is a fair rate of return for a business? Clearly, a monopoly is going to have a view that differs from the public's. Since it is the monopoly that controls the cost and revenue data, the possibility exists that the monopolist may control this information in an advantageous way. The situation is complicated by the problem of trying to establish what a normal profit is for a business that has no comparable private sector counterpart, such as the operation of a municipal airport.

In the absence of regulation, a profit maximizing monopolist has an incentive to be as efficient as possible. Price regulation eliminates this motive. In fact, the profit motive is replaced by a guarantee that the monopoly will receive at least a normal profit. Both average cost and marginal cost pricing have this effect. What is the incentive for a monopoly to introduce new, more efficient production techniques if increasing profits would only lead the regulatory agency to change the price structure so as to return profits to a normal level? The U.S. Postal Service is an excellent example. Management has little incentive for resisting labor's demand for increased protection and job security. Any cost saving that might be a consequence of tougher negotiations would only result in lower regulated prices, as opposed to higher profit. In a similar manner, the benefits of research and development of better sorting and delivery methods are mitigated by the price regulation process.

Figure 13-7: External Production Costs

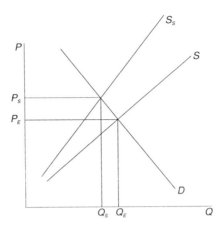

The supply curve S portrays amounts producers are able and willing to supply at various market prices, which reflect only the costs the producers have to pay. If there are other costs, then the social supply curve S_s lies above S. If these costs could be recovered, then P_s and Q_s would be the optimal price and quantity.

Another problem with regulating monopolies is that the agencies set up to protect the consumer from the monopolies end up protecting the monopolies from competition and the consumer.[4] Over time, many regulatory agencies have changed from their intended purpose to one of preservation. Examples include the Interstate Commerce Commission, the Federal Communications Commission, Civil Aeronautics Board, and state public service commissions.

Changes in technology arising in the long run tend to increase the competitive environment in which monopolies must operate. The Post Office now competes with express delivery services, and fax transmissions have reduced the need for postal services. Cable television companies may have to compete with local telephone companies in the near future, and small wireless satellite receivers are becoming available. The cellular phone industry is growing rapidly and has the potential to compete with the traditional telephone service.

Economic theory provides some additional insight about the behavior of monopolies. The thrust of the analysis centers on **contestable markets**.[5] Such a market is one in which businesses can enter and exit freely. That is, should any firm decide to enter the market, it can do so without experiencing any competitive disadvantage. Similarly, a firm is free to exit without any cost, which implies that all

4   For a more detailed discussion, see M. Friedman, *Capitalism and Freedom* (Chicago: University of Chicago Press, 1962).

5   W. J. Baumol, "Contestable Markets: An Uprising in the Theory of Industry Structure," *American Economic Review* 72(March, 1982):1-15.

the resources used by the exiting firm can be sold. Free entry and exit involve long-run changes in the number of firms in the market.

Given this competitive structure, how is a firm likely to operate? As discussed in previous chapters, the firm is forced to break even in the long run because of free entry and exit. Suppose an abnormal profit is earned by a firm. This encourages entry, because other firms would like to earn an above average profit. If a firm does not cover its average cost, it cannot continue to operate in the long run. Thus, firms charge a price that equals marginal cost in order to make a profit without encouraging entry. Inefficient firms cannot exist in the long run, because they would be underpriced by competitors.

The market behavior outlined above applies to a monopoly. Even if there is a single producer, if the market is contestable, the threat of entry induces the monopolist to charge a price that is equal to marginal cost. Contestable markets provide a different perspective on the economic need for the regulation of a monopoly. If such a market exists, the monopoly should not require regulation. The real question becomes one of determining how close real world markets come to being contestable. On the one hand, market imperfections such as patents, performance standards, and legal restrictions tend to limit contestability. Technological change, on the other hand, tends to foster contestable markets.

STUDY QUESTIONS

Problems with Regulation

18. What are some of the economic problems associated with monopoly regulation?
19. As a consumer advocate, should you favor or oppose monopoly regulation?
20. What is a contestable market, and how do such markets reduce the need for monopoly regulation?

● Deregulation ●

Problems associated with the regulation of monopolies have culminated in recent years in the deregulation movement. Several industries that formerly operated as regulated monopolies have been opened to competition. Among them are airlines, banking, freight transportation, telephone, and utilities. In each instance, the deregulation has reintroduced competition and brought about price changes, to the benefit of consumers. Whether these benefits last will depend on whether the markets remain contestable.

The Motor Carrier Act of 1935 empowered the Interstate Commerce Commission to regulate interstate trucking. Rates, routes, and licenses to operate were set by the Commission. This had the effect of creating barriers to entry and guaranteeing a rate of return to the trucking industry. The extensive use of trucking to transport consumer goods meant that consumers ultimately paid the cost of the carriers' fees. Trucking was deregulated with the passage of the Motor Carrier Act of 1980. This legislation made it easier for new firms to enter the industry and for new rates to be set. The results have been lower rates and increased competition.

Airline deregulation occurred in the late 1970s. The Civil Aeronautics Board regulates the airline industry, controlling safety standards, certification of new carriers, routes, and rate changes. Deregulation has enabled carriers to lower fares and to expand into the existing routes of competitors without prior board approval. Easing the restriction on competition has resulted in the emergence of a complex rate structure. In addition, major carriers are engaging in fierce competition for passengers traveling between major airports, and commuter carriers are competing for passengers traveling between small airports and between small and large airports. Several airlines have merged, and others have gone out of business as a result of the deregulation. Consumers have benefited from the reduced fares, but the myriad of prices has created an information problem. The benefits of shopping around for the lowest fare can be quite substantial. It has become important to check with several airlines and to ask about special fares before purchasing a ticket.

During the depression of the 1930s, bank failures were considered to be one of the major causes of the depression and a stumbling block in generating a recovery. Fierce competition among banks and the payment of interest on checking accounts were felt to be at the heart of the problem, so Regulation Q was enacted to control the banking industry. Commercial banks were allowed to offer checking accounts, which paid no interest. Other banks, such as savings and loans, could not offer checking accounts but could offer savings accounts, which paid slightly higher rates of interest than commercial banks' savings accounts. All savings accounts had maximum interest rates.

Regulation Q limited competition among banks. The ceiling rates that were set allowed banks to operate under well-defined rules; and as long as market rates of interest for corporate and government bonds were comparable to the regulated rates, the banks could operate as a cartel. But as interest rates rose during the 1960s and 1970s, banks started competing again for depositors. Further competition began in the 1970s when stock brokerage firms began offering investment opportunities (e.g., money market funds) with returns well in excess of the Regulation Q ceilings.

Distinctions between commercial banks and savings and loans are disappearing. Banks can now offer depositors interest rates that are competitive with rates of money market funds. Savings and loans (including credit unions) can offer checking accounts. Commercial banks are also trying to expand into providing investment services for depositors (and enter into direct competition with stock brokerage firms). Competition for credit card accounts is fierce. This environment is leading to bank acquisitions and mergers, resulting in large regional banks that really have national and international interests.

Selecting the optimal regulation is not always a clear-cut choice. The emerging telecommunications industry is a case in point.[6] Certainly, economic analysis indicates less regulation and more competition are desirable. But should one focus on the short or the long run? In addition, some of the consequences of the alternatives are not guaranteed. One choice facing lawmakers centers on telephone companies offering video services over the phone lines. Both phone and cable lines can now provide video and voice services. Therefore, if they compete directly in local markets, consumers should benefit. A proposal is to allow local telephone and cable companies to purchase interests in each other; and in cities with less than 50,000 people, they could merge. This raises the fear that single providers will emerge. Proponents of the provision argue that small markets can only support single providers. Furthermore, they argue emerging technologies (satellites, electric utilities) will provide ample competition in the future. Consequently, lawmakers are confronted with fostering short-run competition with an adverse impact on smaller markets or supporting smaller markets and with the expectation that technological change will create competition in the long run.

---

[6]   A. Murray, "Competition Is at Risk in Telecommunications," *Wall Street Journal*, July 17, 1995.

STUDY QUESTIONS

Deregulation

21. The presence of nonprice competition, even in a regulated market, is evidence that the market is contestable. What nonprice competition can you recall with airlines and credit cards?
22. Why must deregulated markets remain contestable in order for consumers to benefit in the long run?

● Summary ●

The long-run pure competition equilibrium is desirable for consumers, because firms operate at and consumers pay the lowest possible cost per unit. Other forms of market structure generate prices that exceed the marginal cost. The divergence increases as the number of competitors decreases. Average cost pricing and marginal cost pricing are two forms of price regulation. Unfortunately, criteria for identifying monopolies require subjective evaluations. Problems of regulation include determining a normal profit, guaranteeing a normal profit, subsidies, barriers to entry, and assessing the likelihood of technological change. The theory of contestable markets provides an economic argument for the position that monopoly regulation may be unnecessary in these situations.

● Key Terms ●

Average cost pricing: setting a regulated price at the intersection of demand and average cost.
Concentration ratio: the proportion of market sales controlled by the largest firms.
Contestable market: a market in which there is a threat of the entry.
Externality: a benefit or cost arising from the production of consumption of a good or service.
Marginal cost pricing: setting a regulated price at the intersection of demand and marginal cost.
Public good: a good or service for which consumption cannot be restricted to the consumer who made the purchase.
Regulatory agency: a public organization responsible for controlling prices, entry, and extent of competition in an industry.
Subsidy: public funds that supplement revenue or help cover the costs of a business.

Chapter 14

The Value of Time

In the discussions of consumer demand in Parts II through IV, the span of time was limited to one budget period. Part V shows how the traditional model of consumer choice can be modified to accommodate a consumer's decision making over several periods called a **planning horizon**. Two very important options become part of the decision making: borrowing and saving. Since more than one time period is involved, there is no reason to require that a consumer's expenditures equal the money budgeted. One option is for the consumer to save some current income and spend it in a subsequent period. The other option is to allow expenditures to exceed money income for the same period and borrow the difference. This chapter outlines the setting in which these decisions are made. Economic considerations associated with choices about borrowing and saving are explained.

Material presented here is not separate and distinct from the preceding chapters. Economic tools and logic used in earlier sections are applied to decision making over time. A consumer's problem continues to be one of utility maximization subject to a budget constraint. Opportunity costs associated with borrowing and saving are at the heart of the analysis. The consumer decides by comparing his or her willingness to borrow and save to the conditions under which the market allows borrowing and saving to occur. This type of decision making is analogous to moving along a budget constraint in order to reach the highest level of utility.

The introduction of a planning horizon requires the relationships among time, money, and utility be examined. Decision making within one period, as described in Chapter 7, is called **intratemporal choice**, because the focus is on the choices within a single period. **Intertemporal choice** refers to decision making over more than one period.

● Dollars Separated By Time ●

Which seems better to you: $100 right now or $100 a year from today? The universal choice is $100 today. The crux of the question is the effect of time on the valuation of money. Preferring $100 today over $100 in 12 months implies that, although the dollar amounts are the same, they are not equal. If money today is not the same as money tomorrow, then whenever decision making involves values occurring at different points in time, values must be adjusted. For example, suppose $50 is borrowed, and $25 is to be repaid in a year and $25 in two years. The repayments sum to $50, but since money today is not the same as money in a year or two years, an adjustment is necessary in order to accommodate the timing of the repayment.

The utility derived from goods is affected by time in the same way. Comparisons of the satisfaction derived from goods separated by time pose the same difficulty as comparisons of money separated by time. Confronted with the alternatives of a $20 steak dinner today or the same meal in a year, almost everyone would prefer the dinner today. In principle, the same type of accommodation must be made as for the timing of money.

This problem can be eliminated by converting money or utility into a common time period. The mechanism for accomplishing this is the use of interest rates. Interest rates can be used to transfer values from one period to another. After conversion, an interperiod choice problem is similar to the intraperiod choice problems outlined in previous chapters.

A diagram is useful for illustrating the effect of time. Figure 14-1 represents the choice between $100 today and $100 one year hence. The two variables in this problem are the amount of money and when it is received. Time is measured on the horizontal scale. The forward movement of time corresponds to movement to the right in the diagram. Let t represent today and (t + 1) denote one year later. Dollars are measured on the vertical scale. Any point in the diagram refers to dollar values and when they are received. Periods t and (t + 1) both have the same money value, or height, of $100. However, they are separated horizontally by a year's time. This separation causes them to be valued differently.

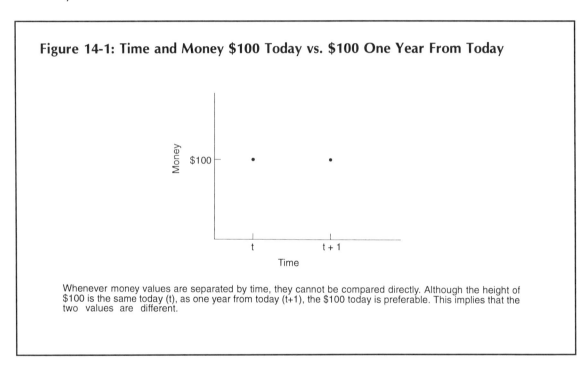

Figure 14-1: Time and Money $100 Today vs. $100 One Year From Today

Whenever money values are separated by time, they cannot be compared directly. Although the height of $100 is the same today (t), as one year from today (t+1), the $100 today is preferable. This implies that the two values are different.

There are three basic reasons why the value of money and the value of consumption are affected by timing. The first is changes in the price level. **Inflation** occurs whenever the market prices of goods rise. This means that more money is required to maintain the same ability to buy, or a given amount of money represents less and less control over goods. The consumer prefers $100 today in part because it will buy more goods today than in a year's time. If inflation during the year is 10 percent, then an extra $10 will be needed next year to purchase the quantity bought for $100 this year.

The effect of changes in the price level can be summarized as follows. Over a specific period of time, the higher the rate of inflation, the greater the amount of money must become in order to maintain the same purchasing power. Also, given a fixed rate of inflation, an increase in the time interval is associated with larger dollar amounts at the end of the interval. Should inflation be 10 percent annually for two years instead of one year, then in two years $121 will represent the same purchasing power as $100 does today.[1]

Suppose there is no change expected in the price level during the year. Given the same choice between $100 today and $100 one hear hence, which would people prefer? Most would still choose the money now. This indicates that there are effects other than inflation associated with the introduction of time. The second reason for the lack of comparability is commonly referred to as **impatience**. Unlimited wants constrained by scarcity cause consumers to be concerned with satisfying needs and desires. People prefer to have utility today rather than tomorrow. This suggests that people require compensation if they must wait. Both the length of the waiting time and the extent of the impatience affect the amount of compensation. As the waiting period increases, so does the compensation consumers require for the delay. As the impatience increases, the compensation also increases.

Risk is the third factor associated with the introduction of time. Uncertainty is something to be considered whenever time enters the decision-making situation. Life is uncertain. Postponing the use of goods involves the risk the consumer might not survive until the later period or the goods might not be available. Similar risks confront businesses and governments. An additional consideration is that the economic setting is likely to change over time, thereby making it more difficult to complete contractual agreements. For example, a recession could cause some people to become unemployed, so they would be unable to buy later. Increases in risk require increases in the compensation involved. Because of inflation, impatience, and risk, the value of time must be incorporated into decision making whenever intertemporal choices are involved. Increases in inflation, impatience, and risk all cause the amount of compensation required to increase. Similarly, increases in the length of time cause the problems of inflation, impatience, and risk to be compounded.

STUDY QUESTIONS

Dollars Separated by Time

1. Explain why dollars separated by time cannot be compared directly.
2. Distinguish among inflation, impatience, and risk.
3. Identify some changes in the economic environment that increase risk as the planning horizon lengthens.
4. The effects of time are not limited to dollar values. Utility derived from goods also is affected by timing. For example, consider the utility derived from a new automobile. Putting aside the question of model changes, would you rather have a new automobile today or wait a year?

---

[1]   How the $121 is generated is discussed in the next section.

● Moving Money Through Time ●

The introduction of time into the analysis creates the need for a mechanism that permits dollar values to be converted from one budget period to another. Figure 14-1 illustrates why this is the case. Since $100 in t is not the same as $100 in (t + 1), they cannot be considered as equal. This lack of comparability is resolved by converting money values in one period to money values in another. Such a transformation eliminates the factor of time and allows for a direct comparison. One way of doing this is to change the $100 in t to an equivalent amount of money in (t + 1).

Since the intent here is to construct an economic setting that allows for an examination of the principles involved without any unnecessary complications, some assumptions will be made. To begin with, assume that the planning horizon is composed of budget periods, each of which is one year long. Only annual rates are considered. For a given situation, interest rates are assumed to be the same in each of the budget periods. That is, no allowance is made for a different interest rate in each of the years in the planning horizon. For example, if the interest rate is 12 percent, it is 12 percent in every period. Interest earned in one period is assumed to earn interest in subsequent periods through **compounding**.

Given these assumptions, the mechanics of transferring money from one time period to another can be outlined. Moving money ahead in time is the equivalent of moving to the right in Figure 14-1. Suppose $100 is placed in a savings account that pays a 10 percent rate of interest, compounded annually. At the end of one year, this account has a balance of $110, which is equal to the initial $100 plus $10 in interest which is computed as 10 percent of the money at the start of the period. The $100 today is the equivalent of $110 one year from today at a 10 percent valuation of time. The relationship is expressed as follows:

$100 + $100(.10) = $110, or
$100(1 + .10) = $110.

Should the money be left in the account for a second year, the closing balance would be $121. The starting balance for the second year is $110, which at 10 percent is transformed into $121. Total interest equals $21 because of compounding. The $10 in interest from the first year earns $1 in interest in the second year:

$110 + $110(.10) = $121, or
$110(1 + .10) = $121.

Figure 14-2 displays this example in diagram form. The initial $100 is transformed into $110 in one year at a 10 percent rate of interest. Moving to the right one period with a 10 percent valuation of time increases the height to $110. The height is $121 for a two-year period. Further movement to the right would cause the subsequent heights to be even more.

Key features of moving money ahead in time can be seen in this illustration. Money, the interest rate, and the length of time are the variables. There is an initial amount of money, an amount of money at the end of the period, and a rate of interest which is constant throughout the investment period. Let Y represent dollars. A subscript for Y is needed to identify the period associated with a particular dollar value. Y_t denotes dollars in period t, Y_{t+3} denotes dollars in period (t + 3) years, etc.

Figure 14-2: An Illustration of Compounding

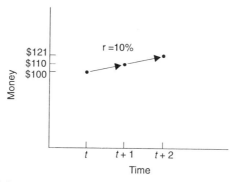

Compounding moves dollar values ahead in time. Assume a 10 percent annual rate of interest and annual compounding. The initial $100 in period t is transformed into $100 in one year ($t + 1$). The extra $10 represents the interest earned. The $110 is transformed into $121 at the end of the second year ($t + 2$). During this second year, interest from the first year earns interest, or is compounded. At a 10 percent valuation, $100 in one year and $121 in two years.

The interest rate is shown as r. Using this notation, the relationship for the one-year investment discussed above can be written in a more general way:

(14-1) $Y_t(1 + r) = Y_{t+1}$.

The second year of the two-year investment is

(14-2) $Y_{t+1}(1 + r) = Y_{t+2}$.

Substituting Y_{t+1} from equation 14-1 yields

(14-3) $Y_t(1 + r)^2 = Y_{t+2}$.

Notice how the exponents of the $(1 + r)$ term on the left-hand sides of equations 14-1 and 14-3 match the subscripts of Y on the right-hand sides. Whatever this exponent happens to be, it is also the subscript. An intuitive explanation is that $(1 + r)$ raised to a power is the transformation mechanism for moving values ahead in time.

Let n represent the number of years ahead that dollars are to be transformed. The general expression—under the conditions of annual budget periods, a fixed annual rate of interest, annual compounding, and a fixed number of years—is shown as equation 14-4. This equation shows what happens to the height (value) of an initial amount of money as it is transferred farther and farther to the right, or ahead in time.

(14-4) $Y_t(1 + r)^n = Y_{t+n}$.

Examination of equation 14-4 reveals that it is consistent with the observations made previously about why dollars separated by time cannot be compared directly. Inflation, impatience, and risk are combined into one valuation of time, the interest rate. The larger r is, the larger Y_{t+n} has to become. For example, if r = 15 percent instead of 10 percent and the initial amount of money is still $10, then Y_{t+1} is $115 instead of $110. A higher rate of inflation necessitates a larger amount of money in a future period just to maintain purchasing power. The higher the impatience, the more compensation required in order to transfer the ability to purchase in period t into the ability to purchase in a future year $(t+n)$. Increases in risk also lead to increases in the future dollar value for compensation. Lengthening the transfer period increases the dollar value, because the larger n is, the larger $(1+r)^n$ must be. The rationale is that an increase in the number of years introduces more time for inflation, impatience, and risk to increase the dollar value.

Quite often, decision making involves determining the value of a future amount of money in a earlier period. The valuation requires computation of what a future amount of money is worth today. For example, suppose a consumer learns that according to a relative's will $5,000 is to be received in two years. What is it worth today? Transferring money backward in time, called **discounting**, is the inverse operation of compounding. It is represented by moving to the left in the preceding figures.

The relationship between compounding and discounting can be explained by returning to equation 14-4. In compounding one begins with an initial dollar value in period t and determines its equivalent in period $(t+n)$. In discounting one takes a dollar value in period $(t+n)$ and determines its equivalent in period t. The reversed causality can be shown by rearranging equation 14-4 into:

(14-5) $Y_t = Y_{t+n}/(1+r)^n$.

The expression $1/(1+r)^n$ is called the **discount factor**. It represents the extent to which one must decrease money in $(t+n)$ in order to transfer it into period t. Y_t is referred to as the **discounted value**, or the current period equivalent of the future value.

An inverse relationship exists between the interest rate and the discounted value. Larger values of r lead to decreases in the discount factor, and declines in the discount factor cause the decline in a given Y_{t+n} to be larger. For example, suppose the interest rate is 10 percent. The $5,000 to be inherited in two years has a discounted value today of $4,132.23.[2] Figure 14-3(a) illustrates the computation. Because two years must elapse before the money is acquired, the $5,000 is equal to (valued at) $4,132.23 two years earlier. A larger interest rate, say 15 percent, generates a larger reduction to $3,780.72.[3]

Increases in the time interval also produce decreases in the discounted value. As n increases, the discount factor must decrease. This leads to a smaller Y_t. Continuing with the above illustration, suppose r equals 10 percent, but the benefactor must wait three years instead of two. The Y_t equivalent is now $3,756.57 rather than $4,132.23.[4] This is shown in Figure 14-3(b).

Now the logic for discounting can be explained. The algebraic properties of equation 14-5 are consistent with the explanation of why the timing of dollar values and consumption is important. Transferring values to earlier periods should involve reductions in value due to inflation, impatience, and risk. Because of inflation during the time interval t to $(t+n)$, any dollar value in the later period must be reduced in order to represent a comparable purchasing power in the earlier period. Impatience is at work, in reverse. Instead of a delay of n periods, the switch in the timing of the valuation is to the earlier period t. Similarly, the risk factor is diminished by such a transfer.

Because compounding and discounting are inverse operations, there is symmetry between moving ahead and backward in time. If $r=10$ percent and $n=2$, then $100 in t is converted into $121 in $(t+2)$. Conversely, $121 in two years discounted at 10 percent per year is $100 today. The symmetry is displayed in Figure 14-4. Whatever causes the height to be greater in $(t+n)$ than in t also must cause

---

[2] $(1/1.1)^2(\$5,000) = (1/1.21)(\$5,000) = \$4,132.23$.
[3] $(1/1.15)^2(\$5,000) = (1/1.3225)(\$5,000) = \$3,780.72$.
[4] $(1/1.1)^3(\$5,000) = (1/1.331)(\$5,000) = \$3,756.57$.

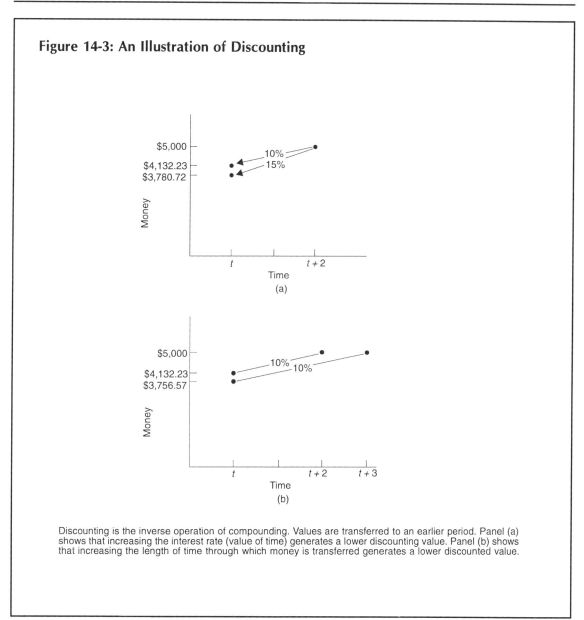

Figure 14-3: An Illustration of Discounting

Discounting is the inverse operation of compounding. Values are transferred to an earlier period. Panel (a) shows that increasing the interest rate (value of time) generates a lower discounting value. Panel (b) shows that increasing the length of time through which money is transferred generates a lower discounted value.

a symmetric decrease in height when discounting occurs. This equivalence implies that it does not matter which transfer process is used. The effect is the same in terms of control over goods—only the direction of the timing differs.

Compounding and discounting provide the requisite tools for handling the effects of time by changing values in one time period to values in another. Through these techniques, a common time

Figure 14-4: Compounding and Discounting

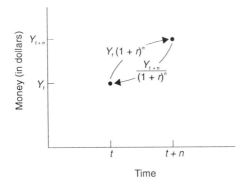

Compounding and discounting are inverse operations. With compounding, an initial value, Y_t, is transformed n periods ahead into Y_{t+n}. With discounting, a future amount, Y_{t+n}, is transformed into a period t value, Y_t.

period can be reached whenever comparisons are needed. Once values have a common time period, they can be compared directly and decisions can be made. The usual procedure is to convert values from various time periods into the current period, designated as period t.

Any decision making involves comparing associated costs and returns, often extending through several periods. These should not be compared as long as they are separated by time. But after they have been converted into a common period, the addition of the related costs and benefits is appropriate. This addition of related discounted values in the same period is called **present value**, PV. Equation 14-6 shows how the present value is computed for an n-period flow, beginning with the current period. Notice that the equation discounts each future value into the current period. Then the discounted values are added together.

$$(14\text{-}6) \quad PV_t = Y_t + Y_{t+1}/(1+r) + Y_{t+2}/(1+r)^2 + \ldots + Y_{t+n}/(1+r)^n$$

Consider the following example. A family has the chance to invest \$500 this period in a new business being started by a neighbor. The neighbor promises to repay the loan as follows: \$150 in one year, \$200 in two years, and \$260 in three years. Should the family make the investment? Figure 14-5 presents the information. Although the returns total \$610, this is not meaningful. Money three years away should not be treated the same way as money only one year away. Furthermore, the \$500 cost occurs today. What needs to be done is to discount all of the returns into values today. Then they can be added together. This present value calculation is shown below, assuming a 10 percent rate of interest. Since the present value of these returns is less than the cost, this particular opportunity should be foregone.

$$\begin{aligned}
PV \quad &= \$150/(1.1) + \$200/(1.1)^2 + \$260/(1.1)^3 \\
&= \$136.36 + \$165.29 + \$195.34 \\
&= \$496.99
\end{aligned}$$

Figure 14-5: A Present Value Illustration

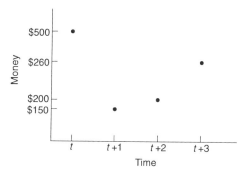

A family is assumed to have an investment option of loaning $500 today to a neighbor. The family is to receive as a return $150 in $(t + 1)$, $200 in $(t + 2)$, and $260 in $(t + 3)$. These future returns must be discounted in today's values before they can be added together. The present value of these returns with a 10 percent rate of interest is $496.99. Since the present value of the returns is less than the cost, the family should not loan the money.

STUDY QUESTIONS

Moving Money Through Time

5. Distinguish among discounting, compounding, and present value.
6. Distinguish between a discount factor and a discounted value.
7. What are some risk, inflation, and impatience factors associated with waiting for the $5,000 inheritance?
8. To familiarize yourself with the effects of interest rates and lengths of time, consider the following:
   a. Suppose $100 is invested for three years at 10 percent. What is Y_{t+3}? Compare Y_{t+3} to Y_{t+2} and Y_{t+1}. How does increasing n affect Y_{t+n}?
   b. What is the discounted value of $2,000 in two years at 25 percent and at 20 percent? Compare the two values. What if the planning horizon increases to three years?

● Two Valuations of Time ●

Interest rates are used to transfer values from one period to another through compounding and discounting. In this context, an interest rate represents the value of time and indicates the number of periods over which time affects values. In reality, there are two basic valuations of time that must be identified in order to outline the essentials of consumer decision making over time. One is the valuation by the consumer, and the other is the valuation by the marketplace.

A consumer's valuation is called the **rate of time preference**. It reflects the individual consumer unit's assessment of inflation, impatience, and risk. The higher the rate of time preference, the higher is the consumer's valuation of goods today over goods tomorrow. Just as the willingness to trade in intertemporal choice is determined by each consumer, the rate of time preference in intertemporal choice is determined by each consumer.

The marketplace also has a valuation of the three effects of time, referred to as the **market rate of interest**. It represents the opportunity cost the marketplace sets for the ability to transform money (and its control over goods) from one period to another. Any funds that become available to the market, such as through consumer savings, represent immediate control over goods, so the market rate of interest is the price the market is paying for current purchasing power. Any funds the market transfers to a consumer, through consumer borrowing, have an opportunity cost, because they could have been lent to others or used for current purchases by the lender. Consequently, the market rate of interest is the market's assessment of inflation, impatience, and risk.

The rate of time preference and the market rate of interest reflect assessments about the effects of time. The distinction between what a consumer is willing to do (the rate of time preference) and what the marketplace allows the consumer to do (the market rate of interest) is very similar to the one discussed in Chapter 7 between the willingness to trade (indifference curves) and the ability to trade (budget constraint). Decision making in an intertemporal setting is based on economic logic similar to that employed for the intratemporal setting. But before this logic can be explained, a little more background needs to be presented about the opportunity costs of intertemporal choice.

Saving (S) is defined as the money income (M) that is not spent on consumption (C). Equation 14-7 represents the relationship for a specific time period. Notice that saving is considered to be a residual, or what is left over after consumption.

(14-7) $S_t = M_t - C_t$

Although this is a straightforward relationship, there are several important principles to bear in mind. Saving is not the same as **investment**. The former arises from not spending, and the latter arises from putting money to a productive use. Viewed from a consumer perspective, the balance in a checking account at the end of a budget period is saving. Placing funds in a savings account, certificate of deposit, or money market fund is investing. Only if the entire money income is not spent can there be saving in period t. Thus, each consumer has an opportunity cost associated with saving. Postponing purchases from one year to another requires compensation for inflation, impatience, and risk. The rate of time preference can be thought of as the amount of compensation the consumer requires for these three factors.

Negative saving, which occurs whenever consumption exceeds money income is **borrowing**. Decisions about whether to borrow hinge on the timing of consumption. A decision to borrow is a decision to switch consumption from a period in the future to an earlier period. For example, borrowing to purchase a car can be thought of as a decision not to wait until enough money has been accumulated to pay cash; the consumer acquires the car sooner and commits future money income to repay the loan. The rate of time preference, then, also represents the price the consumer is willing to pay for having earlier access to market goods. This willingness to pay is due to the reduction in inflation, impatience, and risk stemming from the absence of waiting.

Just as the rate of time preference reflects the consumer's opportunity cost of time, the market rate of interest reflects the opportunity cost of time in the marketplace. When a loan is given to a consumer, the lender is transferring current control over market goods. Consequently, compensation for the effects of time must be provided. Acquiring money from savers provides the marketplace with current control over goods, for which investment institutions pay interest.

There are two ways of evaluating a decision to either borrow or save.[5] One method makes use of the present value approach. The other method involves a direct comparison of the two valuations of time. No matter which is chosen, the solution remains the same.

The present approach has already been illustrated with the $500, three-year investment option. First, one estimates the costs and returns each period for the duration of the investment. These estimates are an assessment of what the market is to provide. In the example at the end of the previous section, current cost was $500, and future returns were $150, $200, and $260. The consumer's rate of time preference was used to convert these market returns, expressed in dollars for the various time periods, into current dollars.

Conceptually, the present value process entails the identification of the anticipated market returns for the duration of the time period being considered. Then these anticipated market returns are valued at the consumer's rate of time preference. In the example, the future returns for three years indicated the terms at which the market would repay the $500. Discounting these returns at the consumer's rate of time preference gave the present value to the consumer of the option. Since there is no reason why the market rate of interest should equal the rate of time preference, the calculation leads to the present value of the returns, which usually is not equal to the present value of the costs.

Borrowing decisions can also be analyzed by the present value approach. The lending institution establishes the market terms for borrowing. These essentially depend on the amount borrowed, the rate of interest, the frequency of payment, and the length of time the borrower has to repay the loan. These factors determine the size of the installments. The decision to borrow can be viewed as involving a comparison the present value of the loan repayments, valued with the consumer's rate of time preference, to the gain due to an increase in current purchasing power.

Imagine that a family has found itself a little short of cash this period and is considering a loan of $700. The E-Z Loan Co. offers to let them repay a $700 loan in three annual installments of $350. If the family has a 15 percent rate of time preference, should the money be borrowed?[6] The present value of the payments, found via equation 14-6, is $799.13.[7] Since this time-adjusted cost to the family is greater than the current purchasing power (return) of $700, the family should not borrow.

The second way for a consumer to make a borrowing or investment decision is through the interest rate comparison method. Consider the option of saving-investing. A consumer's rate of time

---

5   In this introduction to the elements of consumer choice over time, it is assumed that there is only one prevailing market rate of interest that applies to both borrowing and investing. The illustrations abstract from the many interest rate formulas that exist. Rather than becoming sidetracked by the specifics of formula selection, the chapter focuses on the decision-making logic. This logic can be extended readily to closer approximations to the real world.

6   A conceptual discussion of the numerical value of a rate of time preference is presented in the following discussion

7    $(1/1.15)(\$350) + 1/1.15)^2 + (1/1.15)^3(\$350) = \$799.13$.

preference is that particular unit's valuation of time. As such, it represents the consumer's willingness to transfer consumption from the current period to a later period. The market rate of interest represents the compensation the consumer is able to receive in the marketplace. Just as outlined in the models of choice in Chapters 7 and 11, the consumer compares the willingness to trade to the market's ability to trade. If the rate of time preference is less (greater) than the market rate of interest, the consumer should (should not) invest. This is because the marketplace more (less) than compensates the consumer for postponing consumption. For example, if the consumer's rate of time preference is 15 percent and the market rate of interest is 18 percent, the consumer is more than compensated for not consuming by 3 percent.

The same reasoning applies to the decision to borrow. A rate of time preference depicts the consumer's willingness to move future consumption to today. With respect to borrowing, this is the discount the consumer is willing to pay. The market rate of interest represents the discount charged by the market for the ability to switch. If the rate of time preference is less (greater) than the market rate of interest, the consumer should not (should) borrow. This is because the discount the consumer is willing to pay is less (greater) than the discount the market is charging. For example, if the consumer's rate of time preference is 15 percent and the market rate of interest is 18 percent, the market is charging 3 percent more than the consumer is willing to pay for borrowing.

There is no difference between the conclusions drawn by the present value approach and the interest rate comparison method, since both procedures reduce to comparisons of the willingness to trade to the ability to trade. One converts values through time on the basis of the market's valuation and the consumer's valuation, and the other compares the values of time directly. Which procedure should be used in a particular situation depends on how the information about the choices is provided. Some problems, such as the $500 investment and the $700 loan, are amenable to the present value methodology, and others, such as considering the interest rate on savings accounts, are suitable to direct interest rate comparisons. Exercises at the end of this section give illustrations of both.

Now that the intertemporal decision-making framework has been outlined, the issue of assigning a numerical value to a consumer's rate of time preference can be addressed. The illustrations above have used numerical values, but can a consumer indicate a specific rate of interest as a rate of time preference? In reality, the consumer does not have to be capable of saying what the rate of time preference is. For example, would you invest regularly in a savings account that paid 4 percent? Would you do so if the rate of interest was 30 percent? Most answer "no" to the first question and "yes" to the second. In order to answer the questions all, you must compare your rate of time preference to those of the questions. Although you may not be able to state your rate of time preference, you act as though you could. As long as this is the case, the decision-making process outlined above is appropriate. This holds for present value calculations as well. For example, given the option of taking out a loan for a TV, a consumer will consider the terms of the loan dictating the size of the monthly payment. A consumer will discount these future payments to determine if it is appropriate to acquire the TV today.

STUDY QUESTIONS

Two Valuations of Time

9. Explain why a family's decision to invest involves inflation, impatience, and risk.
10. Why is opportunity cost involved in the decision to invest in a money market fund?
11. Why is a consumer more likely to decide to place savings in a money market fund than in a savings account?
12. A family is considering loaning $2,000 to a small business. The proprietor agrees to pay $300 in interest the first year and to pay $2,400 at the end of the second year. If the family's rate of time preference is 20 percent, should the family make the investment?
13. A consumer has the option of buying $1,000 of stock in Advanced Consumer Electronics. In two years, when the money will be needed, the consumer expects to be able to sell the stock for $1,150. Dividends are expected to be $150 per year.
    a. Suppose the rate of time preference is 20 percent. Should the stock be purchased?
    b. If the average annual rate of return for this opportunity were 22 percent, should the stock be purchased?
14. Credit card companies typically charge 18 percent as the annual rate of interest. Given this market rate of interest, are you willing to have an outstanding balance (i.e., borrow)?
15. Some people are concerned that consumers are not saving enough money for retirements. One response has been the introduction of optional supplemental retirement plans. The basic idea is to transfer a portion of a person's salary into special investment accounts. The money is not taxed when it is earned, but rather, is taxed when it is withdrawn during retirement. Use the framework developed in this chapter to explain why consumers would take advantage of the plans. Should all consumers participate?

● Summary ●

Expansion of the analysis of consumer choice to intertemporal decision making requires incorporation of the effects of time. Because of inflation, impatience, and risk, values separated by time must be transformed into a common time period before a meaningful comparison can occur. Compounding and discounting are two ways of shifting values through time. Decisions about borrowing and investing concern the timing of consumption. There are two ways of describing a consumer's decision to borrow and save: the present value of the costs versus the returns and the rate of time preference versus the market rate of interest.

● Key Terms ●

Borrowing: moving control over resources (especially money) to an earlier period.

Compounding: the means by which interest earns interest in subsequent periods.

Discount factor: the amount by which a future value must be reduced when transferred to an earlier period.

Discounted value: current-period equivalent of a future value.

Discounting: transferring values to an earlier time period.

Impatience: preference for having goods today to satisfy utility as opposed to waiting.

Inflation: the rate of increase in prices over time.

Intertemporal choice: decision making involving more than one time period.

Intratemporal choice: decision making restricted to within-period choices.

Investment: the productive use of money.

Market rate of interest: the market's valuation of time.

Planning horizon: time period for which a consumer makes plans about consumption and resource allocation.

Present value: sum of related costs and benefits that have been converted into the current period.

Rate of time preference: a consumer's valuation of time.

Risk: uncertainty associated with future events.

Saving: the difference between money income and expenditures.

Chapter 15

The Demand for Durables and Credit

Durables by their very nature are goods that provide service flows over extended periods of time. This property precludes their explicit inclusion in intratemporal choice models. Notice the reason applies to the three types of demand models: traditional, characteristic, and household production. The durable nature of these goods requires accommodation of a planning horizon in terms of utility generated and resources allocated. Consumers have the option of postponing purchases and continuing to use their existing stocks of durables. Consequently, durable expenditures tend to be more volatile than other categories of consumer expenditure.

Consumer credit is closely associated with consumer durable expenditures. Because of their long service lives and relatively high prices, durables are often purchased with the aid of credit. As a result, an overview of durables must also cover the availability of credit and its effect on the consumer's intertemporal process. More recently, consumers have been using credit cards to purchase a wide variety of goods and services. In addition, repayments in subsequent periods leave less discretionary income to buy goods and services.

This chapter begins with a time-series sketch of consumer durable expenditures and credit use. The objective is to establish the recent history of the relationships among durables, income, and credit. Then attention turns to approaches for incorporating the special features of durables and installment credit into an economic analysis of consumer behavior. The last section presents a consumer-oriented view of the use of credit.

● Durables and Credit Over Time ●

Consumer durable expenditures have risen dramatically during recent decades. This was noted in Chapter 1, in which annual data were presented for 1959-1993. Figure 1-1 and Appendix Table 1-1 showed that current dollar expenditures increased because of economic growth and inflation. Figure 1-2 and Appendix Table 1-1 showed that real consumption expenditures, adjusted for inflation, have risen. This is not surprising, because real disposable income has also increased.

Disaggregating consumption into three major components provides an indication of its changing composition. This was done in Figure 1-4 and Appendix Table 1-1. Relative to real consumption, both real durable and real service consumption rose over the 1959-1993 period, while real nondurable consumption as a percent of total consumption fell.

Part of the explanation for these long-run changes was provided in Chapters 6 and 10. Durables and services have been readily accepted by consumers. They have changed the technology of household production, changed real income, and helped to change the opportunity cost of married women remaining exclusively in household production activities.

Another important characteristic of durables is found in the annual real consumption expenditure data in the Appendix to Chapter 1. Real durable expenditure is much more volatile than nondurables or services. There are ten years for which real durable expenditures were below the previous year's level, whereas this occurred three times for real nondurables and never occurred for real services.

Table 15-1 provides data for subcategories of durable expenditures measured in current dollars for selected years between 1950 and 1993.[1] The data enable one to get a feel for recent consumption patterns of the major components of consumer durables. Column 2 displays personal consumption expenditure, and the third column shows durables. All the expenditures have increased over time. Most of durable expenditures is divided between automobiles and household equipment. The last three columns are the shares of the components of durables. Column 7 is the ratio of durables to consumption, which has fallen slightly over the period. Until recently, other durable expenditures were less than half other two. Automobiles' ratio has fallen slightly, household equipment's share has declined by a larger amount, and other durables' proportion has risen. Another way to see what has occurred is to compare compound annual rates of growth for each series. These are found in the bottom row of the table. Durables, automobiles, and household equipment had lower rates of growth than personal consumption, which is consistent with their falling shares, whereas other durables is the largest.

Table 15-1: Consumer Durable Expenditure By Category, 1950-1993 (billions of dollars).

(1) Year	(2) C	(3) D	(4) A	(5) HE	(6) O	(7) D/C	(8) A/D	(9) HE/D	(10) O/D
1950	192.1	30.8	13.7	13.7	3.3	0.16	0.44	0.44	0.11
1955	257.9	38.9	17.8	16.4	4.6	0.15	0.46	0.42	0.12
1960	332.4	43.5	19.7	18.0	5.8	0.13	0.45	0.41	0.13
1965	444.6	63.5	29.9	25.1	8.4	0.14	0.47	0.40	0.13
1970	646.5	85.7	35.9	65.7	14.1	0.13	0.42	0.77	0.16
1975	1024.9	135.4	55.8	54.5	25.0	0.13	0.41	0.40	0.18
1980	1748.1	219.3	90.3	86.2	42.8	0.13	0.41	0.39	0.20
1985	2667.4	368.7	177.6	128.7	62.4	0.14	0.48	0.35	0.17
1990	3742.6	488.2	202.9	174.2	91.0	0.13	0.42	0.36	0.19
1993	4378.2	538.0	228.0	208.9	101.1	0.12	0.42	0.39	0.19
r	7.5	6.9	6.7	6.5	8.3				

C = personal consumption expenditure, D = consumer durable expenditure, A = automobile expenditure, HE = household equipment expenditure, O = other durable expenditure, r = compound annual rate of growth for 1950 to 1993.

Source: U.S. Bureau of the Census, *Survey of Current Business*, Selected Issues.

---

[1]   A reason for using current dollars is our interest in actual purchases by consumers and their effects on budget constraints.

Consumer credit extends one's current ability to buy at the expense of future purchasing power while the repayments are made. That is, people have the option of switching consumption from a future period, after sufficient money has been accumulated to pay cash, to an earlier period. Most consumer credit is in the form of **installment credit**—money borrowed by consumers and repaid in two or more installments.[2] Such credit is ideal for the purchase of durables, although the use of revolving credit (especially credit cards) has increased dramatically in recent years.

Table 15-2 presents data on installment credit. A key measure of the use of credit is the amount of this type of debt outstanding. **Credit outstanding** is the sum of the balances in the installment credit accounts receivable of lending agencies. The sum represents the amount that remains to be repaid of purchasing power switched by consumers to an earlier period. Total outstandings have grown tremendously since 1945, and the same is true for automobile credit outstanding. Consistent data for revolving credit are shown starting with 1975, and they reveal rapid expansion of the use of credit cards.

Table 15-2: Consumer Installment Credit, Total, Automobile, and Revolving, 1930-1993, Selected Years.

Year	Total	Automobile	Revolving
1930	3.0	1.0	NA
1935	2.8	1.0	NA
1940	5.5	2.1	NA
1945	2.5	0.5	NA
1950	14.7	6.1	NA
1955	28.9	13.5	NA
1960	43.0	17.7	NA
1965	70.9	28.6	NA
1970	102.1	35.5	NA
1975	180.4	55.9	9.5
1980	305.9	116.8	58.4
1985	535.1	208.1	122.0
1990	735.3	290.8	197.1
1993	795.6	281.5	288.0

NA = not available.

Source: U.S. Board of Governors of the Federal Reserve System, *Federal Reserve Bulletin*, selected issues.

---

[2]   This is distinct from revolving credit, which only requires that part of a bill, the minimum payment, be paid each period. The remaining balance is subject to a monthly finance charge. Revolving credit, then, is a type of installment credit.

Debt outstanding from 1945 through 1993 is displayed in Figure 15-1, where the left-hand vertical scale is the reference for this series. Notice how rapidly outstandings grew following the end of World War II. The late 1970s was another period of rapid growth. A decline occurred in the late 1980s, but by 1993 outstandings had started to rise again. Outstandings divided by disposable income is a measure of the effect of installment credit on consumers' budgets, and it is measured on the right-hand vertical scale. This ratio grew very slowly at first, suggesting that consumers' incomes were growing almost as rapidly as their outstandings. However, the ratio began to rise faster in the 1970s and has continued through the 1980s.

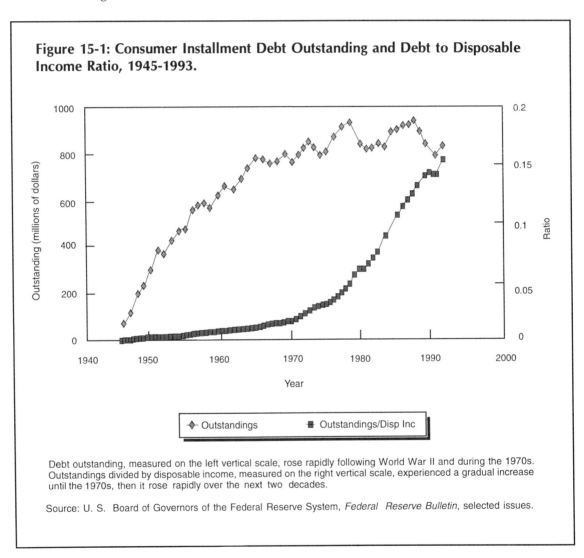

Figure 15-1: Consumer Installment Debt Outstanding and Debt to Disposable Income Ratio, 1945-1993.

Debt outstanding, measured on the left vertical scale, rose rapidly following World War II and during the 1970s. Outstandings divided by disposable income, measured on the right vertical scale, experienced a gradual increase until the 1970s, then it rose rapidly over the next two decades.

Source: U. S. Board of Governors of the Federal Reserve System, *Federal Reserve Bulletin*, selected issues.

Recent trends in the composition of consumer installment credit are presented in Figure 15-2. While credit outstanding has been rising steadily through the 1970s, the 1980s experienced an even faster rise as evidenced by the steeper total line. Since 1975 revolving credit has grown more rapidly than automobile credit outstanding, and by 1993 they were approximately equal. The figure also reveals that the level of automobile credit outstanding has declined slightly since 1990, whereas revolving credit has continued to rise.[3]

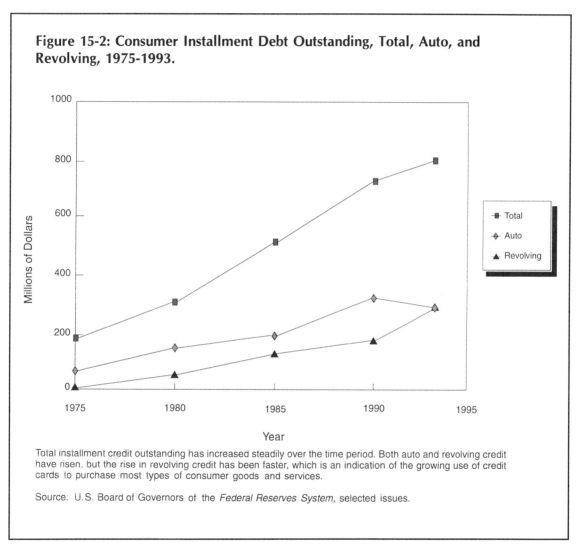

Figure 15-2: Consumer Installment Debt Outstanding, Total, Auto, and Revolving, 1975-1993.

Total installment credit outstanding has increased steadily over the time period. Both auto and revolving credit have risen, but the rise in revolving credit has been faster, which is an indication of the growing use of credit cards to purchase most types of consumer goods and services.

Source: U.S. Board of Governors of the *Federal Reserves System*, selected issues.

Table 15-3 presents the average interest rates for selected types of installment credit. These rates reflect the interactions of borrowers and lenders with respect to their valuations of time, as discussed in Chapter 14. Lower rates for new automobiles versus used and automobiles versus revolving credit are due to the nature of the types of goods purchased. Durables (especially newer automobiles) have

---

[3]   The decline is due in large part to the increased use of leasing arrangements, which are discussed later in this chapter.

relatively high purchase prices and produce service flows over extended periods of time. Long service lives permit durables to become the collateral against default. The trade-in values of previously purchased durables often can be used to make downpayments, and balances due can be covered by loans. Therefore, the risk associated with new automobile lending is lower than for other types of credit. Revolving credit often has little collateral, hence higher risk.

STUDY QUESTIONS

Durables and Credit Over Time

1. Many people argue that the United States is becoming a more consumer-oriented society. How do the data support this position?
2. Why are durables suitable for purchase with the aid of credit?
3. How can the derived demand models be used to explain the growth in the demand for durables?

Table 15-3: Installment Credit Financing Data, 1980-1993.

INTEREST RATES

| | Commercial Bank | | | Auto Finance Co | | AUTOMOBILES | | | |
| | Auto 48 | Personal 24 | Revolving | | | Loan Maturity Average Months | | Amount Financed | |
Year	Month	Month	Month	New	Used	New	Used	New	Used
1980	14.30	15.47	17.31	14.82	19.10	45.00	34.80	$6,322	$3,810
1981	16.54	18.09	17.78	16.17	20.00	45.40	35.80	$7,339	$4,343
1982	16.82	18.64	18.51	16.15	20.75	45.90	37.00	$8,178	$4,746
1983	13.92	16.50	18.78	12.56	18.74	45.90	37.90	$8,787	$5,033
1984	13.71	16.47	18.77	14.62	17.85	48.30	39.70	$9,333	$5,691
1985	12.91	15.94	18.69	11.98	17.59	51.50	41.40	$9,915	$6,089
1986	11.33	14.82	18.26	9.44	15.95	50.00	42.60	$10,665	$6,555
1987	10.45	14.22	17.92	10.73	14.60	53.50	45.20	$11,203	$7,420
1988	10.85	14.68	17.78	12.60	15.11	56.20	46.70	$11,663	$7,824
1989	12.07	15.44	18.02	12.62	16.18	54.20	46.60	$12,001	$7,954
1990	11.78	15.46	18.17	12.34	15.99	54.60	46.10	$12,071	$8,289
1991	11.41	15.18	18.23	12.41	15.60	55.10	47.20	$12,494	$8,884
1992	9.29	14.04	17.78	9.93	13.80	54.00	47.90	$13,584	$9,119
1993	8.09	13.47	16.83	9.48	12.79	54.50	48.80	$14,332	$9,875

Source: U.S. Board of Governors of the Federal Reserve System, *Federal Reserve Bulletin, selected issues.*

● Durables and Consumer Choice ●

Why are durable expenditures more volatile than other categories of consumer expenditure? The answer, of course, is that consumers have the flexibility to "make do" with existing stocks, instead of making additional purchases. This flexibility makes durable expenditures both difficult and interesting to analyze.

Consumers purchase durables in order to derive the concomitant service flows, because the latter generate utility (directly in the traditional demand models or indirectly in the derived demand models). In order to maintain utility in the current period, consumers need to maintain the service flows of durables. But this does not require continued purchases of durables on the part of individual households, because these goods provide the flows over extended periods of time. The consumer can postpone buying durables and continue to use goods purchased previously.

A crucial feature of durables is that consumer demand for them can be separated into two components. One is **replacement demand**. Consumers purchase durables, in part, to replace worn out or obsolete goods. For example, personal computers wear out through use and become obsolete as new and improved components become available. When a personal computer needs to be repaired, an important consideration is whether the unit is worth fixing. If it has been used to such an extent that many components need to be replaced, it may be cheaper in the long run to buy a new machine. Personal computers also become obsolete. A machine with a 286 processor may be working just fine, but new software and operating systems cannot be installed. These personal computers are obsolete and must be replaced in order to take advantage of recent developments.

The second demand component is called **new demand**. A consumer may decide to purchase another durable for any of the reasons outlined in the models of consumer choice. They include preferences, income, and prices. For example, parents could decide that their children should have personal computers to enhance educational opportunities, or use of a computerized accounting package would facilitate household financial planning.

These two components of the demand for durables can be included in a model of consumer choice by modifying the utility function, budget constraint, and (in the case of derived demand) consumption or production technologies to accommodate the intertemporal features of durables. In this text these modifications will be outlined with the aid of causal relationships without delving into the mathematical procedures. The objective here is to just point out the areas in which the models change.

Durables provide service flows. Assume the service flows are related to the quantities available. For example, the cooling capacity an air conditioner provides is a function of the size of the unit. Since durables provide service flows over more than one period, the utility function (and consumption or production technology) must reflect the flows in the current and subsequent periods for the expected lives of the durables. More precisely, current and expected future flows of durables and nondurables must be incorporated.

The budget constraint also needs to be modified to accommodate the intertemporal nature of durables and the use of credit. Money income in a budget period does not have to equal the sum of expenditures. Whenever credit is used to buy a durable, there is a period in which expenditures exceed income, followed by a stream of repayments. An intertemporal budget constraint allows for borrowing and saving within each budget period, but over the planning horizon total income must equal expenditures. The constraint reflects borrowing in one period and the repayments of a loan in other periods. The amount of the repayments depends on the amount borrowed, the length of the repayment period, and the finance charges.[4]

Consumer choice in an intertemporal setting continues to be a matter of utility maximization subject to constraints. The modifications entail defining utility, income, expenditures, and other constraints if the derived demand framework is used, for the planning horizon. Conditions for optimal consumption during the plan are extensions of the criteria identified in Chapters 7-10. A consumer compares the willingness to trade to the ability to trade. Intratemporal decision making involves equating the values of the last dollar spent for goods within that period. Intertemporal choice focuses on the willingness to switch consumption versus the ability to switch, as outlined in Chapter 14. In either setting, the essence of the problem is a comparison of the marginal utilities of the choices and their opportunity costs.

STUDY QUESTIONS

Durables and Consumer Choice

4.   Identify the ways in which durables necessitate changes in the one period models of consumer choice.
5.   Use a rotary (pulse) versus touch-tone telephone as an example to differentiate between the obsolescence and the wearing out of a durable.
6.   Distinguish between replacement demand and new demand for a durable.

● The Growing Use of Credit ●

Data provided in the first section, coupled with the economic perspective of intertemporal choice outlined in the second section, lead to the conclusion that consumers today are more inclined to use credit to purchase not only durables, but a wide variety of goods and services. Consumer preferences have become more disposed toward borrowing, social attitudes have changed, and credit cards have attained widespread acceptance and use. Applying for and receiving credit has become easier, and banks often provide overdraft protection up to specified limits. New and better durables continue to emerge. The length of time to repay loans has been increasing, which helps to keep monthly payments low, so they can be more readily incorporated into budgets. Increasing the repayment period also decreases the present value of the repayments because they are discounted over a longer period of time.

Are consumers overextending themselves with installment debt? Many analysts were concerned about this issue following World War II, and some have become concerned recently.[5] A study by

---

[4]   The appendix to this chapter contains a more explicit discussion of these credit terms.
[5]   For an overview of such studies see: D. Eastwood and C. Sencindiver "A Re-Examination of Consumer Credit Growth," *Proceedings of the 31st Annual Conference of the American Council on Consumer Interests*, 31(1985):169-74.

Enthoven provides a very interesting perspective on the situation.[6] Instead of focusing on the growth of credit per person, he considered a life-cycle approach. The financial situation confronting a consumer unit depends on its stage in the life cycle. Those consumers who are most inclined to borrow are in the early stages of the life cycle. Although these people borrow more, the debt is repaid subsequently, and the family begins to save.

The decision-making can be depicted quite easily in terms of the material presented in the previous chapter. A consumer's rate of time preference is considered to vary with the stage of the life cycle. That is, a consumer's valuation of inflation, impatience, and risk changes as the consumer ages. Valuation of consumption today versus consumption tomorrow is likely to be quite different for a young adult versus a retiree. As consumers enter the life-cycle stage in which rates of time preference tend to be high, they are more likely to borrow, as their valuations of consumption today tend to exceed their valuations of the repayments.

An implication of this perspective is that although outstanding debt may rise, it can be attributed to a specific segment of the population—not to all consumers. Enthoven formulated a mathematical model to simulate the long-run debt to income ratio in such an environment. Assuming that some families are always entering the borrowing stage while others are progressing toward paying off debt, he derived a limiting debt to income ratio of just over 18 percent. In other words, he concluded that total outstanding installment debt relative to disposable income would not exceed the 18 percent limit in the long run. This suggests that consumers would not continuously borrow, and that as a group consumers use debt responsibly.

Enthoven's result is displayed in Figure 15-3. The vertical scale is the ratio of outstandings to disposable income, or the debt to income ratio. Time is measured on the horizontal scale. His model has the debt to income ratio rising over time, but the curve approaches a horizontal line as it gets closer to the long-run ceiling. The starting point of the curve is a period, such as the end of World War II, when outstanding debt was extremely low. Debt rose rapidly following the war, but Enthoven's conclusion was that it would level off in the long run. Evans and Kisselgoff apply Enthoven's model to a more recent period.[7] Their conclusion was that consumers as a group were continuing on a long-run path toward a limiting debt to income ratio.

Notice the outstandings to disposable income ratio displayed in Figure 15-1 seems to be approximated by the D/M curve in Figure 15-3. The post-World War II baby boom cohort may have caused a temporary resurgence in credit growth during the 1970s and 1980s, noted above. This segment of the population entered the stage of the life cycle in which borrowing is more frequent. If the Enthoven model is correct, the resurgence should be temporary, and as this age cohort matures, the aggregate debt to income ratio should fall.

---

[6]   A. Enthoven, "The Growth of Consumer Credit and the Future of Prosperity," *American Economic Review*, 47(1957):913-29.

[7]   M. K Evans and A. Kisselgoff, "Demand for Consumer Installment Credit and Its Effects on Consumption," *The Brookings Model: Some Further Results* (Chicago: Rand McNally, 1968).

STUDY QUESTIONS

The Growing Use of Credit

7. Why are lower income and younger households more likely to use credit?
8. During the late 1970s and early 1980s, inflation was cited as a reason for consumers' "buy now" strategy. Explain why expected inflation can be an incentive to use credit and buy now.
9. What impact is the post-World War II baby boom likely to have on credit use in the next few years?
10. Identify the economic logic for using credit as a utility maximizing option.

Figure 15-3: A Limiting Debt to Income Ratio

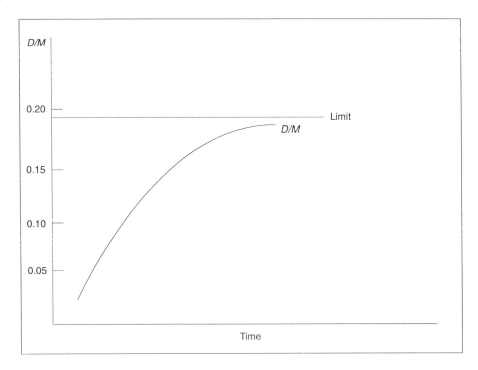

In Enthoven's lifecycle approach to the growth of credit, the ratio of debt to income is portrayed as the curve D/M. The limiting debt to income ratio is a horizontal line. Over time, D/M may approach this limit, but the closer it gets, the flatter the curve becomes.

● Guidelines for Borrowing ●

Borrowing money to acquire capital is considered to be sound practice on the part of business. Since most forms of capital have high purchase prices and long service lives, it is reasonable for a business to repay loans using the returns generated by the new capital. The circular flow diagram in Chapter 2 indicated that consumers, like producers, have dual roles to play, so the same logic should apply to households. Durables are capital. They have long service lives and relatively high purchase prices. Given this perspective, there is economic justification for borrowing to acquire durables. Of course, there are caveats, and these are noted in the following discussion.

A typical consumer unit experiences significant economic change between the time it is created and its termination. Its earned income generally starts off at a low level because of low entry wages in an occupation. Experience, on-the-job training, and additional formal education lead to advancement and increased earned income. Retirement is associated with a decline in earned income. Consumer needs also change over time. Initially, durables are acquired in order to manage the dwelling unit, prepare meals, and have transportation. The cost of children also varies with their ages. When they are very young, they tend to be expensive. Then children become relatively less expensive until they reach their teens. Once children reach their teens, they are very expensive and remain so until they split off to form new households.

There is no reason to expect that the income stream of a consumer unit will match its changing needs. Initially, a consumer unit may need to borrow to acquire furnishings and transportation. Members are likely to save in an attempt to make a down payment for the household's first owner-occupied dwelling unit. Households typically try to save in anticipation of expenses associated with older children and retirement. During the life cycle of the unit, durables also need to be replaced and new ones bought. Credit can be used to match utility more closely to life-cycle earnings over the planning horizon.

Responsible use of credit depends on the consumer's careful evaluation of the costs and returns. The key to the effective use of credit is the recognition that it affects the timing of consumption. In exchange for earlier consumption, future income is committed to repayments. Many consumers view such repayments as the equivalent of savings that they are unable to generate on their own. Lacking the discipline to save, these consumers see repayments as a viable alternative.

Credit costs are determined by three factors which comprise the terms at which the market lends to a consumer. The down payment percent is the percent of the purchase price that must be paid by the consumer when the good is acquired. Often, the down payment can be paid with the trade-in value of the durable being replaced, and in the case of new automobiles rebates can be put toward down payments. The amount borrowed is 1 minus down payment percent, multiplied by the purchase price of the good. The market rate of interest transforms the amount borrowed through time, and the length of the repayment period determines the length of time over which interest is to be compounded.

Studies of consumer credit have found that it is the size of the monthly payment that matters to consumers.[8] The size of the installments depends on the credit terms. Increasing the down payment reduces the amount that is borrowed; thus, the size of the installments is reduced. Raising the market rate of interest raises the size of the installments. Increasing the repayment period allows for more

---

[8]   D. Eastwood, "Consumer Credit and the Theory of Consumer Behavior," *Journal of Behavioral Economics*, 1(Summer, 1977):79-105.

time, so the total borrowing cost is increased. But because more payments are involved, the size of each installment is lowered. With respect to revolving credit, there is no limit to the repayment period. The ability to borrow is set by the rate of interest and the minimum payment that must be made each month. Minimum payments are based on the consumer's outstanding balance for the respective card.

Credit terms have the conceptual effect of determining the slope of the budget constraint. Many different formulas exist for the calculation of the actual size of an installment. All these formulas are consistent with the relationships just described.

As outlined in Chapter 14, there are two ways of describing the decision-making framework. One focuses on present value comparisons, and the other relates the rate of time preference to the market rate of interest. A consumer can evaluate the size of the installments or minimum payments due by using the rate of time preference to discount the payments stream and comparing the present value of the installments to the present value of the utility derived from using the good at an earlier point in time. If the present value of the utility flow exceeds the present value of the installments, credit should be used. The other way is for the consumer to compare his or her rate of time preference to the market rate of interest. If the consumer's rate of time preference is greater than the market rate of interest, the consumer should borrow.

Of course, in order for the consumer to be as well off as possible, the value of the last dollar spent must be known. This is implicit in the present value or interest rate comparisons. Accurate assessment of the marginal utility of a purchase and its consumer's price is essential. Only if it is worth the price should the consumer purchase a good or service, including durables, with or without the use of credit.

The properties of durables make such determinations very difficult. The fact that durables are purchased infrequently fosters the information problem introduced in Chapter 11. Most consumers are not very knowledgeable about durables. Technological changes alter the service flows of durables, so it is hard to assess the marginal utility of new models of existing goods, let alone new products. In addition, the infrequency of purchases makes it necessary to become reacquainted with local retail markets. In many instances replacing a durable is equivalent to becoming familiar with the product for the first time.

Most durables have properties of experience goods. A consumer can best determine the marginal utility of a product after it has been used. Then the usefulness of the good, its features, and the repair record can be evaluated. However, the high purchase price of durables precludes buying and trying several brands. Instead, consumers need to gather information prior to purchase. Advertisements can be of some value if they contain information about price and quality. But testimonials and other aspects of advertising directed toward experience properties should be considered with some skepticism. Product rating services can be extremely useful, as various features considered to be important by experts are compared across brands. Warranties also are important, as durables frequently need to be serviced while under warranty.

The information problems involved in the purchase of durables are complicated by the option of using credit. The cost of borrowing needs to be included whenever credit is an alternative to paying all of the market price. Significant variations in credit terms exist among lenders. (One indication of this is seen in Table 15-3, where the interest rates for various types of durables are shown). A new feature of revolving credit cards adds to the complexity. Lending institutions are offering incentives for using their cards which include credit toward purchases of automobiles, frequent flier miles, and annual cash rebates. These decrease the cost of using the cards, whether or not only the minimum payment is made, and make it harder to assess the benefits of switching consumption.

Leasing is becoming a popular alternative to purchasing or borrowing to buy some goods, especially automobiles. Basically, a **lease** grants the use of the named good for a specific period of time. Ownership is not transferred, and at the end of the lease, the consumer does not own the good. Usually there is no downpayment with a lease. Monthly payments are based on the price of the good minus its estimated value at the end of the lease. Lease payments typically are lower than loan payments because of the estimated resale value. Conditions for leasing require consumers to follow scheduled maintenance, and with respect to cars, there are mileage limits. Failure to meet the conditions may result in additional costs at the end of the lease period. Some leases (open ended) require a payment of the difference between the actual value at the end of the lease and the estimated value. Others (closed end) have no payments if the market value is less than the estimated value, although these leases typically have higher monthly payments than open ended leases. Consumers usually have the option of buying the good at the end of either type of lease.

While leasing is an alternative to paying cash or using installment credit, it can be very difficult to determine the consumer's price. Additional complications include the value of the initial price of the good and estimating the resale value. Furthermore, potential charges at the end of the lease may be large and therefore have serious financial impacts at that time.

What is an appropriate buying strategy in this environment? The consumer needs to recognize the disadvantaged position and work toward eliminating the problems. Learn about the product. Use buyer guides. Have a list of questions, and do not be afraid to ask sales personnel to answer them. Avoid using credit card incentives as part of the rationale for buying. Try to have the payments completed before the service flow ends.

Some budgeting is necessary as well, first determine what percent of the purchase price can be paid out of savings and the current budget and then determine how large a monthly installment and/or lease payment can be accommodated. The two basic components of any budget are fixed and variable expenses. **Fixed expenses** are those that do not vary from month to month. Rent, insurance, and mortgage payments fall under this heading. Also included are monthly installments on outstanding loans, lease payments, and minimum payments due on credit cards. **Variable expenses** are those that can change from month to month, such as food, utilities, and clothing costs. Use financial records whenever possible to determine realistic amounts. All the budget items are added together, and then the total is subtracted from disposable monthly income. The remainder is the available discretionary income, and some of it can be used to make credit and/or lease payments.

It is important to realize that the impact of any new loan is to change the budget by increasing fixed expenses. A rule of thumb used by many counselors is that less than 20 percent of take-home pay should be allocated to loan repayments. Borrowing is not a viable option if the budget constraint is too restrictive or tight. The purchase should be postponed until accumulated savings and/or a larger income make the purchase feasible. Another important consideration is that the acquisition of a durable can affect other budget items. For example, the purchase of a more fuel-efficient car can decrease transportation costs.

Once the consumer has determined how much can be allotted to monthly credit payments, it is possible to consider using credit. Remember that throughout the shopping stage, the ultimate objective is the generation of utility through the acquisition of goods and services. This means that the motivation for the purchase should not be solely the availability of credit. Credit cost is only one component of the consumer's price. The consumer should also evaluate the behavior of the seller/lender. Are these people more interested in the profit from loans than from the sale?

Other credit tips include the following. Watch out for balloon clauses in which the loan has small payments until the last one, which is so large that another loan be necessary. Charges at the expiration of a lease can be large and have impacts similar to balloon payments. Make sure you understand the delinquency charges. These include collection fees, storage costs, and fines. Lease conditions should be consistent with expected use of the good.[9] Be careful about adding new purchases to an existing loan, including homeowner equity loans. Often default means that all the purchases included in the loan are at risk and subject to default charges.

What can you do when confronted with very severe budget problems compounded by credit problems? The place to begin is with the original lender. Determine if it is possible to alter the terms of the loan. But a key point to bear in mind is that the only way to decrease the monthly payments, short of bankruptcy, is to extend the repayments. This lengthens the time involved, and increases in time increase the borrowing cost. The end result, then, is an increase in the consumer's price for the extended use of credit. Lengthening the repayment period has another adverse effect. It increases the likelihood that other durables may need to be replaced and/or emergencies will occur before the end of the repayment period, leading to additional problems.

Another possibility is a bill consolidation loan, through which the existing loans are repaid and a new loan is negotiated. Often, the monthly installments are lower because the repayment period has been lengthened. But the loan may be refinanced at a higher rate of interest, thereby increasing the borrowing cost, the consumer's price, and the risk.

State governments have responded to the disadvantaged position of consumers through the imposition of interest rate ceilings. These are statutory limits on the interest rates that can be charged on consumer loans. However, there are wide variations among states with respect to the actual ceilings and to the types of loans covered. The federal government has addressed the problem primarily through the Truth-in-Lending Act of 1968. It requires lenders to inform prospective borrowers of the annual percentage rate of interest (APR) and the dollar amount of the finance charges for a loan. These efforts are directed toward facilitating the consumer's assessment of the borrowing costs and, thereby, the consumer's price. The ultimate objective is an increase in utility due to a better assessment of the value of the last dollar spent.

STUDY QUESTIONS

Guidelines for Borrowing

11. Why is a consumer at a disadvantage when buying a durable, especially on credit?
12. Why is borrowing for a vacation less desirable than borrowing for a car?
13. Bills from most credit card companies prominently display the minimum payment. Why?
14. Is it a sign of poor money management to have an outstanding balance on a gasoline credit card?

---

[9]   For example, driving patterns should be within the mileage restriction.

● Summary ●

The relationship between consumer durable expenditure and consumer installment credit has been examined in this chapter. Both have grown dramatically. The demand for durables can be separated into replacement demand and new demand. Changes in the utility function and budget constraint must be made in order to accommodate the features of durables in the models of consumer choice. Consumers are usually at a disadvantage when buying durables, particularly when credit is involved. Consequently, consumers need to budget and plan carefully when buying on credit.

● Appendix: Consumer Credit and Consumer Expenditure ●

Evans and Kisselgoff analyzed the quarterly expenditures for new automobiles and parts, A, for the period 1948 to 1963.[10] The credit variable was the estimated size of the average monthly installment for automobile loans. It was calculated as follows. The percent of the purchase price that was financed was 1 minus the down-payment percent (D). This was multiplied by the average purchase price of automobiles (P_A) to yield the average amount borrowed. Further multiplication by 1 plus the finance charge (F) generated the cost of the loan. Dividing by the length of contract on outstanding loans (N) yielded the estimated average monthly installment (M). M was converted into constant dollars by dividing by the implicit price deflator for personal consumption expenditure (P_C). Equation 15A-1 displays the relationship.

(15A-1) $M = [P_A(1-D)(1+F)]/P_C N$

Other variables in the expenditure equation were income (Y), the unemployment rate (U), consumer price index for new cars (P_{NC}), the depreciated stock of automobiles at the end of the preceding period S_{-1}, and a dummy variable for early post-war shortages (D_m).

(15A-2) $A = 42.24 + .08Y - 91.40U - 27.63P_{NC} - .06S_{-1} - .22M - 3.81D_m$

Of concern here is the relationship between M and A. Notice that the coefficient is negative, leading to the inference that increases in the monthly installment decrease A. M increases whenever F increases, D decreases, and/or N decreases. As M increases, it becomes more expensive to borrow. Each $1 increase in the real monthly repayment causes a $.22 decrease in A.

Eastwood and Anderson studied quarterly consumer expenditures for new automobiles and parts for the period 1953 to 1970.[11] Their stock adjustment model did not contain a monthly payment variable because data were not available. Instead, an estimated maturity for new loans was used. The presentation and interpretation of the coefficients of this model are beyond the level of this text. What can be noted is that the coefficient of the length of contract was positive. The inference is that increases in the length of contract alone decrease the size of the installments. This induces consumers to increase their expenditures for new automobiles. The elasticity of contract length was estimated to be .40, or a 1 percent increase in the maturity leads to a .40 percent increase in A.

Kirby and Capps provide an interesting analysis of the relationship between consumer instalment debt and food expenditure.[12] They developed a two equation model in which the first equation

---

[10]   Evans and Kisselgoff, *op. cit.*

[11]   D. Eastwood and R. Anderson, "Consumer Credit and Consumer Demand for Automobiles," *Journal of Finance*, 31(1976):113-23.

[12]   R. Kirby and O. Capps, Jr., "Impact of Consumer Installment Debt on Food Expenditures" *Journal of Consumer Affairs*, 28,1(1994):81-95.

focused on the determinants of the ratio of consumer installment debt to personal disposable income and the second pertained to the effect of this debt ratio on food expenditures. The conceptual tie between the two equations is that the amount of debt, through the necessity of repayments, affects the money available for expenditures in subsequent periods. National data for January, 1980 through December, 1989 were used to estimate the equations.

With respect to the debt to income ratio, the more optimistic consumers were about the economy, the greater the ratio (i.e., consumers tended to increase their borrowing relative to disposable income). The elasticity of the interest rate for borrowing on the debt to income ratio was estimated to be negative and very inelastic (the interest rate has a small effect on the size of monthly payments). The unemployment rate was negatively related to the debt ratio as was the proportion of the population between 25 and 44. In the food consumption equation, the debt to income ratio had a small long-run effect on food expenditures. This led to their inference that higher debt to income ratios in the long run permitted higher levels of food purchases.

● Key Terms ●

Credit extended: new loans.

Credit outstanding: value of installment loans that remain to be repaid.

Fixed expenses: expenses that must be repaid on a regular basis.

Installment credit: loans that are to be repaid in two or more installments.

Lease: a contract which provides use of a good for a fixed period of time, and ownership is not transferred.

New demand: consumer demand for durables based on traditional demand variables.

Repayments: credit entries to the installment accounts receivable.

Revolving credit: credit that does not have a fixed maturity, so only minimum payments have to be made each period.

Replacement demand: consumer demand for durables based on their depreciation and obsolescence.

Variable expenses: expenses that can vary from period to period.

Chapter 16

Housing: Buy or Rent?

The percent of the average consumer's income spent on housing-related expenditures has been growing over time. This category has become the single largest component of the typical consumer's budget. For the period 1937 to 1939, the Bureau of Labor Statistics estimated that 33.7 percent of the average consumer's income was spent on housing; by the end of 1993, this figure had risen to 41.4.[1] Homeownership has also comprised the largest portion of consumers' assets. In 1984 it accounted for 41.3 percent of net worth, and this had risen to 43.0 percent by 1988.[2] Housing is a necessity, because everyone needs some form of shelter. But there is a broad spectrum of types of housing available across a very wide price range, so housing involves much more than just meeting basic needs.

This chapter focuses on key economic considerations associated with the choice of a dwelling unit. The initial section provides an overview of many factors involved in the decision making which include the advantages of homeownership and renting. Economic principles associated with the demand for housing are covered in the second section. These are related to the traditional model of consumer choice and to the intertemporal model. Information problems associated with housing are identified as well. Investment in housing is addressed in the final section. The view presented is that homeownership should be considered as an investment opportunity in addition to its role as a consumption activity.

● The Housing Choice ●

Most localities offer a wide range of housing options. The basic distinction is between renting and owning. Over time, consumers have shown an increased disposition toward homeownership, as reflected in Table 16-1. Less than one-half of all housing units in 1930 were owner-occupied. The decline in this percentage over the next ten years was due primarily to the Great Depression. Since 1940, there has been a steady increase in the percentage of owner-occupied housing units.

The housing decision involves more options than just buying or renting. Within these two categories, there are many variations. Rental units range from apartment complexes to single detached dwelling units, and the rents for each type vary considerably. Owner-occupied housing includes more than single detached houses, and wide price variations occur here also. Recently, even the distinction between rental and owner-occupied housing has become blurred by the emergence of condominiums and cooperatives.

A **condominium** is a type of property in which the consumer owns the individual dwelling unit, but there are common areas (e.g., outside walls, roof, and land) that are owned and operated collectively. Each owner is assessed fees to cover the expenses associated with the common areas. In a **cooperative**, each resident owns shares in a nonprofit corporation, but it is the cooperative itself that

---

[1]   U.S. Bureau of Labor Statistics, *The CHI Detailed Report*, selected issues.
[2]   U.S. Bureau of the Census, *Current Population Reports*, series P-70, No 22.

Table 16-1: Owner-Occupied versus Rental Housing, 1930-1993, Selected Years (percentage distribution).

Year	Owner-Occupied	Renter-Occupied
1930	47.8	52.2
1940	43.6	56.4
1950	55.0	45.0
1960	61.9	38.1
1970	62.9	37.1
1980	65.6	34.4
1990	64.0	36.0
1993	64.6	35.4

Source: U.S. Bureau of the Census, *Historical Statistics of the United States: Colonial Times to 1970*, Part 2 (GPO, 1975) and U.S. Bureau of the Census, *Current Housing Reports*, Series H-150, 1993 Annual Housing Survey (GPO, 1994).

owns the housing complex. Under this arrangement, the consumer leases the individual dwelling unit. Fees are collected to pay the expenses arising from operating the complex.

Consumer needs and desires for the various types of housing depend on the consumer's stage in the life cycle. Single persons and young couples typically reside in rental housing. Married couples with no children generally rent. Consumer units with children usually live in owner-occupied housing. These generalities are supported by the data in Table 16-2. Approximately 65 percent of all occupied housing units in 1993 were owner-occupied. Almost seventy percent of households with two or more persons had owner-occupied housing. When married-couple families are examined by the age of the head of the household, the percentage of owner-occupied housing increases with age. A major reason for this pattern of homeownership is the presence of children. The child-raising phase of the life cycle is associated with the transition from rental housing, usually an apartment or duplex, to single-family housing.

Choosing among the various housing alternatives requires a careful comparison of the advantages of owning a home and the advantages of renting. Some advantages are based on consumer preferences. Others are associated with the budget constraint. The general economic problem of comparing the willingness to trade to the ability to trade can be applied to housing. Identification of the optimal housing choice requires an accurate assessment of the value of the last dollar spent. For a given housing alternative, the numerator is the marginal utility of the housing option, and the denominator is the consumer's price. The remainder of this section identifies the major factors affecting the value of the last dollar spent for a housing choice.

Table 16-2: Owner-Occupied versus Rental Housing by Age of Head of Household, 1993.

| | Thousand of Units | | Percents | |
	Own	Rent	Own	Rent
All Households	61,252	33,742	64.5	35.5
Households with two or more persons	49,899	21,836	69.6	30.4
Married-couple families with two or more persons by age of head				
Under 25	355	942	27.4	72.6
25-29	1,969	1,866	51.3	48.7
30-34	4,099	1,869	68.7	31.3
35-44	10,215	2,502	80.3	19.7
45-64	15,224	1,918	88.8	11.2
65 and over	7,868	824	90.5	9.5

Source: U.S. Bureau of the Census, *Annual Housing Survey for the united States in 1993*, Current Housing Reports, Series H150/93 (1995).

There are several advantages to homeownership that primarily affect utility. A certain amount of status is attributed to being a homeowner. Part of the American dream, especially since the 1930s, has focused on having a single detached dwelling unit. Many federal programs have been created to help consumers reach this goal. Increased security is another factor often associated with homeownership. In an apartment setting, it can be difficult to know your neighbors, and there are likely to be many more strangers on the premises. Greater privacy is another positive feature. Personal freedom is enhanced through homeownership. Whenever a household wants to redecorate or remodel, there is no need to seek a landlord's approval. Consumers often feel that the single detached dwelling unit provides a better environment for children. There usually is more play area, and parents have more control over their own children's contact with others.

Homeownership also possesses some financial advantages. (These are discussed more completely in the next section.) The federal personal income tax system provides two tax advantages to homeowners. The first is the homeowner's ability to include property taxes as an itemized deduction. Renters are unable to do this even though part of their rents represent payments to cover the property taxes on the rental unit. It is the landlord who deducts such taxes. Over time, property taxes have increased dramatically, as local governments have been forced to rely more on this source of revenue.

In many localities, taxes on residential property have become so large that the deduction constitutes a significant financial consideration.

The second tax advantage is the consumer's ability to deduct interest payments on home mortgages. Almost all homeowners borrow money to pay part of the purchase price of the home. Because the dollar amounts of such loans have become quite large, the tax write-off of the interest payments is an important consideration. For example, the size of the average loan for average loan for the purchase of previously occupied, conventionally financed homes rose from $35,000 in 1965 to $79,746 in 1993.[3] These increases have resulted in higher interest expenses, which the homeowner can deduct from gross income, even though other interest payments (e.g., instalment credit) are not tax deductible.

Keeping pace with inflation is a concern with intertemporal decision making. Since 1978 homeownership has proven to be a very good way for consumers to protect themselves partially against inflation. Table 16-3 indicates why. Column 2 shows that the average price of new single-family housing has increased 236 percent over the 15 year period. Part of the increase is due to changes in the size and construction of new homes. The third column makes an adjustment for this by showing the change in the cost of building a standard house.

The **Consumer Price Index** (CPI) measures the change in the cost of a fixed market basket of goods that consumers purchase. It is one of the conventional measures of price changes. Column 4 shows the annual percentage changes in the CPI. A component of the CPI is the purchase price of owner-occupied housing, and column 5 displays the annual percentage changes in this series. Comparing these two columns shows that the price of owner-occupied housing has increased faster than the overall CPI in most years. Those consumers who have become homeowners during this period, in general, have seen the market value of their homes increase faster than inflation. Consequently, homeownership has been a hedge, or protection, against inflation. Furthermore, the federal tax system allows a homeowners to avoid paying a tax on the increased value when the house is sold if a more expensive house is purchased within a certain period of time. Individuals 55 or older also receive a special tax break through a one-time exclusion of up to $125,000 from the sale of a home (some other conditions are noted later in this chapter).

These financial considerations comprise the basis for viewing homeownership as an investment. In purchasing a dwelling unit, a consumer is doing more than purchasing a durable to acquire a service flow. Most consumers are aware of the direct increases in utility and the tax advantages stemming from homeownership, but they do not understand the investment perspective. This is developed in more detail in the last section of the chapter.

Rental housing does provide advantages over homeownership in terms of utility and consumer's price. First, maintenance is the responsibility of the landlord. Those households lacking the skills or inclination to do maintenance find renting advantageous. Another advantage is that the household does not have to tie up its own money in the down payment. There is an opportunity cost associated

---

3   U.S. Bureau of the Census, *Annual Housing Survey for the United States in 1993*, Current Housing Reports, Series H150/93(1995).

Table 16-3: Owner Occupied Housing Costs, 1978-1993.

(1)	(2)	(3)	(4)	(5)
			Annual	
	Average Price of New	Price Index of	Percentage Change[3]	
Year	Single Family Home[1]	Standard New Home[2]	CPI	CPIH
1978	62.5	58.8	7.6	10.2
1979	71.8	67.6	11.3	13.9
1980	76.4	74.6	13.5	17.6
1981	83.0	80.6	10.3	11.7
1982	83.9	82.6	6.2	7.1
1983	89.9	84.6	3.2	2.3
1984	97.6	88.3	4.3	4.9
1984	100.8	90.1	3.6	5.6
1986	111.9	94.4	1.9	5.5
1987	127.2	100.0	3.6	4.7
1988	138.3	103.6	4.1	4.8
1989	148.8	107.5	4.8	4.5
1990	149.8	109.1	5.4	5.4
1991	147.2	110.0	4.2	4.5
1992	144.1	112.1	3.0	3.3
1993	147.7	115.4	3.0	3.0

[1]Thousands of dollars.
[2]Calculated using 1987 = 100.
[3]Calculated using 1982-84 = 100.
CHI = consumer price index for all items; CPIH = consumer price index for shelter.

Source: U.S. Bureau of Labor Statistics, *Consumer Price Index, Detailed Report,* selected issues.

with the funds used by the consumer as a down payment. This money could have been spent or invested elsewhere. Rental housing enables a tenant to be much more mobile. A homeowner must sell one house and purchase another whenever a move is necessary. Not only are real estate fees involved, but it takes time to sell a house. Consequently, consumers who expect to move frequently often prefer rental housing. Another way housing prices can fall in a given geographic area is when a rise in unemployment forces people to move away, thereby increasing the supply of housing available, decreasing the demand for housing, and consequently, the price of housing.

Two other advantages of renting arise from the intertemporal nature of housing. Rental housing is less risky for the tenant. Homeowners face the risk of incurring unexpected maintenance expenditures. For example, should a leak develop in the roof, the homeowner must bear the cost of the repair. The tenant does not have to pay such unexpected expenses. The other risk borne by the homeowner is that of a loss in real estate value. Individual property values depend, in part, on the actions of other owners in the area. Should a neighbor's property become run down for example, all houses in the area are affected. To the extent that changes in neighborhoods can decrease rental property values, homeowners incur the risk of losing money. Renters, on the other hand, do not have any money invested and can relocate more easily.

STUDY QUESTIONS

The Housing Choice

1. Identify the ownership and rental aspects of condominiums.
2. What are the ownership and rental aspects of cooperatives?
3. Why are mobile households likely to prefer rental housing over condominiums and cooperatives?
4. Many companies with locations across the country find it necessary to relocate personnel. Why do many of these companies offer to buy the current homes of their employees when they are transferred?
5. Why are the tax advantages of homeownership considered to be a better break for the wealthy?
6. Identify the financial risks associated with homeownership.
7. Use a supply and demand diagram to trace out the sequence of events when there is a rise in unemployment in a housing market.

● Housing Demand ●

The demand for housing can be discussed in terms of the traditional model of consumer choice. Advantages of the various types of housing can be separated into effects on consumer preferences and effects on the income constraint. Changes in the stage of the life cycle affect the utility derived from rental and owner-occupied housing. As a household ages and grows, preferences change in favor of owner-occupied housing. Factors associated with this change are status, security, privacy, personal freedom, and a better environment for children.

Budget conditions for the household change over time as well. When a household is formed, expenses for the acquisition of durables other than a residence usually preclude making a down payment for an owner-occupied residence. The price of homeownership and the level of income restrict the housing choice to rental units. Through postponed consumption, the household can save enough money to make a down payment on a house. Once the budget constraint permits such a move, the utility maximizing housing option is usually ownership. This transition process is consistent with income data on households. Renters typically have lower incomes than homeowners. For example, the median income for renters in 1993 was $20,725 while for homeowners it was $37,244.[4]

The consumer's price of housing includes much more than just the rent or the **mortgage** (loan agreement between the homeowner and lender). Other costs are incurred when the service flow is

---

[4]   U.S. Bureau of the Census, *Annual Housing Survey for the United States in 1993*, Current Housing Reports, Series H150/93 (1995).

acquired. Utility bills must be included as part of the monthly housing expenses of homeowners—and renters, if costs are not part of the rent. Maintenance expenses are also part of the consumer's price for homeownership. Another important expense is transportation cost, which includes time and money. As the distance among the locations of where one lives, works, and shops increases, the cost of the residence rises. Insurance is another cost that must be considered as part of the consumer's price.

There are two other factors that are particularly relevant to the selection of a housing unit. The first is the perceived quality of the neighborhood. Proximity to traffic tends to decrease the price a consumer is able and willing to pay. Well-maintained neighborhoods are more desirable, as each individual unit receives external benefits. The other factor associated with residential property values is the school system. Households with school-aged children tend to be concerned with quality schools. Neighborhoods that send children to better schools typically have higher property values, because many households are willing and able to pay for the concomitant educational service.

Most consumer units choose owner-occupied over rental housing whenever possible. Usually, when a consumer is able to become a homeowner, it is with the aid of a mortgage. As soon as the income constraint permits such a move, consumers tend to switch the start of the consumption of the owner-occupied service flow to an earlier period through borrowing.

The economics of information framework, outlined in Chapter 11, can be applied to housing. Optimal purchases occur when the consumer is able to evaluate the value of the last dollar spent. As with any other expenditure, the household must be able to assess the marginal utility of the housing service flow and the consumer's price. To the extent that this cannot be done, there is market system failure and purchases are less than utility maximizing.

Price variation is a common feature of any local housing market. There are so many considerations that go into the determination of the consumer's price of a dwelling and into the marginal utility associated with a specific unit that a consumer initially needs to address information problems. Familiarity with a housing market is the best way of ensuring that the optimal choice is identified. At first, the acquisition of information should focus on the types of units available, their market prices, and their proximities to work and shopping. These are primarily search aspects of housing. The search should continue as long as one feels that the additional shopping around is worth the effort. The gain is the benefit of locating alternative dwelling units at different locations, and the cost stems from the opportunity cost of time and the travel cost stemming from the additional search.

Generally consumers can evaluate the marginal utility associated with housing. This is due, in part, to the necessity of housing—everyone needs some sort of shelter, and everyone has experience residing in a dwelling unit. Furthermore, social activities and travel place consumers in a variety of housing situations. Consumers' problems tend to relate to difficulties in assessing consumer's prices, which are discussed below, and the quality of the neighborhood, which can always change as a result of nearby development or road construction.

Most housing market system failure is associated with the consumer's price. The basic problem is to try to determine all of the costs related to the use of a particular dwelling unit. This problem is somewhat different for renters than for homeowners.

A **housing lease** sets the terms for the relationship between the landlord and the tenant. It is important to recognize that most leases are written from the landlord's perspective and are designed to protect the investment the landlord has made. Each lease should be read carefully, as considerable variations in terms can occur. Not only does the lease specify the rent, but it also identifies other components of the consumer's price. These include the terms under which the rent can be raised, the conditions for terminating a lease, and the payment of utilities, and the care of the building and grounds.

The consumer's price for owner-occupied housing is much more difficult to determine. A renter need not be concerned about the long-run value of the property, but homeowners must consider the quality of the structure. A poorly built house means the owner will incur higher than expected repair and maintenance costs. Furthermore, utility bills are affected by building quality.[5] These concerns also apply to tenants of condominiums and cooperatives because repairs and utilities are shared.

For most homeowners housing has properties of a credence good. Few consumers are in a position to supervise on a knowledgeable basis the construction of a residence. Once a house is built, the only way to determine how well it was constructed is to take it apart. Even then, an expert is needed to assess the structure. Credence good problems are addressed through building codes and the licensure of the building trades. Building codes are intended to ensure that the structure is built properly. Licensure is designed to protect the unknowing consumer from improper and unsafe work. Home buyers should be aware, though, that enforcement is difficult. Wide variations in quality prevail in most markets. Prior to searching for a house, a consumer should become familiar with easy-to-read booklets on how to assess a building. These are often provided by realtors and banks.

Given the high purchase price of houses, most consumers borrow to acquire the dwelling. Borrowing poses another information problem. There are many types of mortgages, and their terms vary by lender in addition to the percentage of the purchase price that is financed. The consumer should shop around among lenders to compare various types of loans having fixed and variable rates of interest and different maturities. A home is an extremely durable good, so the security for a loan is the property itself.

When credit is used to fiance the purchase of a dwelling unit, careful valuations must be made of the intertemporal gains and losses. With any mortgage arrangement, the homeowner pays a percentage of the purchase price as a down payment, borrows the rest, and repays the loan in monthly installments. Consequently, those consumers who want to become homeowners must go through a period of saving to afford the down payment. Households that save for this purpose have concluded that they will be adequately compensated for switching consumption to a later period through the receipt of the market rate of interest for their savings and the anticipated use of an owner-occupied dwelling. Once the down payment constraint has been surmounted, the consumer's problem is to find suitable housing for which the monthly mortgage payments, plus other components of the consumer's price, can be incorporated into the budget. The consumer must compare the present value of the stream of mortgage payments to the expected benefits of homeownership.

---

[5]   Renters also are subject to the utility bill concern, but to a smaller degree, because it is easier for tenants to move.

STUDY QUESTIONS

Housing Demand

8. Use an indifference curve diagram to show how a change in the stage of the life cycle is likely to change preferences for owner-occupied or rental housing.
9. Can you identify any neighborhood-community factors that affect property values?
10. Why is deciding whether to buy a home an intertemporal consumer choice problem?
11. Would you expect a family to engage in more search if members were considering homeownership as opposed to renting?
12. Identify the search good properties of owner-occupied and rental housing.

● Housing as an Investment ●

Up to this point, the analysis of housing has emphasized the consumption aspects. A closely related and important consideration is the financial advantage of investing in owner-occupied housing.

Four financial advantages of homeownership have been identified so far in this chapter. Two of them are the special treatments of property taxes and interest expenses in the federal personal income tax system. The third is the hedge against inflation provided by the general rise in the market value of housing over time. Fourth is the special tax treatment of the capital gains of homeownership. The difference between the price paid and the price at which the unit is sold (after making adjustment for physical improvements) is the capital gain, which is taxable. However, the federal tax laws permit owners over 55 years old to deduct up to $125,000 of gain if filing a joint return ($62,500 single), the dwelling unit had been owned and lived in by the person filing for at least three years, and this gain deduction had not been used since 1978. These four advantages of homeownership also accrue to owners of condominiums and cooperatives.

Another important investment aspect of owner-occupied housing stems from a process called leverage. With **leverage**, the homeowner's money is used as a basis to borrow additional funds. For example, suppose that in 1988 a family purchased a house with a market value of $75,000. After searching for the best credit terms, they paid 25 percent down and then borrowed the remaining 75 percent. The down payment was $18,750, and the amount borrowed was $56,250. After living in the house several years, the family had to move. The house was sold for $85,000, and the family was left with a net gain (i.e., after paying real estate fees and settlement costs) of $10,000. Now the family has $28,750 to use as a down payment for another house. If 25 percent is the down payment requirement, they can now purchase a house with a market price of $115,000 by borrowing $86,250. Each additional $1 of gain the family received through the appreciation of the house becomes the equivalent of $4 in the marketplace through borrowing (leverage).

The view of homeownership as an investment is based on the tax advantages and the increased value of housing over time. Consider the life cycle of the typical household. Given that the consumer unit would like to own a home that it cannot yet afford, what is the best way to attain the desired dwelling unit? The answer is to invest in lower priced housing. The family must save enough to be able to make a down payment for a first house. One way to acquire the down payment is to save part or all of the second income of the dual working or dual career family. The first house need not necessarily be adequate for family needs over the life cycle. The increase in market value of the first house and the ability to leverage the gain may enable the family to attain its desired housing in an efficient manner.

Support for this view is found in the research of Alberts and Kerr.[6] They estimated the rate of return for homeowners under various down payment percentages and income tax conditions for the 1970 to 1974 housing market in Utah. Estimated rates of return were compared to the estimated average return on a portfolio of common stock for the same period. Their conclusions were that homeownership was profitable and provided a better rate of return than the stock portfolio.

Two very important caveats need to be noted. One is that the process of leverage also works in reverse. If the price in the example fell, each $1 of the loss would be associated with a $4 loss in purchasing power. This means that consumers who invest in housing must be extremely careful to choose housing units that will appreciate in value. The other caveat is that in order for leverage to be utilized, the family must borrow more money. Consequently, the monthly mortgage and other housing costs rise. The best way for a family to accommodate larger payments is to have an increase in income. Such an expectation is not unreasonable for a family in the early stages of its life cycle.

STUDY QUESTIONS

Housing as an Investment

13. If the down payment percent is 20 percent, how much leverage does a down payment of $19,000 represent?
14. Is a decrease in the down payment percent good or bad for home buyers? Explain.
15. How has the emergence of the dual working and dual career family facilitated homeownership?

● Summary ●

Housing needs and desires change with the life cycle. Young and mobile households typically rent. Families with children usually are homeowners. There are advantages associated with each type of housing tenure. The demand for housing primarily depends on consumer preferences and income. Information problems specific to the housing market result from infrequency of purchase, unfamiliarity with local housing, and credence good characteristics. In addition, most potential home buyers confront consumer problems associated with borrowing. Homeownership can be viewed as a type of investment, given the tax advantages and the increased value of housing over time.

---

[6]   W. W. Alberts and H. S. Kerr, "The Rate of Return from Investing in Single Family Housing," *Land Economics*, 57(1981):230-42.

● Appendix: Housing Demand Applications ●

The characteristics approach to the study of consumer demand, outlined in Chapter 10, assumes that utility is derived from the characteristics that goods possess. This model leads to a typical demand equation in which the price a consumer is able and willing to pay is a function of the characteristics of that good. A study by King has applied this approach.[7] Housing demand was assumed to provide four characteristics: structural features, interior and exterior quality, interior size, and lot size. The study examined housing prices in the New Haven, Connecticut, metropolitan area for the period 1967 to 1970. Among the empirical results were estimated outlay elasticities for the four characteristics. These were 2.04 for structure, 1.72 for quality, 0.64 for space, and 0.54 for site. The fact the elasticities for structure and quality were greater than 1 indicates that expenditures for these features tend to be quite responsive to percentage changes in outlay. The fact that the elasticities for space and quality were less than 1 indicates that expenditures for these features rise more slowly in proportion to outlay.

Butler estimated hedonic demand equations for owner and rental housing.[8] Data for the St. Louis metropolitan area for 1967 were used. Among the estimated equations was the one reported below. Because the dependent variable is in log form while the independent variables are not, the exact interpretation of the coefficients is not straightforward. However, the signs of the coefficients do reflect the directions of the causal relationships. Increasing the number of rooms increased the rent. As the age of the structure increased, the rent decreased. Somewhat poor plumbing decreased the rent, as did the unsound plumbing.

$$logR = 4.38 + 0.14 \, RM - 0.01 \, A - 0.41 \, S - 0.17 \, U$$

where R = rent, RM = number of rooms, A = age of unit, S = somewhat poor plumbing, and U = unsound plumbing.

Cronin derived a utility maximizing model for housing search.[9] Although an examination of the specific results is beyond the focus of this text, it can be said that these results indicate that the amount of search depends on the cost of information. As lower cost sources of information are used, higher levels of search take place. This is consistent with the presentation in Chapter 11. A decrease in information cost, by itself, leads to an increase in the value of the last dollar spent on information. This encourages more search.

A study by Sheiner has examined the relationship between housing prices and the savings of renters who are in the early stages of their life cycles.[10] These consumer units were in the 25-34 age group and were part of a representative national sample of households in 1984. The study tested the hypothesis that if a renter wants to become a homeowner, then increases in housing prices should lead to increases in savings in order to meet the downpayment. Results led to the inference that house prices had a positive effect on the net wealth accumulated by renters in this life cycle stage.

---

[7]   A. T. King, "The Demand for Housing: A Lancastrian Approach," *Southern Economic Journal* 42(1976):1077-87.
[8]   R. V. Butler, "The Specification of Hedonic Indexes for Urban Housing," *Land Economics* 42(1976):96-108.
[9]   F. J. Cronin, "The Efficiency of Housing Search," *Southern Economic Journal* 48(1982):1016-30.
[10] L. Sheiner, "Housing Prices and the Savings of Renters," *Journal of Urban Economics* 38,(1995):94-125.

● Key Terms ●

Condominium: a property in which the dwelling unit is owned by the consumer but common areas are collectively owned.

Consumer price index: a price index based on a fixed market basket of goods and services purchased by consumers.

Cooperative: a housing complex in which residents own shares of the property.

Housing lease: an agreement that establishes the relationship between a renter and a landlord.

Leverage: use of one's own money as a basis for borrowing additional funds.

Mortgage: a credit agreement between a homeowner and a lender.

Chapter 17

Three Investment Decisions

There are three intertemporal decision-making situations that you are likely to confront as a consumer at one time or another over your life-cycle. They are going to college, buying insurance, and purchasing common stock. In fact, because you are reading this book you probably have already considered the first one. The situations may seem to be unrelated, but the intertemporal model can serve as a useful framework for analyzing each situation. Furthermore, the principles identified in this chapter can be used as the basis for understanding the economics associated with other investment decisions.

● A College Education ●

Does it pay to go to college? Are the time, effort, and other resources required to earn a bachelor's degree justified in terms of the anticipated benefits? The human capital perspective argues that one should attend college only if it is a profitable investment—if the present value of the return is greater than the present value of the cost. One way to consider the problem is to imagine a high school senior who is trying to decide whether to attend a four-year college. Decision making over time is involved, because the costs will be incurred during the next four years and the returns will be received over the rest of the individual's life. Since these costs and returns are separated by time, it is necessary to convert them into a common period. Assume, for simplicity, that the prospective college student does not have to borrow.

Direct costs to the student include tuition and educational materials. The largest cost to the student is the opportunity cost of foregone earnings. Instead of going to college, the prospective student could go to work right away. If a college student has part-time employment, this opportunity cost can be reduced, but then other trade-offs are involved, such as reduced course load, study time, and/or leisure time. Grades could be affected as well. These possibilities complicate the situation significantly, so the usual empirical procedure is to avoid them by considering only a full-time student without any marketplace employment.

Educational costs do not include expenditures attributed to normal living activities, such as room and board, clothing, travel, and entertainment. Even if the student lives at home, these costs arise, and in this case they are absorbed by the family. Because these costs occur whether or not the individual attended college, there is no basis for including them as college-related expenses.

In addition to direct costs, there are costs that are incurred by the public. Federal, state, and local governments all contribute to colleges. This is true not only of public institutions but also of private colleges, which receive public support through grants from all levels of government, as well as from corporations and nonprofit organizations. These funds help to reduce the tuition and fees any student must pay. Local governments, in particular, incur costs as a result of the provision of public services. For example, more police protection is required, streets must be repaired more frequently. Public costs of higher education are substantial. These costs would be incorporated into an overall economic analysis, as they reflect resources that are transferred to colleges. But when costs for the prospective student are analyzed, these public costs are not considered because they are borne by society, and the student's social cost is very small.

What are the benefits of going to college? One of the direct returns is the increased earning potential a typical college graduate has over a high school graduate. Table 17-1 provides data on median incomes for persons 25 year and older, by sex and years of education, for 1970, 1980, and 1990. The data indicate that as education increases, so does median income. This is true for all persons, male, and female; for full-time year round workers; and for those in the 25-34 age group. (Although the data for other age groups are not presented, earnings differentials are similar.)

Table 17-1: Median Incomes of Persons 25 and Older by Sex and Education, 1970, 1980, and 1990 (thousands of dollars).

| | High School | | | | College | | | | | |
| | 1-3 Years | | 4 Years | | 1-3 Years | | 4 Years | | Over 4 | |
	Male	Female	Male	Female	Male	Female	Male	Female	Male	Female
Total										
1970	7.3	2.4	8.8	3.4	9.9	3.7	12.1	5.4	13.4	7.9
1980	11.5	5.4	15.0	7.4	15.9	8.2	23.3	10.6	27.8	14.0
1990	15.1	7.0	21.8	10.7	27.2	14.7	37.9	20.4	42.5	27.0
Full-time year round										
1970	8.9	4.8	10.1	5.8	12.1	7.0	14.7	8.4	17.5	9.7
1980	15.5	9.4	18.3	11.0	20.5	12.6	26.4	14.9	31.2	18.0
1990	20.9	14.4	26.5	18.3	31.6	22.2	39.1	28.0	49.1	33.8
Full-time year round, 25-34 years of age										
1970	8.0	4.5	9.0	5.7	10.4	6.4	12.0	7.9	13.9	8.6
1980	14.0	9.2	17.4	11.3	18.4	13.0	21.0	14.7	23.5	17.0
1990	14.0	6.9	20.1	11.8	23.0	15.7	29.1	22.0	30.5	25.7

Source: U.S. Bureau of the Census, *Current Population Reports*, Series P60, selected issues.

Another important direct return from a college education is social development. College social life, which in intertwined with the formal education, fosters a change in the individual. Perhaps the best way to recognize this is to recall the first time you saw your high school friends again after you entered college. Interests often change to such an extent that it is difficult to interact in the same way with old friends.

A college graduate also receives direct returns from the social status and personal confidence derived from the achievement. Society, in general, values education, and a college graduate is accorded some status which is not given to a high school graduate. The college diploma also is an indication that the individual has been able to complete a rather formidable task successfully, and there is a great deal of personal satisfaction associated with the accomplishment.

Society also benefits when people go to college. Better educated people tend to be more concerned citizens and more informed voters. Another benefit is that to the extent college graduates are more productive in the marketplace, production costs are reduced. An additional public return is the increased cultural activities made available because of the presence of the college community.

While the public returns are important for society, they do not accrue directly to the prospective student. Consequently, the public returns are not considered by the individual when deciding whether to go to college. Only the direct returns that have a bearing on the individual are germane to that person's evaluation of the profitability.

Estimates of whether it pays to go to college have been based on the human capital perspective of the high school senior. This means that only the direct costs and returns are considered. Table 17-1 provides a convenient starting point for outlining how these costs can be estimated. The opportunity cost of not working while in college can be approximated by the median salary of a person having a high school diploma. Tuition costs, as well as estimates of fees and expenses, can be acquired from specific institutions, or average costs provided by college associations can be used to estimate the four-year cost. Earnings differentials by age, sex, and educational attainment can be used to project the lifetime earnings differential of a typical college graduate over a high school graduate.

Several caveats need to be noted. One is that the observed earnings differential can reflect more than educational differences. For example, if students who go on to college tend to have more motivation and ability, the earnings differential reflects this tendency as well as the effect of the college education. Limiting the analysis to the earnings differential omits the other returns and costs identified above. These omissions can lead to distortions in the estimated profitability, because it is unlikely that omitted returns would be equal to omitted costs. Another caveat is that the data pertain to representative high school and college graduates. Considerable variation exists among individuals, so the use of medians or averages can be misleading for personal evaluations.

Finally, in order to use earnings differential projections over a working life, one must assume that both the high school and the college graduate are always working. Unemployment decreases the earnings of any individual, and, therefore, the returns from any educational attainment. Figure 5-3b provided some indication of the employment experiences of high school graduates versus those men and women who attended or graduated from college. As the education level increased, the unemployment rates declined. These data suggest that simple earnings differential projections probably understate the monetary returns to the college graduate, because the person who graduates from high school but does not go on to college has a higher likelihood of being unemployed during a working life than does a college graduate.

Sidestepping the caveats noted above, empirical studies of the returns from a college education generally conclude that it is profitable. One such study is that by Monk-Turner.[1] Based on the human capital perspective, prospective students and parents should be concerned with the profitability of additional education beyond high school. Two of the choices are to attend a two year community college or a four year college. Monk-Turner examined the wages of high school graduates who went to community or four-year colleges ten years after graduating from high school. Her sample contained information on race, sex, IQ, some characteristics of the person's family, region, and type of college

---

[1]   Elizabeth Monk-Turner, "Economic Returns to Community and Four-Year College Education," *Journal of Socio-Economics*, 23,4 (Winter, 1994):4441-7.

attended. The rate of return after ten years for each additional year of education for typical students who went to four-year colleges was 7.9 percent, and the one for community colleges was 5.4 percent. These results lead to the inference that it is more cost effective to attend a four-year college. In addition, Monk-Turner argued the estimated returns to either decision are underestimated because the earnings differentials tend to increase throughout a person's working life.

To the extent that employment considerations comprise the motivation for attending college, a prospective student should try to ensure that the skills acquired are designed to facilitate employment. With this perspective in mind, it is useful to take a moment to identify why there is an earnings differential, aside from the ability caveat noted above. Several factors are involved. Part of the reason is that the graduate acquires information that is valuable to business. This is particularly true for some academic fields, such as accounting, marketing, or engineering. Improved communications skills derived from the college experience are valuable as well. Having a college degree also indicates to a potential employer that the graduate has better problem-solving skills than the typical high school graduate. The best way to recognize this is to reflect on the exams taken in high school versus those taken in college; the degree of difficulty is considerably different. Many businesses are willing to pay more for college graduates' skills and then spend additional funds for the on-the-job training programs. Finally, successful completion of a college education is a positive indication to an employer that the graduate has the motivation to begin and finish a complex and time-consuming task.

STUDY QUESTIONS

A College Education

1. How would borrowing affect the profitability of a college education?
2. How would a scholarship affect the profitability of a college education?
3. Suppose a family is considering whether the wife should return to college to earn an MBA degree. What are the key economic variables associated with this decision?
4. Explain what the costs and returns are for the decision to go on to graduate school.

● Insurance ●

Insurance provides a way of covering the risk, or probability of loss, stemming from certain consumer activities. Driving a car is an example. There is no way to engage in this activity without incurring a risk. While there are many types of insurance, with considerable variation among the types, there are some common features. These features provide a basis for evaluating all kinds of insurance through the value of the last dollar spent.

The fundamental idea behind insurance is to collectively share the risk of loss. An illustration provides the best way to become familiar with how insurance works. Assume a family lives in a house valued at $60,000. Suppose the risk that a fire will completely destroy the house at some time during a one-year period is 1 in 1,000. This implies that the expected loss for any one homeowner of a $60,000 house is $60 per year. A group of homeowners could share the risk by forming a pool. If 1,000 homeowners each contributed $60, then there would be enough money in the pool to cover the loss of one house, and the probability that this would occur if virtually 1. Because each homeowner is contributing to the pool, the risk to each is covered.

All insurance works on this basic principle. In order for insurance to be workable, four conditions must hold, and they can be explained with reference to the fire insurance example.[2] First, the probability of a loss has to be known. This is necessary so the expected loss can be determined. Insurance companies spend large sums of money just to identify these probabilities, which are reevaluated regularly.[3]

The second condition is associated closely with the first. The probability of a loss should be small. There is no precise definition of small. An annual premium of $6,000 is required if the probability that a fire will completely destroy a house is 1 in 10. Not only is the premium relatively large; but when the probability is high, a legitimate question arises as to whether or not the consumer should be incurring such a risk.

The third condition is that many individuals must be members of the pool. This is necessary to keep the **premium**, the annual charge for insurance, close to the expected loss. Returning to the fire illustration, if only 100 members belonged to the pool, each would have to pay $600 in order for there to be enough money to cover the loss of a house. Since this exceeds the expected to loss of any one homeowner by $540, it would not be economically sound to join such a small pool.

Fourth, the probability that any one member of the pool will lose should be independent of the risk to other members. That is, a loss by one person should not be related to losses of others in the pool. Suppose the opposite were true. If the risks were interdependent, then when one person lost, others would be at a greater risk. In effect, the risk would not be spread out, and there would not be enough money in the pool to cover the higher probability of a loss.[4]

As long as the four conditions hold, consumer activities can be insured. The decision to insure hinges on a comparison of the market terms for the particular type of insurance and the consumer's valuation of the protection. Insurance companies set market terms on the basis of the expected value of the loss. Then some additional fees are added on to cover the cost of providing the insurance service. The premiums comprise the market price in the denominator of the value of the last dollar spent. The numerator is the consumer's marginal utility derived from the insurance. Decision making over time is involved, because the premiums are paid prior to the period being covered. Prepayment is necessary, because there is no point in paying the insurance when the loss has occurred or the period of coverage has expired.

Assessing the value of the last dollar spent can be a difficult procedure for consumers because of information problems. Insurance is an infrequently purchased service. This means that consumers are at a disadvantage when dealing with insurance agents. Most of the difficulty centers on assessing the marginal utility of the protection, because the cost represented by the premiums is fairly straightforward. Almost all types of insurance are worthwhile, and they enable consumers to cover the risk associated with normal activities. However, there are wide variations in policies, and it is important for the consumer to understand the terms of each policy. Prior to purchasing an insurance policy, the consumer should read it carefully and make sure every clause is understood in addition

---

[2]   Michael R. Behr and Dennis L. Nelson, *Economics: A Consumer Perspective*, (Reston, VA: Reston Publishing Co., 1975).

[3]   This is why insurance premiums tend to change annually.

[4]   This is one reason why some insurers have stopped issuing policies in south Florida following the destruction caused by hurricane Hugo.

to knowing exactly what is covered. This is crucial if one is to assess the utility provided by the protection. A consumer needs to be aware that the insurance agent is going to emphasize the probability of loss in an effort to affect the perceived marginal utility of the policy.

The basic features of insurance can be used to evaluate the various types. Life insurance is an example. Although there are many types of life insurance, there are only two broad classes. One is term life insurance, and the other, for lack of a better phrase, is referred to as invest-life insurance. **Term life insurance** covers the risk associated with the survival of the insured person from one point in time to another. Should the insured person live to the end of the term, the policy expires. Premiums paid are based on the amount of insurance and the probability that the individual will live to the end of the term. This class of life insurance is identical to other types of insurance in the sense that the premiums reflect the expected loss and the policy expires at the end of the term.

Investment-life insurance does more than just cover the risk of living throughout the term. Premiums exceed the expected value of a loss plus insurance company costs. The excess is used to build up a fund called the **cash value**, which is given to the beneficiary at the end of the period being covered. That is, should the insured person live to an agreed-upon date, the insurance company acts as if the individual had died and pays the beneficiary. Notice that investment-life insurance policies always require that someone be paid. Whether or not the insured dies during the covered time, the beneficiary must be paid.

Two purposes are served by investment-life insurance policies. One is to cover the risk of living, and the other is to invest. Consequently, such policies must be evaluated on a two-part basis. For the insurance aspect, the consumer should determine the value of the last dollar spent. For the investment aspect, the relevant consideration is the opportunity cost of the excess premium. Could this money have yielded a higher return it had been invested elsewhere? A study by the Federal Trade Commission provides part of the answer. The commission's estimate of the average rate of return for conventional investment-life insurance policies was 1.3 percent.[5] This is way below the return a consumer could have received by placing the excess premiums in a savings account, let alone in other investment opportunities. The low return on conventional policies makes insurance companies reluctant to provide policy information useful for consumer decision making. Consumers need to be very careful when assessing and comparing policies.[6]

A major factor causing the low return was the insurance companies' conservative management. Insurance companies tended to be extremely careful in their use of excess premium monies. However, this is changing. High interest rates, coupled with greater awareness on the part of consumers of what they are purchasing, have caused new types of investment-life insurance policies to be created. More aggressive investment programs have also increased the financial health of some insurance companies but hurt others, so that prospective and current policy holders need to monitor the activities of insurers.

Viewed from a consumer perspective, the choice between investment-life and term insurance depends on several factors. One is the self-discipline of the consumer. An advantage of the investment-life insurance policy is the premiums are a form of forced saving. Setting aside current income to provide for future consumption may be difficult for consumers. Those who have the self-discipline to

---

5   Lewis Mandell, *Consumer Economics* (Chicago: Science Research Associates, 1981):297.

6   A procedure for evaluating existing life insurance policies is in Joseph M. Belth, "Is Your Life Insurance Reasonably Prices?" *The Insurance Forum* 9(June, 1982):168-8.

save on their own must consider whether they will be able to invest the equivalent of the excess premium profitably.

How much life insurance a person should have is another issue. The fundamental idea is to protect against the loss of income. Certainly those spouses who generate a marketplace income need to protect other members of the consumer unit against a sudden loss in purchasing power. Additionally, protection against the loss of home-produced utility should be considered. The utility of the consumer unit is at risk through potential loss of this utility as well. A consumer unit must value all the sources of utility and determine how much term insurance is warranted. This depends on the age of the insured and the amount of the potential loss of utility. There are no hard and fast rules.

A final point is appropriate regarding insurance for children. The view of insurance outlined above leads to the conclusion that most children should not be insured. Generally, they do not provide significant marketplace or home production utility, so there is little risk of loss. But investing for children as they grow up to provide them with a financial start when they go out on their own is a different matter. Such a purchase should be considered purely as an investment, separate from insurance.

Extended warranties for consumer durables can be considered as a type of insurance. Deriving service flows increase the likelihood of repairs. These policies are difficult to assess. The chance of using them is rather low when durables are new, so policies that cover short periods of time relative to the period of use are more suspect. Also the ability of the owner to make repairs and/or to have access to preferred repair shops which may be excluded by the warranty can decrease the value of extended warranties.

STUDY QUESTIONS

Insurance

5. Identify consumer activities that have risks associated with them.
6. When shopping around for insurance, some consumers pay a lawyer to examine the competing policies. Why is this reasonable consumer behavior?
7. Explain why it is to the insurance agent's advantage to emphasize the probability of loss in selling insurance.
8. Why is it unreasonable for a family to have life insurance for children but reasonable to have health/accident insurance for them?
9. Why is it reasonable for a family to buy life insurance for a spouse whose activities are devoted completely to home production?

● Stock ●

Nearly every consumer unit at some point during its life cycle is in a position where it can consider postponing consumption. Even with the advent of pension plans, investment options should still be considered as a means of saving for rainy days, for large future expenditures such as a college education, or for retirement. A casual glance at the business section of any newspaper reveals that there are many different types of investment options from which to choose, such as savings accounts, mutual funds, money market funds, stocks, bonds, and real estate. A common feature of some of these options is that their market prices change over time. These changes affect the returns consumers receive from postponing consumption.

Perhaps the best known of the options characterized by changing market prices is stock. Everyone, no doubt, has heard of fortunes won and lost in the stock market. To the uninitiated, purchasing stock to make money seems to be almost mystical This need not be the case, as the principles of intertemporal decision making can be used to identify the essential features of stocks. The following discussion outlines these features with regard to common stock. Other investment opportunities with changing market prices can be evaluated in a similar manner.

A corporation is a specific form of business organization. One of the special features of corporations is the ability to issue stock. **Stock**, which represents ownership of the corporation, is divided into individual units called **shares**. Conceptually, the process can be characterized in the following manner. Individuals get together and decide to organize the production of a good or service. After meeting some legal conditions, they are able to form a **corporation**. In order to buy the factors of production needed to produce the good or service, the corporation must acquire money. One way the corporation can do this is to sell shares of stock. The money so acquired enables the corporation to purchase necessary resources. In exchange, the stockholders become the owners of the corporation. Should the company earn a profit, the board of directors can decide to distribute these profits to the stockholders in the form of **dividends**.

A key feature of the corporation is the limited liability of the stockholders. This means that if the corporation should go bankrupt, the most any stockholder can lose is what was paid for the stock. No matter what the debt position of the corporation is when it goes out of business, the stockholders are not liable for any outstanding debts. When the company is liquidated the shares have no value, so the stockholder's loss is limited to the amount paid to acquire the shares.

As long as the corporation remains healthy, its shares are desirable. If for some reason one stockholder wished to sell shares, the corporation does not have to buy them back. Instead, the stockholder can sell them to another investor. The corporation also can receive permission to sell additional shares to the public. Stock markets serve as clearing houses for those who want to buy and sell shares of companies.

There are two ways in which a stockholder is compensated for giving up money in exchange for ownership in the corporation. One is through dividends (D). Dividends usually are paid quarterly on a per share basis. The other type of compensation stems from changes in market prices. After the stock is purchased, its price per share in the market may change. If the stock appreciates in value, the stockholder can gain additional compensation by selling the stock. For example, suppose you purchase one share of stock the Downeast Consumer Company for $100.[7] During the ensuring year, a total of $15 in dividends is paid. After this year has elapsed, you decide to sell the share of stock. Assume that the market price is $100, so you receive $100. The market rate of return you have earned is 15 percent ($15/$100).

If the market price when you sell the share is different from the price you paid to own the share, the difference must be included in the computation of the return. If P_P denotes the price paid to own the stock and P_R denotes the price received when it is sold, the difference $(P_R - P_P)$ is the amount of money that has been made through the change in the market price. A positive difference means that the stock has appreciated in value and is referred to as a **capital gain**. A negative difference is

---

[7]   This example just considers the before-tax return to a consumer.

associated with a decline in the market value and is called a **capital loss**. The total rate of return (RET) for the purchase of a share of stock that is held for a year is shown in equation 17-1.

(17-1) $RET = [D + (P_R - P_P)]/P_P$

If the price received for the share of Downeast Consumer had been $105 instead of $100, the rate of return would have been 20 percent. On the other hand, if the price received been $95, the rate of return would have been 10 percent. Changes in the market price of stock clearly have a tremendous effect on the rate of return. In fact, most the attention the stock markets receive focuses on changes in the prices of the shares.

Applying the logic developed in Chapter 14, a consumer should purchase a stock whenever the anticipated market rate of return exceeds the rate of time preference. The consumer's problem is to identify those companies whose dividends and capital gains are expected to compensate for postponing consumption. While both factors are crucial in determining the profitability of an investment, which one to emphasize depends to a large extent on the consumer's stage in the life cycle. Dividends tend to fluctuate to a much smaller degree than market prices. Capital gains, while they can be substantial, are a much riskier way of generating returns, and it often takes a considerable length of time to realize them.

During retirement consumers have little or no earned income and may need to rely on a steady unearned income. People who look to stocks for a steady income should acquire shares in corporations with stable earnings. Stock in such corporations is less likely to generate significant capital gains in the short term, but the stability to the dividends is desirable for this group of consumers.

Younger consumers are in a different situation. Since they can rely on earned income for an extended period, steady dividends are less important. Rather, preference can be given to those stocks that are thought to have potential for capital gains in the long run. Shares in such companies are called growth stocks. Investing in growth stocks is riskier, but this risk is offset by the possibility of larger returns.

Anticipated expenditures also can be a motivation for investing in stocks. For example, a family may know that in a few years college expenses will arise. One thing the family can do is to consume less today and buy those stocks that they believe will rise most rapidly over the next few years. Here again, the focus is on capital gains as opposed to dividends.

How is the consumer able to anticipate what is likely to happen to stock prices? Essentially, this is the information problem associated with the stock market. The age-old advice of "buy low, sell high" is correct, but how is the typical investor to do this? Changes in stock prices depend on many factors, such as the industry in which the company operates and the competitive position of the company in the industry. The growth potentials of the industry and the company are important, too. Noneconomic factors such as political events also affect stock prices.

Supply and demand analysis can provide a clearer perspective on this market. A positively sloped supply curve suggests that as the price per share of a given stock increases, more and more holders of that stock conclude that their shares ought to be sold while the price is high. The market demand curve is negatively sloped, reflecting the relationship that the lower the price the greater the demand becomes, because more people are of the opinion the stock's price will increase. Both the supply and demand curves have the potential to shift as a result of changes in the determinants, such as risk and price expectations. Because the determinants do in fact change regularly, the market prices of stock change constantly.

There are several sources of information available to assist the prospective investor in forecasting the direction of price changes. The communications media offer television and radio programs directed toward investors. Daily, weekly, and monthly newspapers and magazines are devoted to financial interests. Stock brokerage firms employ large research staffs to determine when to buy and sell specific issues. Other investment analysts operate independently of the stockbrokers. Independent analysts typically sell their information to clients through newsletters or by directly managing investment funds. Some research firms have publications that regularly evaluate the performance of every company listed on the major stock exchanges.

Confronted with such an environment, the consumer must be as knowledgeable as possible about all aspects of investment in stock, including the mechanics of the various ways of actually purchasing stock. Advances in computer technology along with the Internet have made it possible to consumers to monitor their portfolios constantly. Financial software coupled with connections to the information super highway can retrieve stock and bond prices. This means that consumers can track their investments from almost anywhere. Furthermore, they can make decisions about buying and selling stocks and bonds without having to go to a broker's office.

A consumer first must determine how much money is required to meet life-cycle needs. Then attention can focus on identifying companies whose stocks the consumer believes are most compatible with these needs. This is when all the investment information is put to use. The selection of which stocks to purchase should involve a consideration of the trade-offs among risk, capital gains, and dividends. The process is nothing more than trying to forecast the market rate of return and purchasing those stocks that are expected to provide returns greater than the consumer's rate of time preference.

STUDY QUESTIONS

Stock

10. Since risk is involved, why is there no insurance against loss from the ownership of stock?
11. Why is it necessary to have an investment strategy when one is considering the purchase of stock?
12. Identify some short-, intermediate-, and long-term investment considerations for a young couple living in rental housing.
13. How would your answer to question 12 change for a family consisting of a middle-aged couple with a 13-year old daughter and an 8-year old son?
14. Suppose you were interested in buying a duplex so you could live in one side and rent the other. How could the economic considerations outlined in this section be useful?
15. Consider the market for Downeast Consumer stock. How would the supply and demand curves for shares be affected by favorable rumors about a new product the company is developing?

● Summary ●

Deciding whether to get a college education, buying insurance, and investing in stocks present consumers with intertemporal choice situations. The decision to go to college is based on an evaluation of the present value of the costs and the returns. Recent research has concluded that the present value of the returns of a college education is positive and larger for four-year colleges than for community colleges. Insurance provides a way to pool the risk associated with various future activities. The cost of insurance reflects the expected value of a loss, except in the case of investment-life insurance, where the excess cost serves as a form of saving. Buying common stock is another way of investing. Dividends and capital gains are the market returns for holding stock. Market supply and demand curves for a stock shift for many reasons. These shifts make it difficult to forecast what the price will be in the future.

● Key Terms ●

Capital gain: a positive difference between the price received and price paid.
Capital loss: a negative difference between the price received and price paid.
Cash value: accumulated premiums in excess of the term cost of life insurance.
Corporation: a type of business that receives special legal privileges and can raise money through selling stock.
Dividends: corporate earnings distributed among shareholders.
Insurance: a way of covering the risk associated with some consumer activities.
Investment-life insurance: life insurance that covers the risk of dying within a fixed period of time and also builds up a cash value.
Premiums: charges for insurance coverage.
Shares: individual units of stock.
Stock: units of ownership of a corporation.
Term life insurance: life insurance that covers the risk of dying during a fixed period of time.

• Index •